RELIGIOUS EXPERIENCE

CRITICAL CATEGORIES IN THE STUDY OF RELIGION

Series Editor: Russell T. McCutcheon, Department of
Religious Studies, University of Alabama

Critical Categories in the Study of Religion aims to present the pivotal articles that best represent the most important trends in how scholars have gone about the task of describing, interpreting, and explaining the place of religion in human life. The series focuses on the development of categories and the terminology of scholarship that make possible knowledge about human beliefs, behaviours, and institutions. Each volume in the series is intended as both an introductory survey of the issues that surround the use of various key terms as well as an opportunity for a thorough retooling of the concept under study, making clear to readers that the cognitive categories of scholarship are themselves historical artefacts that change over time.

Published

Syncretism in Religion: A Reader
Edited by Anita M. Leopold and Jeppe Sinding Jensen

Ritual and Religious Belief: A Reader
Edited by Graham Harvey

Defining Hinduism: A Reader
Edited by J.E. Llewellyn

Religion and Cognition: A Reader
Edited by D. Jason Slone

Mircea Eliade: A Critical Reader
Edited by Bryan Rennie

Defining Buddhism(s): A Reader
Edited by Karen Derris and Natalie Gummer

Defining Islam: A Reader
Edited by Andrew Rippin

Myths and Mythologies: A Reader
Edited by Jeppe Sinding Jensen

Defining Judaism: A Reader
Edited by Aaron W. Hughes

Readings in the Theory of Religion: Map, Text, Body
Edited by Scott S. Elliott and Matthew Waggoner

RELIGIOUS EXPERIENCE

A READER

Edited by
Craig Martin and Russell T. McCutcheon
with Leslie Dorrough Smith

Published by Equinox Publishing Ltd.

UK: Unit S3, Kelham House, 3 Lancaster Street, Sheffield S3 8AF
USA: ISD, 70 Enterprise Drive, Bristol, CT 06010

www.equinoxpub.com

First published 2012

ISBN: 978-1-84553-097-6 (hardback)
ISBN: 978-1-84553-098-3 (paperback)

British Library Cataloguing-in-Publication Data
A catalogue record for this book is available from the British Library.

Library of Congress Cataloging-in-Publication Data
Religious experience : a reader / edited by Craig Martin and Russell T. McCutcheon with Leslie Dorrough
Smith.
        p. cm. — (Critical categories in the study of religion)
    Includes bibliographical references and index.
    ISBN 978-1-84553-097-6 (hardback) — ISBN 978-1-84553-098-3 (pbk.)
  1. Experience (Religion) I. Martin, Craig, 1976- II. McCutcheon, Russell T., 1961- III. Smith, Leslie
Dorrough, 1975-
    BL53.R443 2012
    204'.2—dc23
                                                2012002500

Typeset by JS Typesetting Ltd, Porthcawl, Mid Glamorgan
Printed and bound in the UK by MPG Books Group

CONTENTS

Preface   vii

Sources   ix

1. Introduction   1
    Russell T. McCutcheon

Part I: The Background of Experience

2. Raymond Williams   19
    "Experience," from *Keywords: A Vocabulary of Culture and Society*

3. Robert Desjarlais   24
    "Rethinking Experience," from *Shelter Blues: Sanity and Selfhood
    among the Homeless*

Part II: The Autonomy of Experience

4. William James   37
    "Lecture 2: Circumscription of the Topic," from *The Varieties of
    Religious Experience: A Study in Human Nature*

5. Charles Taylor   55
    "James: Varieties," from *Varieties of Religion Today:
    William James Revisited*

Part III: The Universality of Experience

6. Joachim Wach   71
    "Universals in Religion," from *Types of Religious Experience:
    Christian and Non-Christian*

7. Diana Eck   88
    "Bozeman to Banaras: Questions from the Passage to India," from
    Encountering God: A Spiritual Journey from Bozeman to Banaras

Part IV: The Explanation of Experience

8. Wayne Proudfoot   109
    "A Classic Conversion Experience" and "Explaining Religious
    Experience," from *Religious Experience*

9. Ann Taves   122
    Excerpt from "Conclusion," from *Fits, Trances, and Visions:
    Experiencing Religion and Explaining Experience from Wesley to James*

Part V: The Unraveling of Experience

10. Robert H. Sharf   131
    "Experience," from *Critical Terms for Religious Studies*

11. Joan Wallach Scott   151
    "The Evidence of Experience," from *Critical Inquiry*

Conclusion: The Capital of "Experience"

12. William James in Late Capitalism: Our Religion of the Status Quo   177
    Craig Martin

Some Afterwords ...

13. I Have a Hunch   199
    Russell T. McCutcheon

    Bibliography   203
    Index   211

PREFACE

Talk of "religious experience" has been a part of religious studies for some time. German theologian Friedrich Schleiermacher (1768–1834) argued as far back as 1799 that the core of religion is an awe-inspiring *experience* of God. His work was influential on a wide variety of key figures in the history of religious studies, notably including William James (1842–1910), Rudolph Otto (1869–1937), Joachim Wach (1898–1955), and Mircea Eliade (1907–86). This vein of scholarship teaches us that religious experience is the essence of religion, and that the "outward" things—like creeds, texts, rituals, and so forth—are always secondary manifestations of religious experience. A person might tell a narrative about a religious experience, she might invent a ritual to memorialize it, but these things are always and necessarily secondary (temporally and in importance) to the original experience itself.

Why would religion scholars argue that experience is at the core of religion, especially when we lack empirical evidence both of gods and of the universal experiences they are supposed to have evoked? In part Schleiermacher's theory was motivated by his need to defend Christianity against materialist philosophers who had virtually done away with supernatural claims. Then-popular philosopher Immanuel Kant (1724–1804) drew a picture of the nature of the universe that left little if any room for divine beings; Kant believed in a god of sorts, but argued that there is nothing we could know about him. Kant's religion was therefore stripped of many of the things important to Schleiermacher and other Christians of his day. As far as they were concerned, Kant had taken the heart out of Christianity. In response, Schleiermacher argued that the core of religion is an experience of God that is *completely independent* of philosophy or philosophical knowledge. He would allow Kant to paint the Christian god out of the philosophical picture, but Schleiermacher would bring his god back in by saying that we have *direct experiences* of this god—on Schleiermacher's account, the fact that we can't philosophically know something about God is irrelevant. For Schleiermacher, we can *intuitively know* such a god exists, through experience, in a way that bypasses philosophy and Kant's critique. In sum, Schleiermacher's assertion of the centrality of religious experience was a defensive gesture designed to win back for Christian theology some of the ground lost to modern philosophy.

Despite the fact that we have many good reasons to reject Schleiermacher's claims about religious experience—as several of the essays in this book attest—the idea that religious experience is at the core of religion persists to this day. Few today use the term, as Schleiermacher did, to defend Christian doctrine, but we—the editors—would argue that the rhetoric of "religious experience" continues to be used to advance other social agendas, some of which are discussed in the following pages. This volume is therefore designed to introduce readers to the problem of "religious experience"—we have included essays that argue for or assume the existence of universal religious experience, as well as essays that call into question the idea.

The critics we have included hail from a wide range of disciplines: Wayne Proudfoot is an analytic philosopher of religion, Raymond Williams was a literary critic, Robert Desjarlais is an anthropologist and ethnographer, and Joan W. Scott is a feminist historian. The concept of experience, it is worth noting, has come under fire not only from within religious studies but across the humanities and social sciences in general.

Part I includes two essays we have chosen because they raise critical questions we hope will frame the volume. Parts II and III contain essays written by scholars who take for granted the existence and possible universality of religious experience. Parts IV and V include essays by scholars who have begun to call into question the rhetoric of "experience." Readers will notice that for Parts II through IV, the essays chosen include a "classic" essay as well as a more contemporary contribution that falls within the same tradition. Charles Taylor, for instance, assumes the sort of centrality of experience as did William James before him, Diana Eck assumes the universality of experience as did Joachim Wach, and Ann Taves remains as committed as Wayne Proudfoot was to explaining (and perhaps explaining away) experience.

We are skeptical of talk about religious experience, and we believe that questions such as "why would people talk about religious experience" are more interesting than questions about the nature of "religious experience." Hence the concluding chapter ignores the question of the existence of "religious experience" altogether, and instead considers what people might gain or lose by rhetorically opposing "religious experience" to so-called "organized religion." The short afterword, "I Have a Hunch," closes the volume by satirizing scholarship gone awry.

The citation styles for the following essays have been converted to a uniform style, and editors' notes have been added to help readers unfamiliar with some of the historical figures and technical terms that appear below.

The editors would like to acknowledge Leslie Dorrough Smith for writing the introductions to each chapter, introductions that nicely focus the reader's attention on some of the key issues in each essay. We would also like to thank Kim Davis and Melanie Williams (then undergraduate students in the Department of Religious Studies at the University of Alabama) for assisting with scanning and formatting many of the essays at a very early stage of producing this volume. We would also like to thank Janet Joyce, Tristan Palmer, and Val Hall at Equinox Publishing for their support and patience in seeing this volume through to completion. Thanks also go to the presses that have allowed us to reprint copyrighted essays, as well as the authors who gave us permission to do so.

SOURCES

Raymond Williams. 1983. "Experience." In *Keywords: A Vocabulary of Culture and Society* (rev. ed.), 126–9. New York: Oxford University Press. Copyright © Raymond Williams 1976, 1983. Reprinted with permission of Oxford University Press.

Robert Desjarlais. 1997. "Rethinking Experience." In *Shelter Blues: Sanity and Selfhood Among the Homeless*, 10–17. Philadelphia: University of Pennsylvania Press. Copyright © The University of Pennsylvania Press 1997. Reprinted with permission of the University of Pennsylvania Press.

William James. 1911. "Circumscription of the Topic." In *The Varieties of Religious Experience: A Study in Human Nature*, 26–52. New York: Longmans, Green, and Co.

Charles Taylor. 2002. "James: Varieties." In *Varieties of Religion Today: William James Revisited*, 3–29. Cambridge, MA: Harvard University Press. Copyright © The President and Fellows of Harvard College 2002. Reprinted with permission of Harvard University Press.

Joachim Wach. 1951. "Universals in Religion." In *Types of Religious Experience: Christian and Non-Christian*, 30–47. Chicago IL: University of Chicago Press. Copyright © The University of Chicago 1951. Reprinted with permission of the University of Chicago Press.

Diana Eck. 2003. "Bozeman to Banaras: Questions from the Passage to India." In *Encountering God: A Spiritual Journey from Bozeman to Banaras*, 1–21. Boston, MA: Beacon Press. Copyright © Diana L. Eck 1993, 2003. Reprinted with permission of Beacon Press.

Wayne Proudfoot. 1985. Selections from *Religious Experience*, 102–7 and 216–27. Berkeley, CA: University of California Press. Copyright © The Regents of the University of California 1985. Reprinted with permission of the University of California Press.

Ann Taves. 1999. "Conclusion." In *Fits, Trances, & Visions: Experiencing Religion and Explaining Experience from Wesley to James*, 348–61. Princeton, NJ: Princeton University Press. Copyright © Princeton University Press 1999. Reprinted by permission of Princeton University Press.

Robert Sharf. 1998. "Experience." In *Critical Terms for Religious Studies*, Mark C. Taylor (ed.), 94–116. Chicago, IL: University of Chicago Press. Copyright © The University of Chicago 1998. Reprinted with permission of the University of Chicago Press.

Joan Wallach Scott. 1991. "The Evidence of Experience," In *Critical Inquiry* 17(4), 773–97. Copyright © The University of Chicago 1991. Reprinted with permission of the University of Chicago Press.

"But merely because there exists a 'religious experience,' if you will, that is grounded in some manner (is there, by the way, an experience that is not?), it by no means follows that the reality which grounds it should conform objectively with the idea the believers have of it."

Emile Durkheim, *The Elementary Forms of Religious Life* (1995, 420)

1

INTRODUCTION

Russell T. McCutcheon

In the evening, I went very unwillingly to a society in Aldersgate Street, where one was reading Luther's Preface to the Epistle to the Romans. About a quarter before nine, while he was describing the change which God works in the heart through faith in Christ, I felt my heart strangely warmed. I felt I did trust in Christ, Christ alone for salvation; and an assurance was given me that he had taken away *my* sins, even *mine*, and saved *me* from the law of sin and death.   (Wesley 1988, 249–50)

So wrote John Wesley (1703–91), in what scholars call his conversion narrative, concerning an experience that reportedly took place during a meeting (somewhat like a modern day Bible study) in London on the evening of Wednesday, May 24, 1738. At that time, Wesley, the son of a clergyman, was himself a Church of England minister who had recently returned from a (not altogether successful) three-year assignment as a missionary in Savannah, Georgia (at that time a British colonial possession). Reporting that he had "continual sorrow and heaviness of heart" on the days preceding that evening meeting in late May, Wesley recounts in this famous journal entry how—as that evening's speaker was addressing Martin Luther's commentary on Paul's letter (or, from the Greek, epistle) to the early Christians who were in Rome—he had experienced a "strange warming" of his heart—a phrase that has become famous, especially among historians of Methodism, the originally British but now worldwide Protestant denomination that John and his younger brother Charles (1707–88) went on to establish. According to his journal, this sentiment or feeling—something which, in this tradition, is clearly differentiated from the cognitive (but still no less interior and thus personal) content of knowledge, often termed "belief"—was followed by an awareness of the role that Jesus Christ had played, through his life, death, and resurrection, in guaranteeing Wesley's own salvation from, as he puts it, "the law of sin and death."

Although many other examples could be supplied, we have here one of the better known accounts of an interior sentiment or affectation (that is, a feeling or emotion) that, to the person who reports having had it, is said to defy explanation; for it is said to carry with it what they might describe as a fullness or an immediacy of awareness that makes it stand out as unique and thus distinguishable from the other sorts of experiences that people regularly report having—such as the experience of hunger, thirst, joy, boredom, or even fear. Despite what insiders from a variety of cultures may call such exemplary moments in their awareness—if they do in fact possess a framework within which such things not only count *as* things worth paying attention to but also stand out as worth reporting—in the academic study of religion scholars commonly call such sentiments "religious experiences," and those who study them have, for some time, been interested in comparing such reports, looking for the various similarities and differences in the content and form of such reported experiences, all in hopes of drawing conclusions about how religion works.

So, with this initial piece of data in hand—our data being Wesley's journal entry concerning the "strange warming" of his heart—a simple question presents itself: what are we to do with the fact that some people report having had such experiences? Moreover, just what *is* an experience and what sense does it make to talk, as many scholars do, about such things as *unmediated experiences*—that is, internal states or dispositions that are said to result from nothing observable in the empirical world (unlike, say, the experience of heat which is presumably *mediated* by sensory preceptors and neurons as you grab the hot handle on the frying pan)? For that matter, what *is* a strange warming of the heart? What might cause it? What's more, what does it mean to have a heavy heart? Was Wesley speaking metaphorically (better put, *writing* metaphorically, for we cannot forget that all we have is a text and, despite our tendency to hear a human voice behind it, no one is actually speaking here—an important point to which we will return), as in when people commonly associate their heart with emotions, such as claiming to have a broken heart? Or was he speaking literally about sensations taking place in his upper chest, as in when people today talk about experiencing heartburn? Somehow, I suspect that the latter doesn't quite capture what most people think Wesley was trying to put onto paper—though, could psychological or physiological studies help shed light on what *caused* his experience? After all, as the noted US neurologist, Oliver Sacks, has phrased it, "with no disrespect to the spiritual, … even the most exalted states of mind—the most extraordinary transformations—must have some physical basis or at least some psychological correlate in neural activity" (2007, 41). But if Wesley was writing metaphorically—a technique we commonly use to place two otherwise unlike things beside each other, to say something about the one by transferring properties of the other—then to what were his metaphors "warming" and "heart" actually referring?

These are the sorts of questions that have occupied the attention of many scholars, and may very well be the questions that many of the readers of this book wish to pursue; but before attempting to answer any of them—and those looking for a start on such answers would do well to read Ann Taves's important survey of the literature (2005), along with Martin Jay's detailed survey of various uses of the notion of experience in modern scholarship and literature (2005), as well as Jensine Andresen's edited collection of essays for a sample of how some cognitive scientists are today approaching the topic (2001)—we ought to step back and consider a few things. For example, is it even correct to assume, as those who try to answer such questions commonly do, that such a thing as language (e.g., whether spoken in words or, as in Wesley's journal, written in a text) *refers* to something outside of itself, as in when we assume that "cup" (whether the sound you hear when it is said or the shapes you see when it is read) *refers* to some property internal to that object on my desk (that is, the very property that makes it a cup and not a bottle or a pen), or when we assume that the quoted words that opened this Introduction *correspond* to an utterance that came from a historical agent named John Wesley, who lived in England more than a couple hundred years ago. In fact, is it even correct to assume that his words—and perhaps this is why we call them *his* words—correspond not simply to an utterance that somehow flowed from his lips or, in the case of our quotation, from his pen, but that they also correspond to a meaning that he presumably had in his head (notice how meanings are in the head while emotions are in the heart)? Reading these words—*his* words—is therefore commonly thought to provide the careful reader with access to a meaning—*his* meaning—that Wesley had in mind when putting pen and ink to paper; a private meaning only he possessed, akin to his private experience, but that he fortunately exhibited publicly through the medium of language. This is the old "What did Shakespeare mean when he wrote…?" approach to studying meaning—the common approach that we easily find in everyday life (and many high school and college courses). According to this model, writers and speakers *express* (a key word—words matter!) their meanings in a code (in our case, it is called the English language, which is symbolized in arrangements of characters that we call letters or in combinations of spoken sounds that we call phonemes) that, when heard or read properly, enables a listener or a reader over two hundred and fifty years later to know what someone named Wesley experienced and then meant when he spoke about his heart's strange warming. Without this assumption that something eternal lurks behind and thereby animates the letters and the sounds, something that links the reader to the writer and the listener to the speaker (what theorists would simply call the *sign* that links the *signifier* to the thing being *signified*), it would make little sense to ask about what either Shakespeare or Wesley meant when he wrote either this or that, for both of them are long gone and all that remains is a text in front of us today—the collection of signs in ink on paper or pictured in shades of light and dark on a computer screen—that has passed through innumerable editorial hands and before countless eyes prior our own.

But is this the way experience, language, and meaning-making actually work? Is experience something inside a person, owned by a person, and is meaning somehow disengaged from the words on a page and the sounds that we hear, such that the sounds and the ink can come and go but the meaning they represented remains forever? If so, then the text of Wesley's quotation might function like an arrow leading away from his experience, on that fateful evening in May, and to the reader, wherever and whenever he or she may be, efficiently communicating across time something unique about this strange feeling that he had. But if meaning and experience *do not* work in this fashion, if they are not some inner, pure, and eternal thing, exclusive to the subject and only later symbolized publicly in fallible language, then too quickly moving from reading words on a page, overhearing words spoken orally, or watching people doing things, to concluding that texts, sounds, and behaviors provide direct access to some inner world of timeless significance is a serious error in scholarship.

To rephrase: perhaps we could say that if you follow the common sense model of meaning-making (which is often called the correspondence or the referential theory of meaning), then claims of religious experience will likely be understood as signaling a pre-verbal, pre-linguistic, and thus pre-cultural moment that is later expressed publicly, but done so only to varying degrees of satisfaction (which is none other than the old, "I can't quite put it into words" approach to how meaning works) by means of those social conventions we call languages. However, if we adopt an alternative theory about how meaning-making takes place, and, by doing so, further complicate meaning's relation to those internal states or dispositions that we commonly know as either experiences or beliefs—a theory to be discussed below in more detail—then we will have to take seriously that, as phrased by the Austrian philosopher, Ludwig Wittgenstein (1889–1951), "the expression of belief, thought, etc.," such as Wesley's journal entry, "is just a sentence;—and the sentence has sense only as a member of a system of language; as one expression within a calculus" (1965, 42). To put it another way, notations on a page or sounds coming from the mouths of people do not necessarily refer to anything outside of themselves; that is, they may simply be notations and sounds that refer to nothing other that the rules of the symbol systems in which they occupy a place (e.g., grammar)—rules that we, as the people who develop and use them, employ to distinguish which markings and which sounds get to count as language and which are seen and heard as mere marks and sounds. If this is the case, then markings and soundings are not neutral collections of signs that re-present (as in the sense of presenting something anew) an otherwise unavailable inner world, thereby making it available, in translated form, to outsiders. And if so, then they do not provide the reader or the listener (no matter how careful they may be in their descriptive and interpretive work) with direct access to any pre-verbal or pre-cultural meanings that were once in someone else's head. Simply put, there is no way to answer "What did Shakespeare mean when he wrote…?"

If this alternative approach to meaning-making is used, then the question "Do you know what I mean?" may not be about the meaning at all, regardless of what the person asking the question may think it is all about. Instead, such a statement may be an invitation to determine whether speaker and listener share the same set of linguistic rules—what Wittgenstein called a calculus or what we might as well just call a grammar, whether linguistic or perhaps social (as in behaving correctly, as other members of the group do in this or that situation). And thus the common reply, "Yeah, I know what you mean," may merely establish that that the listener and the speaker do indeed share the same rules. And by sharing the same rules they have established that they are members of the same group, sharing common likes and dislikes.

Case in point: consider the widely parodied "eh?" (pronounced "ay") which is often used by Canada's English speakers (a trait picked up from the British, but which is also found, though not as prominently, in US English). Waiting at a bus stop, it would not be unusual to hear someone say, "Nice weather, eh?" But the person saying this is not, in fact, posing a question. For, despite the upward inflection as their sentence ends, one would never expect to find "eh?" used at the end of a sentence that put forward a controversial claim—one that risks the sort of disagreement that marks a break or a gap in social life.

That is to say, the linguistic signal "eh?" *functions* (as opposed to *means*) for Canadians much as "or what?" functions in American slang, as in "Is this great weather, or what?": they are both occasions to solicit agreement from the person with whom one is having a conversation—"Yeah, it's great weather" is therefore the expected, and thus the correct, answer. And by correct I simply mean the answer that signals your participation in the group—the group's expectations for weather on an autumn morning, perhaps, or the group's expectations for what sort of behavior can reasonably be expected to take place between strangers waiting at a bus stop. Important to recognize is that this exchange is therefore not about the weather (much like questions such as "How are you doing?" are not about how you are doing but, generally, are simply a way of saying hello; the correct answer, regardless of your disposition, is therefore "Fine"), for the observation on the quality of the weather simply provides an occasion for group affirmation and group build- ing. "Eh?" is therefore a way to invite, perhaps even to force, agreement and thus solidarity by putting forward a claim already known to have the agreement of your conversation partner—it is already known because you each already know the other to be a member of your group, sharing your tastes, your sensibilities, your expectations, and most impor- tantly, your language. Despite being strangers, you are both waiting for the same bus, after all. This agreement therefore is a mark of shared social affinity: "Are we both in the group who thinks that the weather is pleasant today?" to which someone answers, "Yes, we are peers." "Eh?" questions are therefore simply occasions for massaging the group and your place within it.

If queries about the weather may not actually be about the weather, then could expe- rience talk not actually be about supposedly pristine, internal things called experiences either? For if we follow Wittgenstein, then regardless of what people making claims of having had an experience may think, their claims (like all language) may be nothing more or less than evidence that the writer or the speaker are properly schooled in using their group's language rules—and using the rules does nothing more or less than use the rules, thereby reproducing and reinforcing them, and in the process reproducing and reinforcing the identity of the group that results from those who collectively use them.

In this model, the sounds of speech and the markings of texts do not refer to any- thing outside of the fact that the speaker and listener, the writer and reader, are equally competent to put their shared rules into practice—much as readers of this text are doing right now—and doing this so well that the fiction of meaning is created as a result. In this case—recalling an earlier example—if I write "cup" (as I have just done, and which readers have just read) it may tell us nothing about some essential feature of an object on my desk that makes it naturally distinguishable from other objects also on my desk; instead, writing and reading "cup" may tell us everything about our (that is, the writer's and the reader's) common place within a rule system which distinguishes "cup" from "cap"—not to mention "cop," "cot," "cut," "cat," etc—distinctions that we reproduce and teach to newcomers because we find them useful, not only because this system of distinc- tion helps us to find something to drink with but, more importantly perhaps, because they facilitate our cooperative activities with others in our group and allow us to identify those who are not in the group. Participating in such systems is therefore a way in which we continually reinvent ourselves as a specific sort of "we" and mark certain things in the world as significant to us.

Of course, this alternative theory of language will probably frustrate those who employ the common sense view of words as neutral signs that directly correspond either to intangible ideas (e.g., justice) or things (e.g., cups) in the real world. But for others, the fact that users of our language system have so successfully schooled each other in "seeing" a cup when hearing the sounds represented by "cup," and a cat when hearing the sounds represented by "cat"—sounds and symbols repetitively driven into us from an extremely young age, by those around us, those who made us what we are today—makes language, meaning, experience, and social identity all the more interesting things to study. For despite my assurance that a *cow* is a cow and that it says *moo*, I also happen to know (because I've seen others do it to their children) that well-meaning (but no less coercive) adults leaned into me, as a very young child, and repeatedly told me, likely with great enthusiasm—"The cow says moo. The cow says moo"—while probably pointing just as repeatedly to a drawing in a child's story book or to an object outside the car window. Would that sketch in the book, that object on the other side of the farmer's fence, have naturally been something worth paying attention to *without* being forced to take notice of it, without being given a name for it, and without repeatedly being told of a whole series of interconnected relationships that it had with other names ("farmer," "farm," "horse," "barn," "pasture," "milk," etc.)? In fact, much like that farmer's fence, not only creating a set of identities by separating farm from not-farm but, in doing so, helping us to conceptually and physically group together and organize all that falls within it as somehow being inherently related (i.e., the well, the tractor, the chicken coop, the shovel, the bags of corn seed, and the pig sty are now all part of "the farm"), being taught any series of interconnected relationships is a way that an identity is made, inasmuch as one acquires the tools (in other words, the structure, the grammar) to determine what is like what and who is like whom. For example, when placed into the correct framework, a flag, a song, a series of holidays, certain events in the past, and certain institutions can all come to create the impression of a uniform national identity. But without initiation into this or that particular linguistic and social calculus, would I have *experienced* the cow and its moo? Would I *feel* French or Greek or Mexican or American? Would I *believe* that I was or was not a farmer? Or, without initiation into the use of that particular calculus, would the moments that together conspired to create that sense of identity instead be irrelevant, and thus unnoticed, in a hectic world in which I had come to pay attention to yet other things by means of relationships perhaps unimaginable to those intent on "seeing" certain objects *as* cows and hearing certain sounds *as* moos?

Apparently, experience is a lot more complicated than was first apparent when reading that quotation from John Wesley, for it now seems that the internalization of a previous calculus, developed long before we arrived on the scene and taught to us by others, ensures that none of my experiences are simply my own; instead, what gets to count as an experience is determined for us by others, by the grids given to us and by means of which we determine what is and is not significant to us. Thus, instead of talking about "his experiences" and "his meanings," as we did earlier when discussing what Wesley wrote, we might better phrase it as *our* experience and *our* meaning, inasmuch as the frameworks that determine what gets to stand out *as* an experience and what gets to count *as* meaningful are public and therefore collective (such as the usually unnoticed grid that allows us to pay attention to some long gone social actor named John Wesley, while ignoring countless other people who undoubtedly had rich lives in the eighteenth century). And it is not just that "cup" or "cow" do not necessarily point to something internal to those things we call cups and cows, for everything that has just been said (or, again, should I say written?) equally applies to *all* of the other words in the preceding paragraphs. For example, whether I used it in my own text, or whether used by Wesley—as in the phrase, "I felt my heart strangely warmed"—we may have no choice but to ask: To what does "I" and "my" refer? Does it point to something unique inside of me (such as my identity, my subjectivity, my self) or merely to shared assumptions and social rules common among those who constitute my peers—assumptions about what gets to count as an individual?

Taking a serious look at how we talk about experience may therefore be the way in to a whole range of hugely important issues.

* * *

The essays selected for this volume, all of which are intended for a reader new to these issues but motivated enough to tackle some complex issues, explore this very complexity. Therefore, readers expecting to find a selection of articles in the vein of Wesley's journal—that is, a collection of articles narrating religious experiences that people claim to have had—will likely be disappointed, for after the selections included in Parts II and III of the book (in which the essays in each part offer a so-called classic and then also a contemporary example of the widespread view of religious experience being uncaused by other sorts of experiences [i.e., autonomous] and yet universally shared among all human beings), the volume turns to a selection of essays that call into question these very assumptions, making not religious experience the focus of study but, instead, the social effects of making such claims. It's for that reason that the collection opens with Raymond William's brief but crucial study of the two senses in which the word "experience" has been used in the English language—what he terms experience past and experience present. The modern sense of experience as naming a private affectation or sentiment of fullness and immediacy—what Williams calls experience present, which is just as Wesley used the term and much as many people today now use the term—is a fairly recent linguistic invention. So Williams also draws attention to another notion of experience as naming the cumulative result of past situations. In fact, it is this older sense of the term, as naming something public and observable, that occupies the majority of *The Oxford English Dictionary*'s many different definitions for the word (citing examples from as early as the fourteenth century). So, despite the popularity today of assuming that experience denotes an interior disposition available only to the participant—such as those who might nostalgically look back on their school days, longing for "the student experience"—we still have no difficulty understanding a job ad that specifies that applicants need to have "work experience." In this case, experience names something that accumulates over time (hence Williams names it experience-past), something empirical and therefore public (for I can hear whether you know how to play the piano and I can taste whether you know how to cook), something that can be done with the body (such as the skills required of the job), something that I can observe so as to confirm whether you have it or not. So while I can see whether you know how to do long division, I certainly can't see Wesley's strangely warmed heart.

Two items are crucial to entertain at this point. First of all, whereas experience-present is said to be private and unavailable for empirical (that is, sensory) confirmation (i.e., one cannot confirm that Wesley's heart was indeed "strangely warmed"), experience-past is very public and therefore available for empirical confirmation (i.e., one can easily verify whether a novice professor has teaching experience). These two different usages of the term therefore seem to be the opposite of one another. Second, if we accept Wittgenstein's assessment of claims of belief as being nothing more or less than utterances that can be heard and sentences that can be read, then claims of experience-present are, after all is said and done, just that—*claims* and, as claims that can be understood, they must operate by the shared calculus that we call language, rules that are thoroughly public and social (after all, neither you nor I invented the grammar that we use to make sense of this very text). The point? What some see to be experience-present can instead be understood as but one more instance of experience-past. To put it another way, the ability to have an experience, much less to report that one has had one, may itself be evidence of one's prior participation in a certain sort of social world, one comprised of specific rules that can themselves be observed, taught, recorded, and compared to the rules of other social worlds. What some might understand as the supposed immediacy of experience-present may actually be but an internalized residue of an earlier social world (its calculus), invented by others and that, through the actions of others, has been imprinted on us—or better put, *within* us.

Now, of course, this is not the way that the people who make disclosures about their experiences usually think of them—and the question is whether their self-representations (e.g., I think this, I saw that, I meant something else) limit how scholars can examine people's claims and the actions about which they may make claims (e.g., I did this because…). Case in point: I have no doubt that John Wesley was not assuming that his claim to having had an unique experience at a meeting on Aldersgate Street was nothing but an example of how arbitrary signs are connected up in complex systems to form language—a system which is meaningful only so long as more than one person accepts the arbitrary arrangements and combinations that we know as text and grammar. Not at all! Instead, I presume that he, much like the person who assumes "cup" somehow points directly to that thing still sitting on my desk, took for granted that his journal entry was somehow in step with a stable reality in the world, one to which only he happened to have direct access. After all, it was his own heart that was strangely warmed, was it not? But is this description of his assumptions entirely correct? For, come to think of it, if he really did believe that only he had access to this interior disposition then what sense would it make for him to come home, put pen to paper, and write about it, for writing places indicators of this supposedly private disposition into a public domain? So while he likely, and quite sincerely, understood himself to have undergone something unique to himself, that cannot be the whole story.

What if, to begin with, we assumed that the private place from which Wesley's feeling originated was, at least he might say, not limited to him. What if it was private yet somehow shared by others, such as those also attending that evening meeting, or those who might someday read his published journals? What if we assumed, much like those who today talk about Human Nature as being something unique to each individual (i.e., to each "I") yet shared by *all* individuals (i.e., by the "we")—thereby making everyone equally individual *and* equally members of that family we know as humanity—that the site of Wesley's private disposition of assurance was also present, though just as private, within everyone else? Now, it starts to make sense for him to write about it, while still being unable to put "it" into words adequately, for now the internal thing which his writing *expresses* might be something of relevance to people other than Wesley himself.

So if we're trying to be descriptively accurate when coming across people using the term "experience" in that sense that Williams termed experience-present, we likely have to address two things that these people seem to assume: (1) that although their sense of an interior sentiment is autonomous, or disconnected from being caused by the mundane or empirical things of usual day-to-day life, it is nonetheless also (2) universally shared by (all or at least some) others who are likewise thought to have a similar private, interior space (what scholars sometimes call subjectivity) where such emotions reside. And this is just what we see happening when, in response to the question "Know what I mean?" we commonly see someone reply by simply shaking her head, up and down or side to side. And as if by magic, without the so-called meaning ever being put on the table—placed in public, for scrutiny and possibly for dispute—something seems to have been mysteriously transported, as if by telepathy, between these two otherwise distinct hearts and minds. Yes, I know what you mean.

Throughout the history of that field that we know as Religious Studies, the Academic Study of Religion, Comparative Religion, or even the Science of Religion (the last two names for the field were once more popular than they are now), we come across scholars who, much like the people they study, presume just this: that their object of study is an internal yet universal state (whether emotional, as in an experience or faith, or cognitive, as in a belief) that can only be accessed by means of its various expressions or—using a term favored by those known as phenomenologists of religion (descriptivist scholars interested in doing comparative work, looking for cross-cultural similarities)—its manifestations. These manifestations are generally found in specific sorts of narratives (called myths), certain types of behaviors (called rituals), and a host of other media, from art to hand gestures (all called symbols). In fact, these three items, myth, ritual, symbol, were once (and, in some university curricula, still might be) the basis for common course titles, in which the variety of manifestations studied in a semester were thought to betray a common core, or, using a term often used in philosophy, what is usually termed an essence.

Likened to the core of an onion—inasmuch as it is the only thing remaining when one peals back its many layers—the essence is that without which something would not be what it is. For example, we might say that the color of the onion—or so the argument goes for those who define things (like onions or cups on my desk) by identifying their essence—does not make it an onion, for red onions are no more or less onions than those that are yellow or white or green (which we also call scallions). Color comes and goes (i.e., color is contingent), suggesting that it is not a necessary, or essential, trait of the onion.

Perhaps size, shape, or taste is a better candidate for an onion's necessary trait. Or perhaps the way we use them? Where they are grown? A little thought on the subject makes it clear that none of these features is required for something in the world to count as an onion, for different onions taste differently, have different shapes and sizes, and can be used in any number of ways—but that doesn't mean that any of them are less of an onion. Much as an onion's empirically observable characteristics (size, shape, color, etc.) can all differ, though the item is still an onion, many scholars of religion have assumed that, like the onion-ness that remains when its various observable layers are each removed, there is a nonempirical core that remains once religious beliefs', behaviors', and institutions' unnecessary (that is, changeable) traits are gone.

This strategy for defining something as a this and not a that usually goes by the name of essentialism; in the study of religion, in which we find so many different variations in people's beliefs and actions, the essentialist approach has, for the past few hundred years, settled on private experience as the true essence of all religion. And because the inner world is so often thought to take priority over the outer world, these initial, pre-social experiences come to be understood as the source, the cause, of all that follows them; first comes faith, as the scholar of religion Wilfred Cantwell Smith (1916–2000) might have phrased it, and only then come the traditions and the institutions. Therefore, despite the many observable differences in the claims people make, the way they do things, and the sorts of groups they form to pass along their traditions, beliefs, and rituals, much as with onions there must be something in common (or so it is thought) in order for us to recognize all of these things *as* religious. And that thing they all share turns out not to be a *thing* at all; instead, it is an internal state, an intangible disposition, a subjective immediacy of awareness, that all people are said to have and thus to share. Though expressed in a multitude of ways, that which motivates these varied expressions, that which is first felt internally and only then manifested externally, is said to be common and thus necessarily shared.

One of the better known examples of an early scholar of religion adopting this approach was the German Protestant scholar Rudolf Otto (1869–1937). Working in an intellectual tradition not unlike that of his predecessor, the German Protestant theologian Friedrich Schleiermacher (1768–1834), sharing important assumptions about the empirical unavailability of experience in common with his contemporary, the American psychologist William James (1842–1910), and setting the stage for the later work of such scholars as the influential Chicago historian of religions, the Romanian-born Mircea Eliade (1907–86), Otto concluded that those things which we call religious are religious not because of any external or observable trait that they may or may not have—for, after all, place that thing called an altar in a different setting, and do different things with it, and you won't likely continue to think it's an altar but simply a table or a desk. Instead, items in the empirical world simply provide an occasion or a site for the expression of what he held to be a prior and timeless inner awareness that is projected, outward from the individual and into the world. And for Otto this inward awareness is an experience of the numinous, a term he coined from the Latin word *numen* (presence or power), naming one's inner awareness of being in the presence of the compelling yet fearful mystery of it all.

That it is awfully difficult to study a mystery (after all, where does one begin and how does one know where to end?) seems to have been overlooked by the many people influenced by Otto's work. However, the problems do not stop there, for there are other implications of this still common position for scholarship on religion. For example, in the (often quoted) opening lines of chapter 3 of his important book, *The Idea of the Holy* (as the title was translated from the 1917 German original, *Das Heilige*), Otto writes the following:

> The reader is invited to direct his mind to a moment of deeply-felt religious experience, as little as possible qualified by other forms of consciousness. Whoever cannot do this, whoever knows no such moments in his experience, is requested to read no farther; for it is not easy to discuss questions of religious psychology with one who can recollect the emotions of his adolescence, the discomforts of indigestion, or, say, social feelings, but cannot recall any intrinsically religious feelings. We do not blame such an one, when he tries for himself to advance as far as he can with the help of such principles of explanation as he knows, interpreting "aesthetics" in terms of sensuous pleasure, and "religion" as a function of the gregarious instinct and social standards, or as something more primitive still. But the artist, who for his part has an intimate personal knowledge of the distinctive element in the aesthetic experience, will decline his theories with thanks, and the religious man will reject them even more uncompromisingly.　　(Otto 1958 [1917])

Drawing on the common analogy of art and religion—inasmuch as people sometimes assume both to be concerned with unique feelings that cannot be fully explained by appealing to any of their observable causes—Otto's position is clear: *to be, or to feel, is to know.* Those who do not possess "an intimate personal knowledge of the distinctive element" of the object under study therefore have no choice but to remain silent when it comes to discussing it. Such scholarship on religion is deeply influenced by an intellectual movement we know as Romanticism—a philosophical, artistic, musical, and literary movement that originates in some eighteenth-century Europeans' negative reactions to the scientific rationalism of the Enlightenment. Religion cannot be explained—or so the argument goes—it can only be felt. Practiced in this way, the study of religion amounts to a form of participation, inasmuch as the scholar is assumed to share in the experiences of the people under study—at least enough to feel and understand them enough to represent them accurately.

But in what other area of the university, in which other scholarly discipline, would we play by such rules? For must one be an ancient Greek to study ancient Greece? Must one be a communist to study communism? What about marine biologists and what they study? No doubt there are those in other fields who, along with Otto, think that being a participant gives one a privileged viewpoint. For instance, take the more recent academic fields that are today called area studies, where one can easily find professors who maintain that, for example, women have a privileged insight when it comes to the curriculum of a Women's Studies class. But perhaps, instead of studying the supposed content of experience, as with a previous generation of scholars, we ought to shift the ground as we did with the Canadian "eh?," just as recommended by Wittgenstein, and take seriously that claims of experience are just that, *claims* and, as claims, they are public, they follow rules, they are negotiable and contestable, and these claims themselves are the things that are *doing* something rather than being a passive sign (that is a description) of something else. And because they are doing something, those making the claims are social actors and their claims are a form of action that can be studied. And it is this doing, the establishing of a zone of social privilege—the thing that results from claims about the unique nature of "women's experience" or the "American experience"—that ought to attract scholars' attention. Of course those making the sorts of claims that we find in Wesley's and Otto's texts more than likely wish their beliefs, behaviors, and institutions to be treated in a special way (aside: to set apart is among the ancient Latin roots of the modern word "sacred"), but I do not think that scholars ought to be bound by the wishes of the people whom they study. In fact, this is *the* issue that operates in the background of the following essays; this volume's position on this point ought to be clear from its opening epigraph from the early French sociologist, Emile Durkheim (1858–1917).

But readers should not just take Durkheim's word for it; so just why are people not the experts on their own experiences? While I could cite a number of examples to persuade readers that experience is a social product, that without a grid provided for them from the outside (let's say, by a writer such as myself, removed from the world they take for granted), they may not be *experiencing* themselves in either this or that way in the present moment (say, *as* a reader, *as* a student, *as* a teacher, *as* a female, *as* a male, etc.), consider instead a brief but useful example from Wendy Brown's book, *Relating Aversion: Tolerance in the Age of Identity and Empire* (2006). Brown, a political scientist, is interested in the history and current effects of what is now an almost taken for granted theme of life in modern social democracies: that we must *tolerate* each other's differences. That there are some things which many—though, significantly, not all, and *that's* the point!—of us agree we must *not* tolerate (such as those behaviors we label as crimes) makes it evident that the limits of toleration (or, to put it another way, the boundaries of the group which tolerates and of what is tolerated) are contestable, that they change over time, and that they must therefore be tweaked, repaired, built, and rebuilt.

With this in mind, consider Brown's example of the Museum of Tolerance in Los Angeles, part of the Simon Wiesenthal Center. A portion of the museum is devoted to exhibits documenting the horrors of Nazi Germany's attempt to eliminate Europe's Jewish population—exhibits that, as with many modern museum exhibits, prompt visitors to move through carefully recreated settings, to interact with multimedia presentations, and thereby to be enveloped by an ever-growing narrative about events in the past and the significance they ought to be seen as having in the present. "The installation culminates," Brown writes,

> with our literal descent into a concentration camp-like space, replete with barbed-wire; entrances that separate the adult and able-bodied from children, the aged, and the infirm; and uneven rough cement floors. We issue into the cold, cavernous

space of a gas chamber where, for a very long time, we watch images of the camps as actors read the words of inmates and survivors.   (Brown 2006)

"At this point," Brown concludes, "we are no longer mere witnesses to the Holocaust but are *inside* the experience" (139). In support of her point, Brown quotes two previous visitors, writing in the guest book at the end of the exhibit: "I had read some things about the Holocaust, but had never seen it first hand," writes one, and another says, "now I know how it must have felt."

But there's just one problem, a particularly nagging problem, when it comes to the manner in which these visitors have experienced the terrors of the Holocaust. As Brown rightly observes, none of the visitors has actually seen anything other than the museum exhibit first hand, for "what we are seeing is staged rather than real"; "this 'experience' is a facsimile," (138, 139). The awareness that so sincerely moved the museum's visitors— what to them more than likely is perceived as vivid, authentic, and therefore rationally persuasive and emotionally compelling—was, the observer and the museum curators both know, manufactured for them, over half a century and a world away from the events that the exhibits claim to represent; it was done so by the same sort of careful planning and attention to detail that one finds in any modern multimedia exhibit, whether it be a museum, an amusement park, or a motion picture. The visitors have quite obviously never left sunny LA; yet to those writing in that guest book, they have somehow been transported back in time, to some core moment a world away—a moment unchanged despite being recreated in a museum exhibit. Could there be any better example of the manner in which experiences are conjured within pre-fabricated grids and settings, making experience an artefact of a prior social world?

But to press the point still further, what are we to make of the presumption that, whether or not we can access it, there is a pristine "core moment" somewhere out there, in the dimly lit past? Could it be the case that this very sense of an original, even if we agree that it is irretrievably separated from us in time, is just as much a product of a calculus in the present, comprised of specific expectations, assumptions, sets of interests and needs that may have little or nothing to do with their so-called origins? For instance, consider that group commonly known in US history as "the founding fathers." What did they found? Certainly not the contemporary country known as the United States of America, for the nation-state that exists today was beyond the wildest dreams of political actors in the mid- to late eighteenth century. Certainly, from the point of view of the present, their long past actions were *necessary* to establish the new nation-state (e.g., their writing a constitution), but they were hardly *sufficient*, for none of those social actors could anticipate issues in the future (which indicates the crucial role of the US Supreme Court in bridging the gap between distant past and unanticipated future, for this is the body responsible for apply-ing a late-eighteenth-century text to ever-changing present-day circumstances). Their unknown future (they lacked foresight) became our known past (because we possess hindsight), thereby allowing us to look backward in time *as if* those past actions led to our present. But because the contemporary moment is comprised of countless present situa-tions, each populated by and indicative of the desires of countless different social actors in any number of different situations and all looking backward in time for some hint of justification for the particular present *as they wish it to be*, we can see how that thing that we once understood simply as a uniform and tangible past actually turns out to be filled with innumerable actors doing a variety of things for any number of reasons. The past, then, becomes an almost limitless repository from which contemporary actors can pick and choose, to suit their purposes. No doubt, many things were begun in 1776, but should one desire to draw attention to the longevity of certain US political institutions, then a relatively small number of events in that year stand out as significant—significant because of the current desire, not significant in and of themselves. In precisely this way one can argue that the past is an ever-changing construction of the present—ever-changing because the present is so diverse and is itself always changing (that is, the present has a nasty habit of continually becoming the past, which opens the way for yet another unanticipated future to become a new present).

To apply some of this, consider one of my own school's football players, interviewed last season on the local evening news, at a press conference prior to Alabama's annual October game against the University of Tennessee—our arch rivals. When asked what it was like to play a game in Knoxville's famed Neyland Stadium—with over 100,000 cheering fans, all wearing orange and white—he replied by saying that the only thing that he could compare it to was "what the gladiators and lions experienced in the Roman coliseum." Much as with the museum's visitors, we must not overlook the fact that, despite his claims, no actual time travel has taken place; instead, this player's sense of being in ancient Rome was likely a product either of Hollywood special effects magic (had he seen Russell Crowe star in *Gladiator*?) or the imagination of historians hoping that their reading of such things as ancient inscriptions, statues, and architecture might hold up their weighty claims about such things as "the Roman experience." Moreover, today "ancient Rome" comes to stand for so many different things, all because of the many events that have transpired long after it and which were necessarily unknown to the people who actually lived in that place during that time (such as seeing Rome as but one of many so-called "great civilizations" that have risen and fallen over the past several thousand years, including many whose life spans long post-dated Rome's own inevitable decline). So it seems very likely to me that, for this football player in 2006, the English sign "gladiator" (the Latin *gladiatōrēs*, swordsmen, comes from *gladius*, meaning sword) more than likely signifies something that is very different from what it may have meant for the slaves, criminals, war prisoners, and some free men as well who were put in the position of having to fight for their lives. What it meant for such people is, I would suggest, largely if not completely lost to time. The result is that all we have left is someone in the present using such signs as "gladiator" and "ancient Rome" to accomplish social work in the here and now.

But whether grounded in the fictions of Hollywood or of scholarship, we must not overlook that this player's presence on that field in Knoxville apparently becomes understandable to him—becomes something we might call an *experience*—only once it is juxtaposed to a facsimile, somewhat akin to those who, in the immediacy of the shocking attacks of September 11, 2001, were only able to make sense of that day's events by comparing the chaos of the real to facsimiles and fabrications: "It was like a movie," they all said when interviewed by reporters on the scene, no doubt referring to Hollywood's long tradition of disaster films set in busy US cities (everything from 1974's *Earthquake* and *The Towering Inferno* to *Independence Day* [1996], *Armageddon* [1998] and *Deep Impact* [1998]). This confirms not only that, as scholars of religion are apt to say, we must not confuse our map of the territory (such as a description of an action, which is a mere representation) with the territory itself (what constitutes the original presentation of the act), but also that there is in fact no territory, no original, and thus no direct experience of a real world, without the application of a prior, constructed map that not only exists at a distance from that which it eventually represents but, *more importantly perhaps,* whose use actually transforms the generic, chaotic, and thus unknowable limitless background—somewhat akin to white noise or the brute and unorganized stuff of existence—into a delimited and thus manageable domain that can be conceptualized and only then experienced and known, so that one can now experience oneself as being either "in place" or "out of place," either "early" or "late," either one of "us" or one of "them."

So the question is whether, as scholars, we are content to take the museum visitors' and the football player's claims of experience at face value, simply collecting and cataloguing them, or whether we are interested in how they could come to experience and understand themselves, and their relations to others, in just this way. If the former, then we'll go on assuming either that something in the exhibit captures the essence of what it must have been like to be a victimized Jew in late 1930s and early 1940s Germany or that something on the football field captures the essence of the brutal ancient coliseum. But it seems that we have good reason for *not* doing this—after all, as scholars, we know that even if such originals ever did exist, they are both long lost to history; we therefore have no standard against which to compare these people's claims, preventing us from ever knowing how accurate they really are. It is something akin to the troubles of the earlier example, of "You know what I mean?" followed by an agreeable head nod—such action effectively bypasses ever really testing just what the meaning is.

So, just as Wittgenstein suggested, the head nodding, the museum visitors writing in the book, and the college football player likening himself to an ancient fighter, might not actually be about the supposed one-to-one correspondence between the claim and the thing that it is said to represent. If so, then perhaps Wesley's report of his having experienced a strangely warmed heart had little to do with what he might have thought he felt and what he might have thought it meant. Perhaps the British historian of the English working class, E. P. Thompson (1924–93), in his groundbreaking book from 1963, *The Making of the English Working Class* (1980), was onto something in thinking that the early appeal of Wesley's Methodism was to be found in England's dire social context at that time—for example, the terrible living and working conditions of the Industrial Revolution, which was then beginning to transform a previously dispersed, rural, agriculturally based economy to a condensed metropolitan manufacturing economy. Perhaps this was the social context—much as Wesley's "continual sorrow and heaviness of heart," as he phrased it in his journal, provided psychological context for his own experience—that allowed people at that time to come to experience themselves *as* sinners, *as* needing trust, assurance, and salvation from torment and death. Perhaps this is what prompted them to attend

Wesley's highly popular and emotionally ecstatic tent meetings in which their emotional lives, individual value, and group solidarity were expressed and wildly celebrated by means of what Thompson, provocatively applying Karl Marx's (1818–83) well-known critique of religion as an "opiate of the masses," describes as "a ritualized form of psychic masturbation" (Thompson 1980, 405).

So, having begun with Wesley's disclosure, we close with a scholar's analysis of the social, political, and economic conditions that might allow one to feel a heart's strange warming. If readers have stuck with me so far and are now able to entertain experience as the seemingly private residue of an all too public thing—something that has a history and which can be understood to be a product of a prior calculus (whether it be linguistic or socio-political)—then we have come some distance; and it is now time to turn the argument over to those whose work has been collected in this volume. Ending this Introduction with Wesley and Thompson is therefore a good place to let these other writers begin, for there may be no more compelling example of just how different scholarship on experiential claims may be when compared to the claims themselves, indicating that, despite the apparent sincerity of the people making claims about their feelings, sentiments, dispositions, faith, and even beliefs, something other than what they think may be going on. Determining just what that "something else" is I leave to the following authors.

PART I

THE BACKGROUND OF EXPERIENCE

2

RAYMOND WILLIAMS

"Experience," from *Keywords: A Vocabulary of Culture and Society*

Raymond Williams (1921–88) was a Welsh scholar, novelist, and media/culture critic who, among his many accomplishments, is recognized as one of the earliest scholars of the field of Culture Studies. Williams pioneered the notion that culture is a fundamentally ordinary phenomenon: a series of complex, yet completely commonplace, ideological struggles that permeate the whole of society. In making this statement he intended both to rescue the term from its relegation to an elitist realm of arts and literature focused solely on aesthetics, and to simultaneously demonstrate how these very ordinary struggles are also at the center of such arts, literature, and aesthetics.

Williams was born in Wales, the son of a railway worker. Trained at Cambridge, he interrupted his education, including his extracurricular involvement in the student-led branch of the Communist party, for military service in the British Army during World War II. After his return to Cambridge, he completed a degree in English and worked for several years in the field of adult education. In 1973 Williams was named Visiting Professor of Political Science at Stanford University, and after this held a post as Professor of Drama at Cambridge for close to a decade.

In his professional life Williams is noteworthy for having been a professor of drama who was also a playwright and a media critic who, through his influential work in television, also participated in the creation of the medium. His humble beginnings proved greatly influential in his many writings, from his fiction works concerned with agrarian surroundings and working-class themes, to his cultural critiques that pushed past traditional media theory, asking how economic and political forces transformed the production, transmission, and reception of drama and television.

But perhaps his greatest contribution to the study of culture is his understanding of the material heart of cultural development. A socialist through and through, Williams' theory of cultural materialism is, in part, an elaboration of Marx's historical materialism. Simply put, Marx argued that the economic realm—fundamentally, how people labor to survive and the conditions under which this labor is exerted—is the key element that determines the shape of society. The larger ideological realm (including arenas like politics, law, morality, and religion), or "superstructure," is thus anchored and shaped by economic and material concerns. Hence all human relationships and beliefs are, to Marx, epiphenomena, or the secondary result, of a primary economic reality. It is worth noting, however, that in the last few decades some scholars—including Williams—have argued that this "vulgar Marxism" is only one side of Marx's view of culture, although a popular one. These scholars have argued that this overly simplistic view of economics and culture is to some extent warranted by some of Marx's claims, but that he also has more sophisticated things to say on the matter.

Williams disagreed with the vulgar Marxist notion that culture is epiphenomenal, seeing it instead as an inescapable, all-encompassing system of ideological struggle equally capable of influencing the economic, material realm. Nevertheless, Williams fully embraced the proposition that material factors directly affect and shape the rise of cultural phenomena. These sorts of inquiries were influential in what is perhaps one of his best known works, *Culture and Society, 1780–1950* (1958). In this critical history of the development of the concept of culture in British literature, Williams demonstrates how the term "culture" came to have multiple meanings as a result of the dual influences of democracy and industrialization in England. A prolific writer, Williams published many books or book-length volumes across his lifetime. In addition to *Culture and Society, 1780–1950*, several other works are noteworthy for their description of his model of cultural materialism, and the intersections between culture and literature more broadly. A sampling includes *The Long Revolution* (1961), *The Country and the City* (1973), *Keywords: A Vocabulary of Culture and Society* (1976), and *Marxism and Literature* (1977).

The following essay is excerpted from *Keywords*. Meant as something like an appendix to *Culture and Society, 1780–1950*, *Keywords* is also etymologically focused; that is, it delves into the cultural and historical forces that create language. This essay, simply entitled "Experience," offers a look at the factors leading to the creation of the term since the eighteenth century, arguing that there have been two primary meanings attached to the word "experience," which Williams calls "experience past" (as in, "I have prior experience teaching courses on the New Testament") and "experience present" (as in, "I am experiencing warmth from the sun on my face"). It is only the latter, he concludes, that is linked to the talk of "immediacy" and "authenticity" we see in discourses on "religious experience." In setting up this distinction he provides the reader with an important framework for understanding the very central methodological concerns and questions that define all human-based fields of study, and provides a historical basis for the inquiry that defines this present volume.

"EXPERIENCE," FROM *KEYWORDS*

The old association between experience and experiment can seem, in some of the most important modern uses, merely obsolete....The problem now is to consider the relations between two main senses [of experiences] which have been important since the late eighteenth century. These can be summarized as (i) knowledge gathered from past events, whether by conscious observation or by consideration and reflection; and (ii) a particular kind of consciousness, which can in some contexts be distinguished from "reason" or "knowledge." We can give a famous and influential example of each sense.

[Edmund] Burke, in the *Reflections on the Revolution in France* (1790), wrote:

If I might venture to appeal to what is so much out of fashion in Paris, I mean to experience...

This is a conservative argument against "rash" political innovation, stressing the need for "slow but well-sustained progress," taking each step as it comes and watching its effect. We can see how this developed from the sense of experiment and observation, but what is new is the confident generalization of the "lessons of experience": particular conclusions as well as particular methods. Someone in Paris might have replied that the Revolution itself was an "experience," in the sense of putting a new kind of politics to trial and observation, but for all those older implications of the word it seems certain that this would have been overborne, at least in English, by the riper and more gathered sense, then and now, of "lessons" as against "innovations" or "experiments."

That is experience past. We can see experience present in T. S. Eliot ("Metaphysical Poets," 1921):

a thought to Donne was an experience, it modified his sensibility.

What is implicit here is a distinction between kinds of consciousness; to some people, it seems, a thought would *not* be an experience, but a (lesser) act of reasoning or opinion. Experience, in this major tendency, is then the fullest, most open, most active kind of consciousness, and it includes feeling as well as thought. This sense has been very active in aesthetic discussion, following an earlier religious sense, and it can come to be contrasted, over a wide area, with the kinds of consciousness involved in reasoning and conscious experiment.

It is evident that the grounds for reliance on experience past ("lessons") and experience present (full and active "awareness") are radically different, yet there is nevertheless a link between them, in some of the kinds of action and consciousness which they both oppose. This does not have to be the case, but the two distinct senses, from the late eighteenth century, have in practice moved together, within a common historical situation.

It is very difficult, in the complexity of the emergence of these senses from the always latent significances in much earlier uses, to mark definite phases. The general usefulness of experience past is so widely recognized that it is difficult to know who would want to challenge it while it remains a neutral sense, permitting radically different conclusions to be drawn from diversely gathered and interpreted observations. But it is of course just this which the rhetorical use against experiment or innovation prevents. It is interesting that [William] Blake, at almost the same time as Burke, used experience in a much more problematic way: less bland, less confident; indeed a troubled contrast with innocence. So far from being an available and positive set of recommendations, it was bought with the price of all that a man hath ("Four Zoas," II). No specific interpretation of experience can in practice be assumed to be directive; it is quite possible from experience to see a need for experiment or innovation.

This might be easier to agree with than the problem of experience present. It is clear that this involves an appeal to the whole consciousness, the whole being, as against reliance on more specialized or more limited states or faculties. As such it is part of that general movement which underlies the development of [the category of] culture and its directly associated terms. The strength of this appeal to wholeness, against forms of thought which would exclude certain kinds of consciousness, as merely "personal," "subjective," or "emotional," is evident. Yet within the form of appeal … the stress on wholeness can become a form of exclusion of other nominated partialities. The recent history of this shift is in aesthetics (understandably so, when we recall the development of aesthetics itself), but the decisive phase was probably in a certain form of religion, and especially Methodism.[1]

The sense develops from experience as "being consciously the subject of a state or condition" (Murray 1933, 4) and especially from the application of this to an "inner," "personal," religious experience. While this was available within many religious forms, it became especially important within Protestantism, and was increasingly relied on in later and more radical Protestant movements. Thus in Methodism there were experience-meetings, classes "held for the recital of religious experiences." A description of 1857 records that there was praying, and exhorting, and telling experiences, and singing … sentimental hymns. This is then a notion of subjective witness, offered to be shared. What is important about it, for a later more general sense, is that such experiences are offered not only as truths, but as the most authentic kind of truths. Within theology, this claim has been the matter of an immense argument. The caution of Jonathan Edwards—"those experiences which are agreeable to the word of God are right"[2]—is among the more moderate reactions. It is clear that in the twentieth century both the claim and the doubts and objections have moved into a much wider field. At one extreme experience (present) is offered as the necessary (immediate and authentic) ground for all (subsequent) reasoning and analysis. At the other extreme, experience (once the present participle not of "feeling" but of "trying" or "testing" something) is seen as the product of social conditions or of systems of belief or of fundamental systems of perception, and thus not as material for truths but as evidence of conditions or systems which by definition it cannot itself explain.

This remains a fundamental controversy, and it is not, fortunately, limited to its extreme positions. But much of the controversy is confused, from the beginning, by the complex and often alternative senses of experience itself. Experience past already includes, at its most serious, those processes of consideration, reflection, and analysis which the most

---

1. [Ed. note] Methodism was originally a nickname given to a British Protestant Christian revival movement that arose from the Church of England in the early to mid-eighteenth century. Along with others, the brothers John (1703–91) and Charles (1707–88) Wesley are considered its principle founders. The movement, which today can be understood as one of the originators of modern evangelicalism found throughout the world, focused on preaching to working-class people and emphasized doing good works, education, social reform, as well as nurturing one's faith, expressed early on in the form of ecstatic camp meetings.

2. [Ed. note] Jonathan Edwards (1703–58) was the best known US theologian of the mid-eighteenth century; President of Princeton University, he was an influential minister and missionary in the early US colonies who is known today for his sermons—including the infamous "Sinners in the Hands of an Angry God"—and the role he played in a US religious revival movement in the mid-eighteenth century known as the Great Awakening.

extreme use of experience present—an unquestionable authenticity and immediacy—excludes. Similarly, the reduction of experience to material always produced from elsewhere depends on an exclusion of kinds of consideration, reflection, and analysis which are not of a consciously separated systematic type. It is then not that such kinds should not be tested, but that in the deepest sense of experience all kinds of evidence and its consideration should be tried.

3

ROBERT DESJARLAIS

"Rethinking Experience," from *Shelter Blues: Sanity and Selfhood Among the Homeless*

Robert Desjarlais is a professor of anthropology at Sarah Lawrence College, specializing in how cultures construct both experience and subjectivity, how language operates in complex societies, and social understandings of illness and healing. His ethnographic fieldwork in places as disparate as Nepal and Boston have led to the publication of several studies dealing with these interests, which include *Body and Emotion: The Aesthetics of Illness and Healing in the Nepal Himalayas* (1992); *Shelter Blues: Sanity and Selfhood Among the Homeless* (1997); and *Sensory Biographies: Lives and Deaths Among Nepal's Yolmo Buddhists* (2003).

This excerpt from *Shelter Blues* considers how one comes to analyze and explain experience, an issue of particular importance to Desjarlais as he studied the lives of forty homeless (and often also mentally ill) individuals living in Boston. Desjarlais presents the reader with a complex, interwoven look at how homelessness and mental illness are understood in American society, concluding that these experiences are not the simple result of one homeless person's isolated, interior state, but are, instead, determined and formed by an intricate web of cultural images of illness and personhood, as well as political and economic forces.

Thus while he is interested in the face value of the phenomenon of homelessness and mental illness, Desjarlais' investigation does not, out of necessity, end there. In this aptly entitled essay, "Rethinking Experience," Desjarlais offers background on the different theoretical models that have been used to approach the category of experience. By assuming that human experience is constructed—that it is "a process built sharply out of cultural, historical, political, and pragmatic forces"—Desjarlais paves the way to present the experiential world of the homeless as one that is significantly formed and manufactured by society. In this sense, he begins to shape an argument on the significance of the context of experience, a topic treated at greater length in later essays within this volume.

Desjarlais accomplishes this, in great part, by tracing how the term "experience" has been both constructed and understood, much like the Raymond Williams essay before this. Both scholars are vitally concerned with showing how the supposed "authenticity" of experience stems from very particular ways of understanding the human individual, notions that, although perhaps seemingly obvious to people today, are ideas that have a relatively recent and political history. As Desjarlais notes, this vantage point has been harshly critiqued by other scholars who claim that arguing for or even highlighting the constructed elements of experience constitutes a form of "violence" against the people one studies, inasmuch as it undercuts a sense of unique human agency, authenticity, and even "truth." Whether this latter perspective is a valid rationale is, of course, the crux of what Desjarlais, Williams, and other scholars in this volume discuss.

Addressing the topic of the social construction of experience is a critical discussion within all disciplines that study human behavior. If social constructivists are united in their assumption that various human factors create social realities, Desjarlais' investigation, although not explicitly about religion, nevertheless unearths some interesting methodological questions for the student of religion. For instance, if all humanistic fields struggle with gauging and even knowing what experience is, how and what experiences are valuable for study, and whether experiences are even accessible to those not having them, is there anything unique about "religious" experience? Does it bear any truly distinguishing traits?

In this essay Desjarlais sets up a distinction between epistemic concerns (how do we know about experience?) and ontic concerns (what is experience?). He argues that those who appeal to experience as authentic inadequately separate the epistemic from the ontic: they take for granted that experience is ontologically fundamental (it simply exists prior to discourse about experience) and that subjects can simply and directly know it as such. By contrast, Desjarlais raises the possibility that how we know experience constitutes experience in the first place—perhaps the epistemic (how we know experience) is prior to the ontic (what experience is). In addition, he goes on to argue that the "depth" and "multilayered complexity" of experience for modern Westerners is a product of modern Western culture, and is not readily found in other cultures. He concludes by pointing out that despite the "multilayered complexity" of experience, it is usually referred to as having a "unity"—and Desjarlais suggests that both the "depth" and "unity" may in fact be a product of the *narration* of experience.

"RETHINKING EXPERIENCE," FROM *SHELTER BLUES*

Explorations of "experience" are never straightforward ... for once we begin to clarify its nature, we run into a host of problems. The intimate, experiential side of homelessness or any other abjection is just as mythic and just as cultural as the public, horrific side. There are also questions of how one goes about knowing what other people experience and the rhetorical uses to which expressions of experience are put. In turn, any attempt to build effective theories of experience is complicated by the fact that people's lives can entail very different ways of being. The category of experience is riddled with cultural assumptions, political tensions, pragmatic moves, rhetorical pitches, and subjective vicissitudes.

Rather than shy away from such riddles, however, I want to address them as directly as a zigzagging ethnography will permit. In so doing I want to sketch a way of thinking about social life that treats the category of experience not as a universal, natural, and supremely authentic entity—as many take it to be—but as a process built sharply out of cultural, historical, political, and pragmatic forces. Experience, often held to be the most fundamental aspect of being human, is here taken to be one form of life among many.

Behind this approach lie two fundamental concerns found in any study of "human experience." The first centers on the epistemic status of experience: How do we know what we know about experience, and what kind of knowledge does experience entail? The second relates to the ontic status of experience, or what experience, as an act, process, or entity, is assumed to be.

The first concern often boils down, in anthropology at least, to the idea that the native "experiences" to which ethnographers refer are supremely authentic ones—or at least more authentic and truthful than social relations, cultural discourses, or theoretical models. While references to the relation between experience and language, culture, or beliefs pepper many anthropological writings, few ethnographers address experience in more than abstract terms. When these writers try to hammer out the contours of experience, the wrinkles tend to take several characteristic forms. Some anthropologists draw on the concept of experience to provide the "missing term," as the historian E. P. Thompson wrote, through which "structure is transmuted into process, and the subject re-enters into history" (Thompson 1978, 170). Some rely on it because it appears relatively free of the baggage that concepts like "self" or "mind" or "affect" carry (see Kleinman and Kleinman 1995, for instance). Some anthropologists are interested in the cultural pattern-ing of sensory experience, using experience as a correlative of the felt and the sensorial (see Stoller 1989; Howes 1991). Others advocate phenomenological or "experience-near" approaches that try to cut through cultural discourses to touch upon "lived" experience (see Jackson 1989; Wikan 1991). Still others try to get at the moral aspects of everyday life, with experience involving an intersubjective medium of daily engagements (Kleinman and Kleinman 1995).

While these orientations call for diverse theories and findings, all stem from Romantic sensibilities toward the incongruous and nearly unfathomable aspects of everyday life. They follow from Franz Boas's distinction between physical and historical-cosmographic methods, whereby "physicists" sought to "bring the confusion of forms and species into a system," and "cosmographers"—considering the phenomenon itself "without regard to its place in a system"—sought to "penetrate into its secrets until every feature is plain and clear" (Boas 1940, 644–5; see Stocking 1989). Boas, [Edward] Sapir, and [Clifford] Geertz have advocated the latter, ideographic approach, as have many American anthropologists. Yet, as the philosopher Charles Taylor notes, experientialist approaches also echo a "wide-spread aspiration" in post-Romantic thought "to retrieve experience from the deadening, routinized, conventional forms of instrumental civilization" (Taylor 1989, 469; see also Gadamer 1975, 63). Here, experience is held to be a truer aspect of life, rich enough to defy conceptual models. The sentiment accompanying this notion has passed from [Friedrich] Schiller to [Wilhelm] Dilthey to contemporary anthropologists, who claim that theo-retical and medical models fail to account for the intensely felt and personal dimensions of human life and suffering (see, for example, Bruner 1986; Jackson 1989; Wikan 1991; DelVecchio Good et al., 1992; and Kleinman and Kleinman 1995).

For several scholars, lived experience is "the primary reality": "What comes first is experience" (as phrased by Bruner 1986, 4–5). Those who study "experiential truths" thus find they are investigating the most authentic, and most human, of anthropological categories (as phrased by Jackson 1989, 133). In contrast, those anthropologists who do injustice to a society's plane of felt experience stand accused of "doing violence to the authenticity of the flow of lived experience" (Kleinman and Kleinman 1995, 117). Much of the impetus for "an anthropology of experience," as some call it, lies in the attempt to avoid such violence. Michael Jackson, for instance, does not want to "risk dissolving the lived *experience* of the subject into the anonymous field of discourses" (Jackson 1989, 1). The emphasis is on felt realities rather than cultural categories, the near rather than the distant, and the sensate more than the semantic. The sensate implies immediacy, which in turn is said to carry authenticity.[1]

In the end, however, this logic is haunted by a problematic collapse of ontology and epistemology,[2] of being and knowing, in which the supposed realities of experience are given the status of facts by the statements of anthropologists. The problem with taking experience as a uniquely authentic domain of life—as the first and last court of appeal—is that we risk losing the opportunity to question both the social production of that domain and the practices that define its use (after all, questioning cultural assumptions and social constructions is basic to anthropology). Connotations of primacy and authenticity lend legitimacy to the anthropologist's craft, but they can simultaneously limit inquiries to descriptions of the terrain of experience when what we need are critical reflections on how the terrain comes about (see Williams 1979, 164–70; Scott 1991). Asking about experience can tell you about some things, such as how the everyday takes form, just as asking about labor relations or clan lineages can tell you about other things. None of these questions implies any supreme authenticity, merely fields of inquiry. I take the concerns, doings, and lifeworlds of shelter residents as one such field of inquiry.

---

1. In works of this kind, experience is sometimes encountered as a verb—one can be led "to experience" something (Wikan 1991, 295)—but is most often used as a noun, particularly as something one "has" (Bruner 1986, 5). The focus is on experience as a commodity-like entity because many scholars are interested in experience as primary data. The partiality has a history. For William James (1912, 10), experience was a "double-barred" word that included both *what* men did and suffered and *how* men acted and were acted upon. Working in the wake of James, philosophers like John Dewey (1926) and Michael Oakshott stressed the integral nature of this duality, but at a certain expense. Writing in 1933, Oakshott finds that "'Experience' stands for the concrete whole which analysis divides into 'experiencing' and 'what is experienced.' ... [T]he character of what is experienced is, in the strictest sense, correlative to the manner in which it is experienced" (1985, 9). Given this, he deduces that "it would, then, be possible to build up one's views of the character of experience either from the side of experiencing, or from the side of what is experienced; and it would be superfluous to do both, for whatever is true of the one side will be true of the other." One consequence of this outlook is that one can remain content with studying "what is experienced" without questioning how "experiencing" comes about. The word can thus soon become one of James's "single-barred words," like "thing" or "thought," as it generally has been in American anthropology. Indeed, the tendency to reify experience might itself be rooted in Anglo-Saxon language and culture: Norwegian anthropologist Unni Wikan tells me that her native languages hold no ready equivalents for the English noun "experience."

2. [Ed. note] Ontology and epistemology name two branches of philosophy; the former is concerned to investigate theories of being and ultimate reality, whereas the latter is interested in investigating theories of knowledge, as in how one comes to have knowledge about the world. Ontology inquires about the nature of the world, and epistemology inquires about how we can know anything about the world.

Other anthropologists have raised similar issues, such that perspectives on the study of experience generally divide anthropologists into two camps. There are those who advocate an anthropology of experience that investigates, chiefly through phenomenological means,[3] domains of life—pain, bodies, emotions—which one can only poorly apprehend through cultural analysis; and there are others who find that such an anthropology is both epistemologically unfounded, since one can never really know the felt immediacies of another person or society, and irrelevant to more important social and political concerns. Nevertheless, the word is of such value that even scholars critical of experiential approaches acknowledge that without it or something like it "cultural analyses seem to float several feet above their human ground," as Clifford Geertz puts it (1986, 374; see also Scott 1991). Experience, it seems, is a crucial element of contemporary academic thought in the United States. To try to write about humans without reference to experience is like trying to think the unthinkable.

This raises concerns about the ontic status of experience, for despite the apparent necessity of experience, as something that can and must be thought, its universality remains in question. We must ask if the act of experiencing is as essential or as commonplace as many take it to be. In listening to the debates noted above, for instance, one gets the sense that everyone knows what is meant by experience. But the word is rarely defined, and when it is defined, it typically involves a generic "we" (as in "We experience..."). That the category of experience goes undefined or is couched in universalist terms suggests that it is taken as a fundamental and unchanging constant in human life. The situation is similar to the one [Martin] Heidegger faced in [his book] *Being and Time*. Experience, like Being, is seen as one of the most universal and emptiest of concepts. It requires no definition, "for everyone uses it constantly and already understands what he [sic] means by it," and it "has taken on a clarity and self-evidence that if anyone continues to ask about it he is charged with an error of method" (Heidegger 1962, 2).

In contrast to Heidegger, however, I want to argue that experience is not a primordial existential given but rather a historically and culturally constituted process predicated on certain ways of being in the world. Experience is the result of specific cultural articulations of selfhood (namely, a sense of self as possessing depth, interiority, unity, stability, and the capacity for transcendence) as well as certain social and technological conditions that foster and legitimate that sense of self.

The etymology of "experience" suggests how the concept has evolved in European thought. The modern English word "experiment" apparently best preserves the original meaning of "experience," although the latter also meant at first "putting to the test."[4] From

---

3. [Ed. note] Phenomenology is a branch of philosophy that addresses that which presents itself to the human senses, as opposed to speculations on the ultimate truth or reality of the phenomenon in question. Adapted by scholars of religion in the early twentieth century, the phenomenology of religion is a field in which descriptive and comparative work is undertaken while the ultimate truth of the object of study (such as someone's claim to have seen the Virgin Mary) is, as a phenomenologist might say, "bracketed" and set aside.

4. Ayto (1990) reports that "experience," like "experiment" and "expert," comes from the Latin *experiri*, a compound verb, formed from the prefix *ex-* [meaning] "out" and a prehistoric base *per-* denoting

this came an understanding of experience as "actually observed phenomena in order to gain knowledge of them," which in turn led to the more subjective "condition of having undergone or been affected by a particular event" (Ayto 2001, 213).[5] The modern subjectivist connotations of experience appear to be a recent innovation; the idea that to experience is to feel, suffer, or undergo is first recorded in 1588 (Barnhart 1988, 357). The implied interiority parallels the evolution of Western concepts of the self, particularly in terms of the "language of inwardness" that has increasingly come to characterize human agency in the West since [Saint] Augustine (Taylor 1989). Similar to the trajectory of the dominant form of selfhood in the West, which is widely believed to have been initially marked by exterior relationships to one's environment and later to have been moved toward a moral, reflexive agent, experience evolved from a verb denoting an external engagement with or "testing" of one's surroundings to a template marking a person's subjective awareness of that engagement.

Through time that awareness has grown increasingly introspective. In 1938 [Lucien] Lévy-Bruhl observed that:

> Our current notion of experience bears the mark of certain mental habits that are peculiar to the civilizations of the West. Since classical antiquity it has been elaborated over the centuries by generations of philosophers, psychologists, logicians, and scientists.... The essential role of experience, as it has been described and analyzed by this tradition, from Plato and his predecessors down to [Immanuel] Kant and his successors, is to inform the sentient and thinking subject of the properties of creatures and objects with which it places him in relation, to make him perceive movements, shocks, sounds, colors, forms, odors, etc., and to permit the human mind, which reflects on these data and on their conditions, to construct a representation of the world. The general notion of experience that has been thus developed is above all "cognitive." (Lévy-Bruhl 1938, 8–9)

While twentieth-century musings have identified affective dimensions in experience, experience is now generally held to be a subjective, reflexive process that rests securely on a person's cognitive abilities to reflect on and make introspective sense of his or her engagement with the world. As Lévy-Bruhl, [Alfred Irving] Hallowell, [R. Godfrey] Lienhardt, and other anthropologists have pointed out, however, human functioning need not depend on such reflective assessments; rather, it can assume a range of non-introspective forms (see Lévy-Bruhl 1938; Leenhardt 1979; Hallowell 1955; Lienhardt 1961; Crapanzano 1977; Kleinman and Kleinman 1995). Experience involves only one, rather inward-looking arrangement of human action among many.

The stress on interiority ties into the affirmation of ordinary life that has earmarked humanistic thought and literature and relates to the Romantic sensibility that the most

---

"attempt, trial" that meant "to try, test." Turner (1982, 17) notes that *per-* also relates to the Latin *periculum*, [meaning] "peril, trial, danger," through the suffixed extended form *peri-tlo*.

5. [Ed. note] Though the author cites Ayto 1990, see also Ayto 2001.

authentic truths lie in our selves (Taylor 1989). A focus on the truths of personal revelations relates closely to modern religious concerns, particularly the Pietist emphasis on religious devotion,[6] with personal experience, as "a state of mind or feeling" (as the *Oxford English Dictionary* defines it in this context), forming an integral part of the inner religious life. The inner states cultivated through such devotion reveal truths worth talking about. Raymond Williams notes, for instance, that nineteenth-century Methodists held "experience-meetings," or classes "for the recital of religious experiences" (Williams 1983, 128). Today as well, experience is rooted largely in individual agency. A person "has," "learns from," or "discloses" an experience. Privacy, individuality, and reflexive interiority are intrinsic to experience; no one else can experience my toothache, although someone might empathize with my suffering. Experience thus readily equates with a person's "inner life" or "consciousness" and is often considered synonymous with "subjectivity" (Geertz 1986, 373).[7]

The idea of interiority encourages some to try to understand the "very marrow" or "essence" of experience and leads others to suggest that "experience is sensual and affective to the core and exceeds objectification in symbolic forms" (as Good puts it [1993, 139]; [Ed. Note: Desjarlais (1992) is responsible for the "marrow" image]). The excessiveness of experience points to a second distinguishing feature: it possesses hermeneutical depth.[8] The sense of depth, like that of interiority, ties into forms of meaning and selfhood common to the modern West. Erich Auerbach identifies the roots of some of these forms in the opening chapter of his magisterial *Mimesis*, wherein he details how the narrative form of the Greek Homeric poems differs from that of the Judaic biblical writings of the Old Testament (Auerbach 1953, 3–23). Auerbach finds that Homer narrates the travels of Odysseus in such a way that all phenomena are represented as world-immanent. They are given objective, fully externalized form, fixed in a time and place, visible and palpable in all their parts, connected together in a perceptual foreground, without lacunae or "unplumbed depths," and with both people and things clearly depicted and brightly and uniformly illuminated. The biblical narratives, in contrast, convey only so much of the phenomena as is absolutely indispensable for the purpose of unfolding the story; all else is left as an obscure, transcendent background. Scripture conveys only the decisive points, leaving it to the imagination to generate connections. Here time and space, though mentioned, go undefined and call for interpretation, and the whole "remains mysterious and fraught with tension." Whereas the thoughts and feelings of the timeless characters

---

6. [Ed. note] Pietism is the name given to a seventeenth- and eighteenth-century European religious movement associated with the Moravian Church—a Protestant denomination that originated in the mid-fifteenth century in ancient Bohemia and Moravia (which is today part of the Czech Republic) that emphasized the role of piety, understood as one's inner experience of the Gospel's saving power, over the role played by dogma, creed, and the so-called trappings of ritual and institution.

7. The private aspects of experience make some, like Geertz, wary of experiential approaches in anthropology. Those critical of such approaches tend to question the legitimacy of the research more than the universality and relevance of the concept. Yet, in finding that experience denotes a subjective realm that can only be poorly comprehended, they uphold the view that experience is interior, private, and ubiquitous.

8. [Ed. note] Hermeneutics is a field of study, developed largely in the field of biblical scholarship, concerned with determining the meaning of a text as well as with developing theories of interpretation.

in Homer (who age or change little in their lives) are completely represented, those of the biblical characters remain sketchy. In sum, the individual characters of the Old Testament are more complex than the Homeric personages; they possess various layers of conscious-ness, find themselves in problematic psychological situations, and develop through crises over time.

Auerbach keeps to the study of literary history, yet there are strong affinities with more recently discovered domains. Homer's representations of reality and personhood, for instance, recall recent discussions of forms of language and selfhood in non-Western societies, such as Samoa, and suggest how human beings need not depend on profound interiors or complex psychological dramas (see Shore 1982; Ochs 1988; Duranti 1994). In turn, features of the biblical world of form—such as the opaque presence of unplumbed heights and depths, the multiplicity of meanings, the need for interpretation, and the idea of personal transformation and historical becoming—continue to resound, in attenuated form, in many Euro-American traditions (such as modernist novels, films, psychoanalytic thought, and hermeneutics, not to mention everyday life). Ideas of height and depth, of multilayered complexity, of a surplus of meanings calling for steady interpretation, and of an individual who develops through time lie at the heart of ideas of personal experience in the modern West.

The development of experiential depths has been a progressive one. According to Charles Taylor, while the writings of Augustine, [René] Descartes, and Montaigne brought successively stronger declarations of human "inwardness," only with the expressivist yearnings of [William] Wordsworth, [Friedrich] Hölderlin, and others to discover and articulate our inner nature does this interiority come to possess significant, unfathomable depth—"a domain," that is, "which reaches farther than we can ever articulate, which still stretches our furthest point of clear expression" (Taylor 1989, 289). In modernist times, the grounds of experience, rather than those of selfhood, have possessed the richest depths because experience is often seen as the foundation of human agency (Taylor 1989, 465).[9] The import of experience is inexhaustible because experience, like a text or a work of art, carries a wealth of meanings that can never be conclusively interpreted (for instance, see Ricoeur 1970).

The hermeneutical depths of experience distinguish it from the subject matter of tradi-tional cultural analysis. This kind of experience eludes social science analysis and resists easy symbolization. The idea of an abundant, semiotically rich plane of being entails the view that the only way to study experience fruitfully is to attend to the perimeters of expressions, stories, and social formations in which it is cloaked (see DelVecchio Good et al. 1992, 200; Jackson 1989; Bruner 1986). To say that "thick description"[10] is the best

---

9. As Gadamer (1975, 67) describes the philosophy of Dilthey and [Edmund] Husserl, "essential to an experi-ence [German, *erlebnis*] is that it cannot be exhausted in what can be said of it or grasped as its meaning.... What we call an *erlebnis* in this emphatic sense thus means something unforgettable and irreplaceable, something whose meaning cannot be exhausted by conceptual determination."

10. [Ed. note] Thick description is a term traced to the anthropologist Clifford Geertz; he used it to name descriptions of cultural acts that took into account the "deep," interconnected nature of symbols along with the insider knowledge and expertise required to understand a symbol's actual meaning.

method of analysis here is not to denigrate the available methods but simply to point out the kind of phenomena involved: experience is too complex, too subtle, and too private to be understood through anything but phenomenological ascertainments. Even then, "It's all a matter of scratching surfaces," as Clifford Geertz puts it (1986, 373). Talk of surfaces, cores, and bone marrow suggests a shadow play of interiors and exteriors: we cannot penetrate the vessels of experience. The body is often held to be one such container, with the skin serving as an "envelope" within which, as William Faulkner writes, "the sum of experience" resides (1986, 54).

Despite the immediacy, richness, and contingency that characterize lived experience, experience works on a principle of unity. John Dewey talks about the "inclusive integrity" of experience, while Michael Oakshott ponders its "concrete totality" (Dewey 1926; Oakshott 1985). William James, Dilthey, Husserl, [Maurice] Merleau-Ponty, and others agree that the sum of experience is greater than its parts. [James] Joyce's [character,] Leopold Bloom, [Sigmund] Freud's [patient who dreamt of wolves, known simply as] Wolfman, and [Marcel] Proust's remembrances [from his famous work which chronicled his life in detail, *Remembrance of Things Past*] exhibit and exemplify the integrality of experience; memories, dreams, reflections, anticipations, and sensations combine into a whole in the sudden flash of an epiphany. The appeal to wholeness apparently relates, for many, to a desire to develop a concept that might safely encompass the many features of human agency, such as "thought," "feeling," "perception," "reflection," and "sensation."

Experience builds toward something more than a transient, episodic succession of events. The intransience of experience ties into the fact that it has a lasting and memorable effect on the person who undergoes it. "To undergo an experience with something," Heidegger writes, "—be it a thing, a person, or a god—means that this something befalls us, strikes us, comes over us, overwhelms and transforms us" (Heidegger 1971, 57). By undergoing an experience a person picks up something new: "Experience means *eundo assequi*, to obtain something along the way, to attain something by going on a way" (66). Experience transforms: it "does not leave him who has it unchanged," or so says Gadamer in his specification of a "genuine experience" (German, *erfahrung*) (1975, 100). To have an experience or to learn by experience suggests an education that can accrue in certain skills or knowledge, though this education hinges on a flux of subjective reflections that other kinds of learning (such as operant conditioning) do not. The *Oxford English Dictionary* notes that, since the sixteenth century, experience has involved "knowledge resulting from actual observation or from what one has undergone." Experience is thus the fodder for the kind of psychological developments or becomings that have characterized ideas of personhood in Europe since the Old Testament at least.

"To experience is to go along a way. The way leads through a landscape," writes Heidegger, drawing on the fact that *erfahrung* comes from the Old High German *infaran*, which means to travel, traverse, pass through, reach, or arrive at (Heidegger 1971, 61; Needham [1972, 171] notes the etymology). The landscape is organized along both spatial and temporal lines. Experience, by definition, collects itself through the rhythmic pacings of time. As David Carr, who draws from Husserl, puts it, "Our experience is directed towards, and itself assumes, temporally extended forms in which future, present, and past mutually determine one another as parts of a whole" (1986, 30–31).

Narrative typically helps to forge the sense of temporal integration. The idea that experience accumulates in time through stories builds on musings on the relations between forms of life and narrative orderings of time. From Aristotle to Heidegger to [Paul] Ricoeur, the interpenetration of narrative and experience has grown stronger with the increased importance of literature in the lives of the educated. The present state of the art is that we can only grasp our lives through narrative, although one can and ought to question to what degree this apparently "inescapable" fact applies within as well as outside the modern West.[11]

Experience as a whole is subject to similar queries. In much the same way that the truth of sexuality grew out of an economy of discourses that took hold in seventeenth-century Europe (see Foucault 1978), so discourses of depth, interiority, and authenticity, sensibilities of holism and transcendence, and practices of reading, writing, and storytelling have helped to craft a mode of being known in the modern West as experience: that is, an inwardly reflexive, hermeneutically rich process that coheres through time by way of narrative.

---

11. Charles Taylor (1989, 47) holds that a narrative orientation to life is "inescapable." But since a narrative orientation entails a quite specific understanding of time and meaning, it might be safer to say that a *temporal* orientation is inescapable. See Becker 1979, Rosaldo 1986, and Good 1993 for three studies that systematically inquire into the forms of and conditions for narrativity in, respectively, Javanese, Ilongot, and Turkish societies.

PART II

THE AUTONOMY OF EXPERIENCE

4

WILLIAM JAMES

"Lecture 2: Circumscription of the Topic," from *The Varieties of Religious Experience:*
A Study in Human Nature

The quandaries of which the two previous essays speak come alive with this classic piece by William James (1842–1910), hailed as the father of American psychology, one of the three founders of American pragmatism (along with C. S. Peirce and John Dewey), and one of the country's best known philosophers. Born to affluence in a cosmopolitan, cultured family deeply concerned with both religious and cultural diversity and development, James and his siblings (including famed writers Henry James and Alice James) spent their childhood surrounded by the period's most celebrated thinkers, and were inundated with the finest educational and cultural opportunities available.

James was educated as a medical doctor at Harvard, and went on to spend the whole of his working career there as well, teaching medicine, psychology, and ultimately, philosophy. At a time when the field of psychology was in its early stages, James wrote what were then considered to be groundbreaking treatises on the workings of the human mind, and particularly, the psychological aspects of religion, mysticism, and pragmatism.

Pragmatism, a philosophical position somewhat synonymous with James, asserts that one should measure the validity of a belief in relation to its usefulness or ability to create a satisfactory outcome. Put another way, pragmatism asserts that what is true is linked to what works to create positive results in human experience. Religion was thus, to James, "true" inasmuch as it made life more tolerable and hopeful, and exhorted humans to better moral behavior. James's pragmatism was a natural outgrowth of his functionalist beliefs, which were characterized by the principle of a mind/body connection as well as the adaptive role of mental processes in human survival. His functionalist, pragmatic suppositions were enabled by what he called a "radical empiricism." Unlike more traditional notions of empiricism, which depended on observable, tangible data for scientific study, radical empiricism postulated that mental events are equally as valid as more concrete data in determining the nature of reality. Thus in asserting the scientific validity and essentially adaptive function of mental processes, James was able to construct a pragmatic model of religious belief that claimed empirical value, arguing that what was most irrational was to deny what he saw as an innate, human religious disposition.

A prolific writer, the full expression of this functionalist/pragmatist position is expressed throughout his well-known works, some of which include: *The Principles of Psychology* (1890),

The Will to Believe and Other Essays (1897), *The Varieties of Religious Experience* (1902), *Pragmatism* (1907), and the posthumous publication of *Essays in Radical Empiricism* (1912).

In this excerpt from his classic *The Varieties of Religious Experience*, James outlines his assertions on the nature and authenticity of religious experience. James foregrounds individual, subjective experience as the site of authenticity or "truth." He holds that much of what has been called "religion" is, in fact, nothing more than second-hand bureaucratic and tradition-laden social expressions that undercut and dull what James calls the "direct personal communion with the divine" that first characterized the birth of the movement, and more specifically, the charismatic insight of its founder. It is worth noting that James begins in a pragmatist fashion, simply offering what he believes to be a useful, stipulative definition of religion ("for the purpose of these lectures"), rather than identifying the "real thing" as such. However, he goes on to say that his definition picks out the "more fundamental" stuff, thus implying he has found the "real thing" and thereby explicitly violating the pragmatist approach with which he began.

In later portions of *The Varieties of Religious Experience*, James expands the idea of authentic religion with his famous distinction between the "once born" and the "twice born." The former include well-adjusted, happily religious people who have undergone little personal trauma and who generally have neither encountered nor internalized life's more negative experiences; alternately, the latter represent those deeply aware of the darker side of life, but who have come through this depressive period thanks to religious conversion. The twice born (who James also describes as "sick souls") are not only evidence of the adaptive function of religious belief, but to James, are psychologically more healthy since they have witnessed life from both perspectives.

Hence, for James, there is something particularly authentic about personal, individual religion in contrast to the more corporate manifestations or rituals that are often mistaken for it. In this sense, James grounds the authenticity of religious experience in an individual, internal, mental state.

"LECTURE 2: CIRCUMSCRIPTION OF THE TOPIC," FROM *THE VARIETIES OF RELIGIOUS EXPERIENCE*

Most books on the philosophy of religion try to begin with a precise definition of what its essence consists of. Some of these would-be definitions may possibly come before us in later portions of this course, and I shall not be pedantic enough to enumerate any of them to you now. Meanwhile the very fact that they are so many and so different from one another is enough to prove that the word "religion" cannot stand for any single principle or essence, but is rather a collective name. The theorizing mind tends always to the over-simplification of its materials. This is the root of all that absolutism and one-sided dogmatism by which both philosophy and religion have been infested. Let us not fall immediately into a one-sided view of our subject, but let us rather admit freely at the outset that we may very likely find no one essence, but many characters which may alternately be equally important in religion. If we should inquire for the essence of "government," for example, one man might tell us it was authority, another submission, another police, another an army, another an assembly, another a system of laws; yet all the while it would be true that no concrete government can exist without all these things, one of which is more important at one moment and others at another. The man who knows governments most completely is he who troubles himself least about a definition which shall give their essence. Enjoying an intimate acquaintance with all their particularities in turn, he would naturally regard an abstract conception in which these were unified as a thing more misleading than enlightening. And why may not religion be a conception equally complex?[1]

Consider also the "religious sentiment" which we see referred to in so many books, as if it were a single sort of mental entity.

In the psychologies and in the philosophies of religion, we find the authors attempting to specify just what entity it is. One man allies it to the feeling of dependence; one makes it a derivative from fear; others connect it with the sexual life; others still identify it with the feeling of the infinite; and so on. Such different ways of conceiving it ought of themselves to arouse doubt as to whether it possibly can be one specific thing; and the moment we are willing to treat the term "religious sentiment" as a collective name for the many sentiments which religious objects may arouse in alternation, we see that it probably contains nothing whatever of a psychologically specific nature. There is religious fear, religious love, religious awe, religious joy, and so forth. But religious love is only man's natural emotion of love directed to a religious object; religious fear is only the ordinary fear of commerce, so to speak, the common quaking of the human breast, in so far as the notion of divine retribution may arouse it; religious awe is the same organic thrill which we feel in a forest at twilight, or in a mountain gorge; only this time it comes over us at the thought of our supernatural relations; and similarly of all the various sentiments which may be called into play in the lives of religious persons. As concrete states of mind, made up of a feeling *plus* a specific sort of object, religious emotions of course are psychic entities distinguishable from other concrete emotions; but there is no ground for assuming a simple abstract "religious emotion" to exist as a distinct elementary mental affection by itself, present in every religious experience without exception.

As there thus seems to be no one elementary religious emotion, but only a common storehouse of emotions upon which religious objects may draw, so there might conceivably also prove to be no one specific and essential kind of religious object, and no one specific and essential kind of religious act.

The field of religion being as wide as this, it is manifestly impossible that I should pretend to cover it. My lectures must be limited to a fraction of the subject. And, although it would indeed be foolish to set up an abstract definition of religion's essence, and then proceed to defend that definition against all comers, yet this need not prevent me from

---

1. I can do no better here than refer my readers to the extended and admirable remarks on the futility of all these definitions of religion, in an article by Professor Leuba, published in the *Monist* for January, 1901, after my own text was written. [Ed. note: James is referring to James H. Leuba's often quoted essay which lists more than fifty different definitions of religion: "Introduction to a Psychological Study of Religion," *Monist* 9 (1901), 195–255.]

taking my own narrow view of what religion shall consist in *for the purpose of these lectures,* or, out of the many meanings of the word, from choosing the one meaning in which I wish to interest you particularly, and proclaiming arbitrarily that when I say "religion" I mean *that.* This, in fact, is what I must do, and I will now preliminarily seek to mark out the field I choose.

One way to mark it out easily is to say what aspects of the subject we leave out. At the outset we are struck by one great partition which divides the religious field. On the one side of it lies institutional, on the other personal religion. As M. P. Sabatier says, one branch of religion keeps the divinity, another keeps man most in view. Worship and sacrifice, procedures for working on the dispositions of the deity, theology and ceremony and ecclesiastical organization, are the essentials of religion in the institutional branch. Were we to limit our view to it, we should have to define religion as an external art, the art of winning the favor of the gods. In the more personal branch of religion it is on the contrary the inner dispositions of man himself which form the centre of interest, his conscience, his deserts, his helplessness, his incompleteness. And although the favor of the God, as forfeited or gained, is still an essential feature of the story, and theology plays a vital part therein, yet the acts to which this sort of religion prompts are personal not ritual acts, the individual transacts the business by himself alone, and the ecclesiastical organization, with its priests and sacraments and other go-betweens, sinks to an altogether secondary place. The relation goes direct from heart to heart, from soul to soul, between man and his maker.

Now in these lectures I propose to ignore the institutional branch entirely, to say nothing of the ecclesiastical organization, to consider as little as possible the systematic theology and the ideas about the gods themselves, and to confine myself as far as I can to personal religion pure and simple. To some of you personal religion, thus nakedly considered, will no doubt seem too incomplete a thing to wear the general name. "It is a part of religion," you will say, "but only its unorganized rudiment; if we are to name it by itself, we had better call it man's conscience or morality than his religion. The name 'religion' should be reserved for the fully organized system of feeling, thought, and institution, for the Church, in short, of which this personal religion, so called, is but a fractional element."

But if you say this, it will only show the more plainly how much the question of definition tends to become a dispute about names. Rather than prolong such a dispute, I am willing to accept almost any name for the personal religion of which I propose to treat. Call it conscience or morality, if you yourselves prefer, and not religion—under either name it will be equally worthy of our study. As for myself, I think it will prove to contain some elements which morality pure and simple does not contain, and these elements I shall soon seek to point out; so I will myself continue to apply the word "religion" to it; and in the last lecture of all, I will bring in the theologies and the ecclesiasticisms, and say something of its relation to them.

In one sense at least the personal religion will prove itself more fundamental than either theology or ecclesiasticism. Churches, when once established, live at second-hand upon tradition; but the *founders* of every church owed their power originally to the fact of their direct personal communion with the divine. Not only the superhuman founders, the Christ, the Buddha, Mahomet [sic], but all the originators of Christian sects have been in this case;—so personal religion should still seem the primordial thing, even to those who continue to esteem it incomplete.

There are, it is true, other things in religion chronologically more primordial than personal devoutness in the moral sense. Fetishism and magic seem to have preceded inward piety historically—at least our records of inward piety do not reach back so far. And if fetishism and magic be regarded as stages of religion, one may say that personal religion in the inward sense and the genuinely spiritual ecclesiasticisms which it founds are phenomena of secondary or even tertiary order.[2] But, quite apart from the fact that many anthropologists—for instance, [Frank Byron] Jevons and [James G.] Frazer—expressly oppose "religion" and "magic" to each other, it is certain that the whole system of thought which leads to magic, fetishism, and the lower superstitions may just as well be called primitive science as called primitive religion. The question thus becomes a verbal one again; and our knowledge of all these early stages of thought and feeling is in any case so conjectural and imperfect that farther discussion would not be worth while.

Religion, therefore, as I now ask you arbitrarily to take it, shall mean for us *the feelings, acts, and experiences of individual men in their solitude, so far as they apprehend themselves to stand in relation to whatever they may consider the divine.* Since the relation may be either moral, physical, or ritual, it is evident that out of religion in the sense in which we take it, theologies, philosophies, and ecclesiastical organizations may secondarily grow. In these lectures, however, as I have already said, the immediate personal experiences will amply fill our time, and we shall hardly consider theology or ecclesiasticism at all.

We escape much controversial matter by this arbitrary definition of our field. But, still, a chance of controversy comes up over the word "divine," if we take it in the definition in too narrow a sense. There are systems of thought which the world usually calls religious, and yet which do not positively assume a God. Buddhism is in this case. Popularly, of course, the Buddha himself stands in place of a God; but in strictness the Buddhistic system is atheistic. Modern transcendental idealism, Emersonianism, for instance, also seems to let God evaporate into abstract Ideality. Not a deity *in concreto*, not a superhuman person, but the immanent divinity in things, the essentially spiritual structure of the universe, is the object of the transcendentalist cult. In that address to the graduating class at Divinity College in 1838 which made [Ralph Waldo] Emerson famous, the frank expression of this worship of mere abstract laws was what made the scandal of the performance. "These laws," said the speaker,

---

2. [Ed. note] Nineteenth-century scholars commonly assumed that an evolutionary model derived from such fields as biology and geology could also be applied to study how social groups and institutions change over time; this way of applying an evolutionary model to the study of culture—an application which is largely discredited today—was then known as Social Darwinism. At the time, the search for the pre-historic *origin* (rather than the contemporary *function*) of the modern institution known as religion was assumed to lie in earlier, developmental stages. Scholars disagreed, of course, as to just what these stages were. Common choices were: magic (the effort to manipulate an inanimate natural world); festishism (the belief that inanimate objects possessed power); and totemism (the belief that animate objects, such as animals or plants, represented the group).

execute themselves. They are out of time, out of space, and not subject to circumstance:[.] Thus, in the soul of man there is a justice whose retributions are instant and entire. He who does a good deed is instantly ennobled. He who does a mean deed is by the action itself contracted. He who puts off impurity thereby puts on purity. If a man is at heart just, then in so far is he God; the safety of God, the immortality of God, the majesty of God, do enter into that man with justice. If a man dissemble, deceive, he deceives himself, and goes out of acquaintance with his own being. [...] Character is always known. Thefts never enrich; alms never impoverish; murder will speak out of stone walls. The least admixture of a lie—for example, the taint of vanity, any attempt to make a good impression, a favorable appearance—will instantly vitiate the effect. [...] But speak the truth [...] and all things alive or brute are vouchers, and the very roots of the grass underground there do seem to stir and move to bear your witness. [...] For all things proceed out of the [this] same spirit, which is differently named love, justice, temperance, in its different applications, just as the ocean receives different names on the several shores which it washes. [...] In so far as he roves from these ends, a man bereaves himself of power, of auxiliaries.[;] His [his] being shrinks...he becomes less and less, a mote, a point, until absolute badness is absolute death. The perception of this law [of laws] awakens in the mind a sentiment which we call the religious sentiment, and which makes our highest happiness. Wonderful is its power to charm and to command. It is a mountain air. It is the embalmer of the world. [...] It makes the sky and the hills sublime, and the silent song of the stars is it. [...] It is the beatitude of man. It makes him illimitable. [...] When he says "I ought"; when love warns [warms] him; when he chooses, warned from on high, the good and great deed; then, deep melodies wander through his soul from supreme wisdom. [Supreme Wisdom.—Then] Then he can worship, and be enlarged by his worship; for he can never go behind this sentiment. [...] [A]ll the expressions of this sentiment are sacred and permanent in proportion to their purity. [...] [They] affect us more than all other compositions. The sentences of the olden time, which ejaculate this piety, are still fresh and fragrant. [...] And the unique impression of Jesus upon mankind, whose name is not so much written as ploughed into the history of this world, is proof of the subtle virtue of this infusion.   (1868, 120)[3]

Such is the Emersonian religion. The universe has a divine soul of order, which soul is moral, being also the soul within the soul of man. But whether this soul of the universe be a

---

3. [Ed. note] James is quoting an address Ralph Waldo Emerson delivered to the senior divinity class at Cambridge, MA, on July 15, 1838. It was published in Emerson's 1868 book, *Lectures and Biographical Sketches*. James's quotation does not take into account the various places where he has excised material that is in the original, and it differs in several respects—some significant, such as the substitution of the word "warns" for "warms"—from Emerson's text, at least as it reads in a 1903 edition of his collected works. So the text here has been edited, with Emerson's text appearing within square brackets, with reference to the version of the speech that can be found in *The Complete Works of Ralph Waldo Emerson. Vol. 1 Nature, Addresses, and Lectures*, 122–6. New York: Houghton and Mifflin Co., 1903.

mere quality like the eye's brilliancy or the skin's softness, or whether it be a self-conscious life like the eye's seeing or the skin's feeling, is a decision that never unmistakably appears in Emerson's pages. It quivers on the boundary of these things, sometimes leaning one way, sometimes the other, to suit the literary rather than the philosophic need. Whatever it is, though, is active. As much as if it were a God, we can trust it to protect all ideal interests and keep the world's balance straight. The sentences in which Emerson, to the very end, gave utterance to this faith are fine as anything in literature: "If you love and serve men, you cannot by any hiding or stratagem escape the remuneration. Secret retributions are always restoring the level, when disturbed, of the divine justice. It is impossible to tilt the beam. All the tyrants and proprietors and monopolists of the world in vain set their shoulders to heave the bar. Settles forevermore the ponderous equator to its line, and man and mote, and star and sun, must range to it, or be pulverized by the recoil" (1868, 186).[4]

Now it would be too absurd to say that the inner experiences that underlie such expressions of faith as this and impel the writer to their utterance are quite unworthy to be called religious experiences. The sort of appeal that Emersonian optimism, on the one hand, and Buddhistic pessimism, on the other, make to the individual and the sort of response which he makes to them in his life are in fact indistinguishable from, and in many respects identical with, the best Christian appeal and response. We must therefore, from the experiential point of view, call these godless or quasi-godless creeds "religions"; and accordingly when in our definition of religion we speak of the individual's relation to "what he considers the divine," we must interpret the term "divine" very broadly, as denoting any object that is god*like*, whether it be a concrete deity or not.

But the term "godlike," if thus treated as a floating general quality, becomes exceedingly vague, for many gods have flourished in religious history, and their attributes have been discrepant enough. What then is that essentially godlike quality—be it embodied in a concrete deity or not—our relation to which determines our character as religious men? It will repay us to seek some answer to this question before we proceed farther.

For one thing, gods are conceived to be first things in the way of being and power. They overarch and envelop, and from them there is no escape. What relates to them is the first and last word in the way of truth. Whatever then were most primal and enveloping and deeply true might at this rate be treated as godlike, and a man's religion might thus be identified with his attitude, whatever it might be, towards what he felt to be the primal truth.

Such a definition as this would in a way be defensible. Religion, whatever it is, is a man's total reaction upon life, so why not say that any total reaction upon life is a religion? Total reactions are different from casual reactions, and total attitudes are different from usual or professional attitudes. To get at them you must go behind the foreground of existence and reach down to that curious sense of the whole residual cosmos as an everlasting presence, intimate or alien, terrible or amusing, lovable or odious, which in some degree every one possesses. This sense of the world's presence, appealing as it does

---

4. [Ed. note] James is quoting an essay of Emerson's entitled, "The Sovereignty of Ethics." A slightly later edition of the essay can be found in *The Collected Works of Ralph Waldo Emerson, Vol. X, Lectures and Biographical Sketches*, 193. New York: Houghton Mifflin Company, 1911.

to our peculiar individual temperament, makes us either strenuous or careless, devout or blasphemous, gloomy or exultant, about life at large; and our reaction, involuntary and inarticulate and often half unconscious as it is, is the completest of all our answers to the question, "What is the character of this universe in which we dwell?" It expresses our individual sense of it in the most definite way. Why then not call these reactions our religion, no matter what specific character they may have? Non-religious as some of these reactions may be, in one sense of the word "religious," they yet belong to *the general sphere of the religious life*, and so should generically be classed as religious reactions. "He believes in No-God, and he worships him," said a colleague of mine of a student who was manifesting a fine atheistic ardor; and the more fervent opponents of Christian doctrine have often enough shown a temper which, psychologically considered, is indistinguishable from religious zeal.

But so very broad a use of the word "religion" would be inconvenient, however defensible it might remain on logical grounds. There are trifling, sneering attitudes even towards the whole of life; and in some men these attitudes are final and systematic. It would strain the ordinary use of language too much to call such attitudes religious, even though, from the point of view of an unbiased critical philosophy, they might conceivably be perfectly reasonable ways of looking upon life. Voltaire, for example, writes thus to a friend, at the age of seventy-three: "As for myself," he says, "weak as I am, I carry on the war to the last moment, I get a hundred pike-thrusts, I return two hundred, and I laugh. I see near my door Geneva on fire with quarrels over nothing, and I laugh again; and, thank God, I can look upon the world as a farce even when it becomes as tragic as it sometimes does. All comes out even at the end of the day, and all comes out still more even when all the days are over."[5]

Much as we may admire such a robust old gamecock spirit in a valetudinarian, to call it a religious spirit would be odd. Yet it is for the moment Voltaire's reaction on the whole of life. *Je m'en fiche* is the vulgar French equivalent for our English ejaculation "Who cares?" [or it can be translated as the more declarative "I don't care"]. And the happy term *je m'en fichisme* recently has been invented to designate the systematic determination not to take anything in life too solemnly. "All is vanity" is the relieving word in all difficult crises for this mode of thought, which that exquisite literary genius [Ernest] Renan took pleasure, in his later days of sweet decay, in putting into coquettishly sacrilegious forms which remain to us as excellent expressions of the "all is vanity" state of mind. Take the following passage, for example—we must hold to duty, even against the evidence, Renan says—but he then goes on:

> There are many chances that the world may be nothing but a fairy pantomime of which no God has care. We must therefore arrange ourselves so that on neither hypothesis we shall be completely wrong. We must listen to the superior voices, but in such a way that if the second hypothesis were true we should not have been too

---

5. [Ed. note] Voltaire was the assumed name of François-Marie Arouet (1694–1778), the well-known French intellectual and author of the satirical text, *Candide* (1759).

completely duped. If in effect the world be not a serious thing, it is the dogmatic people who will be the shallow ones, and the worldly minded whom the theologians now call frivolous will be those who are really wise.

In utrumque paratus, then. Be ready for anything[6]—that perhaps is wisdom. Give ourselves up, according to the hour, to confidence, to skepticism, to optimism, to irony, and we may be sure that at certain moments at least we shall be with the truth…. Good humor is a philosophic state of mind; it seems to say to Nature that we take her no more seriously than she takes us. I maintain that one should always talk of philosophy with a smile. We owe it to the Eternal to be virtuous; but we have the right to add to this tribute our irony as a sort of personal reprisal. In this way we return to the right quarter jest for jest; we play the trick that has been played on us. Saint Augustine's phrase: *Lord, if we are deceived, it is by thee!* remains a fine one, well suited to our modern feeling. Only we wish the Eternal to know that if we accept the fraud, we accept it knowingly and willingly. We are resigned in advance to losing the interest on our investments of virtue, but we wish not to appear ridiculous by having counted on them too securely.[7]

Surely all the usual associations of the word "religion" would have to be stripped away if such a systematic *parti pris*[8] of irony were also to be denoted by the name. For common men "religion," whatever more special meanings it may have, signifies always a *serious* state of mind. If any one phrase could gather its universal message, that phrase would be, "All is *not* vanity in this Universe, whatever the appearances may suggest." If it can stop anything, religion as commonly apprehended can stop just such chaffing talk as Renan's. It favors gravity, not pertness; it says "hush" to all vain chatter and smart wit.

But if hostile to light irony, religion is equally hostile to heavy grumbling and complaint. The world appears tragic enough in some religions, but the tragedy is realized as purging, and a way of deliverance is held to exist. We shall see enough of the religious melancholy in a future lecture; but melancholy, according to our ordinary use of language, forfeits all title to be called religious when, in Marcus Aurelius's racy words, the sufferer simply lies kicking and screaming after the fashion of a sacrificed pig. The mood of a Schopenhauer or a Nietzsche,—and in a less degree one may sometimes say the same of our own sad Carlyle,—though often an ennobling sadness, is almost as often only peevishness running away with the bit between its teeth. The sallies of the two German authors remind one, half the time, of the sick shriekings of two dying rats. They lack the purgatorial note which religious sadness gives forth.

---

6. [Ed. note] The Latin phrase best translates not as an imperative, or command, but as a declaration: "prepared for everything," which is usually written *ad omnia paratus*, meaning "I am ready for everything." Thanks to Kirk Summers at the University of Alabama for clarifying this.

7. *Feuilles détachées*, 394–8 (abridged). [Ed. note: this volume, whose title roughly translates as "loose pages," is a collection of Renan's essays, published in 1892. Thanks to Daniel Dubuisson for clarifying the translation of the book's title.]

8. [Ed. note] Translation: "decision or side taken," as in a bias or an opinion formed beforehand.

There must be something solemn, serious, and tender about any attitude which we denominate religious. If glad, it must not grin or snicker; if sad, it must not scream or curse. It is precisely as being *solemn* experiences that I wish to interest you in religious experiences. So I propose—arbitrarily again, if you please—to narrow our definition once more by saying that the word "divine," as employed therein, shall mean for us not merely the primal and enveloping and real, for that meaning if taken without restriction might well prove too broad. The divine shall mean for us only such a primal reality as the individual feels impelled to respond to solemnly and gravely, and neither by a curse nor a jest.

But solemnity, and gravity, and all such emotional attributes, admit of various shades; and, do what we will with our defining, the truth must at last be confronted that we are dealing with a field of experience where there is not a single conception that can be sharply drawn. The pretension, under such conditions, to be rigorously "scientific" or "exact" in our terms would only stamp us as lacking in understanding of our task. Things are more or less divine, states of mind are more or less religious, reactions are more or less total, but the boundaries are always misty, and it is everywhere a question of amount and degree. Nevertheless, at their extreme of development, there can never be any question as to what experiences are religious. The divinity of the object and the solemnity of the reaction are too well marked for doubt. Hesitation as to whether a state of mind is "religious," or "irreligious," or "moral," or "philosophical," is only likely to arise when the state of mind is weakly characterized, but in that case it will be hardly worthy of our study at all. With states that can only by courtesy be called religious we need have nothing to do, our only profitable business being with what nobody can possibly feel tempted to call anything else. I said in my former lecture that we learn most about a thing when we view it under a microscope, as it were, or in its most exaggerated form. This is as true of religious phenomena as of any other kind of fact. The only cases likely to be profitable enough to repay our attention will therefore be cases where the religious spirit is unmistakable and extreme. Its fainter manifestations we may tranquilly pass by. Here, for example, is the total reaction upon life of Frederick Locker Lampson, whose autobiography, entitled "Confidences," proves him to have been a most amiable man.

> I am so far resigned to my lot that I feel small pain at the thought of having to part from what has been called the pleasant habit of existence, the sweet fable of life. I would not care to live my wasted life over again, and so to prolong my span. Strange to say, I have but little wish to be younger. I submit with a chill at my heart. I humbly submit because it is the Divine Will, and my appointed destiny. I dread the increase of infirmities that will make me a burden to those around me, those dear to me. No! let me slip away as quietly and comfortably as I can. Let the end come, if peace come with it.
>
> I do not know that there is a great deal to be said for this world, or our sojourn here upon it; but it has pleased God so to place us, and it must please me also. I ask you, what is human life? Is not it a maimed happiness—care and weariness, weariness and care, with the baseless expectation, the strange cozenage of a brighter

tomorrow? At best it is but a forward child, that must be played with and humored, to keep it quiet till it falls asleep, and then the care is over.   (1896, 313–4)[9]

This is a complex, a tender, a submissive, and a graceful state of mind. For myself, I should have no objection to calling it on the whole a religious state of mind, although I dare say that to many of you it may seem too listless and half-hearted to merit so good a name. But what matters it in the end whether we call such a state of mind religious or not? It is too insignificant for our instruction in any case; and its very possessor wrote it down in terms which he would not have used unless he had been thinking of more energetically religious moods in others, with which he found himself unable to compete. It is with these more energetic states that our sole business lies, and we can perfectly well afford to let the minor notes and the uncertain border go.

It was the extremer cases that I had in mind a little while ago when I said that personal religion, even without theology or ritual, would prove to embody some elements that morality pure and simple does not contain. You may remember that I promised shortly to point out what those elements were. In a general way I can now say what I had in mind.

"I accept the universe" is reported to have been a favorite utterance of our New England transcendentalist,[10] Margaret Fuller; and when someone repeated this phrase to Thomas Carlyle, his sardonic comment is said to have been: "Gad! she'd better!" At bottom the whole concern of both morality and religion is with the manner of our acceptance of the universe. Do we accept it only in part and grudgingly, or heartily and altogether? Shall our protests against certain things in it be radical and unforgiving, or shall we think that, even with evil, there are ways of living that must lead to good? If we accept the whole, shall we do so as if stunned into submission,—as Carlyle would have us—"Gad! we'd better!" or shall we do so with enthusiastic assent? Morality pure and simple accepts the law of the whole which it finds reigning, so far as to acknowledge and obey it, but it may obey it with the heaviest and coldest heart, and never cease to feel it as a yoke. But for religion, in its strong and fully developed manifestations, the service of the highest never is felt as a yoke. Dull submission is left far behind, and a mood of welcome, which may fill any place on the scale between cheerful serenity and enthusiastic gladness, has taken its place.

It makes a tremendous emotional and practical difference to one whether one accept the universe in the drab discolored way of stoic resignation to necessity, or with the passionate happiness of Christian saints. The difference is as great as that between passivity and activity, as that between the defensive and the aggressive mood. Gradual as are the

---

9. [Ed. note] James is quoting from the poet's memoir, *My Confidences: An Autobiographical Sketch Addressed to My Descendants*, which was edited by his son-in-law, the English author and politician Augustine Birrell, and published in London by Smith, Elder & Company in 1896, the year after Locker Lampson's death.

10. [Ed. note] Transcendentalism is a name given to a US philosophical, literary, and religious movement of the mid-nineteenth century, associated with the work of such authors as Ralph Waldo Emerson, that emphasized the role of intuitive knowledge and the belief that God was not apart from but immanent, or within, the world of nature. As such, transcendentalists offered a critique of systematized religious practice (i.e., ritual, institution, tradition, etc.) in favor of what was described as a more personal experience of God's abiding presence.

steps by which an individual may grow from one state into the other, many as are the intermediate stages which different individuals represent, yet when you place the typical extremes beside each other for comparison, you feel that two discontinuous psychological universes confront you, and that in passing from one to the other a "critical point" has been overcome.

If we compare stoic with Christian ejaculations we see much more than a difference of doctrine; rather is it a difference of emotional mood that parts them. When Marcus Aurelius reflects on the eternal reason that has ordered things, there is a frosty chill about his words which you rarely find in a Jewish, and never in a Christian piece of religious writing. The universe is "accepted" by all these writers; but how devoid of passion or exultation the spirit of the Roman Emperor is! Compare his fine sentence: "If gods care not for me or my children, here is a reason for it," with Job's cry: "Though he slay me, yet will I trust in him!" and you immediately see the difference I mean. The *anima mundi*, to whose disposal of his own personal destiny the Stoic consents,[11] is there to be respected and submitted to, but the Christian God is there to be loved; and the difference of emotional atmosphere is like that between an arctic climate and the tropics, though the outcome in the way of accepting actual conditions uncomplainingly may seem in abstract terms to be much the same. "It is a man's duty," says Marcus Aurelius,

> to comfort himself and wait for the natural dissolution, and not to be vexed, but to find refreshment solely in these thoughts—first that nothing will happen to me which is not conformable to the nature of the universe; and secondly that I need do nothing contrary to the God and deity within me; for there is no man who can compel me to transgress.[12]

> He is an abscess on the universe who withdraws and separates himself from the reason of our common nature, through being displeased with the things which happen. For the same nature produces these, and has produced thee too. And so accept everything which happens, even if it seem disagreeable, because it leads to this, the health of the universe and to the prosperity and felicity of Zeus. For he would not have brought on any man what he has brought, if it were not useful for the whole. The integrity of the whole is mutilated if thou cuttest off anything. And thou dost cut off, as far as it is in thy power, when thou art dissatisfied, and in a manner triest to put anything out of the way.[13]

---

11. [Ed. note] Translation: "spirit or soul of the world." Stoicism—named after the porch, or *stoa*, where early students met for instructions—is the name given to an ancient Greek philosophical movement, founded by Zeno (344–262 BCE), that understood philosophical inquiry as a life work which required one to overcome emotional reactions in an effort to live a virtuous life. The text known as *Meditations* written by the Roman Emperor, Marcus Aurelius (who ruled from 161 to 180 CE), demonstrates the influence of the Stoics.

12. Book V, chapter X (abridged). [Ed. note: James is quoting from *Meditations*, written around 167 CE.]

13. Book V, chapter IX (abridged). [Ed. note: James is quoting from *Meditations*, written around 167 CE.]

Compare now this mood with that of the old Christian author of the *Theologia Germanica*:

Where men are enlightened with the true light, they renounce all desire and choice, and commit and commend themselves and all things to the eternal Goodness, so that every enlightened man could say: "I would fain be to the Eternal Goodness what his own hand is to a man." Such men are in a state of freedom, because they have lost the fear of pain or hell, and the hope of reward or heaven, and are living in pure submission to the eternal Goodness, in the perfect freedom of fervent love. When a man truly perceiveth and considereth himself, who and what he is, and findeth himself utterly vile and wicked and unworthy, he falleth into such a deep abasement that it seemeth to him reasonable that all creatures in heaven and earth should rise up against him. And therefore he will not and dare not desire any consolation and release; but he is willing to be unconsoled and unreleased; and he doth not grieve over his sufferings, for they are right in his eyes, and he hath nothing to say against them. This is what is meant by true repentance for sin and he who in this present time entereth into this hell, none may console him. Now God hath not forsaken a man in this hell, but He is laying his hand upon him, that the man may not desire nor regard anything but the eternal Good only. And then, when the man neither careth for nor desireth anything but the eternal Good alone, and seeketh not himself nor his own things, but the honour of God only, he is made a partaker of all manner of joy, bliss, peace, rest, and consolation, and so the man is henceforth in the kingdom of heaven. This hell and this heaven are two good safe ways for a man, and happy is he who truly findeth them.[14]

How much more active and positive the impulse of the Christian writer to accept his place in the universe is! Marcus Aurelius agrees *to* the scheme—the German theologian agrees *with* it. He literally *abounds* in agreement, he runs out to embrace the divine decrees.

Occasionally, it is true, the Stoic rises to something like a Christian warmth of sentiment, as in the often quoted passage of Marcus Aurelius:

Everything harmonizes with me which is harmonious to thee, O Universe. Nothing for me is too early nor too late, which is in due time for thee. Everything is fruit to me which thy seasons bring, O Nature: from thee are all things, in thee are all things, to thee all things return. The poet says, Dear City of Cecrops and wilt thou not say, Dear City of Zeus?[15]

---

14. Chapters X and XI of [Susanna] Winkworth's [1874] translation. [Ed. note: The *Theologica Germanica* is an anonymous text believed to have been written in the fourteenth century and first published by Martin Luther in 1516.]

15. Book IV, section 23. [Ed. note: Cecrops—sometimes spelled Kekrops, and meaning "face with a tail"—is the name of the mythic ancestor and first King of the ancient Greeks, who was himself the son of Gaia (Mother Earth). He was believed to have been half man and half snake and the Acropolis, in Athens, was named in his honor. The City of Zeus was Olympia.]

But compare even as devout a passage as this with a genuine Christian outpouring and it seems a little cold. Turn, for instance, to the *Imitation of Christ*:

> Lord, thou knowest what is best; let this or that be according as thou wilt. Give what thou wilt, so much as thou wilt, when thou wilt. Do with me as thou knowest best, and as shall be most to thine honour. Place me where thou wilt, and freely work thy will with me in all things.... When could it be evil when thou wert near? I had rather be poor for thy sake than rich without thee. I choose rather to be a pilgrim upon the earth with thee, than without thee to possess heaven. Where thou art, there is heaven; and where thou art not, behold there death and hell.[16]

It is a good rule in physiology, when we are studying the meaning of an organ, to ask after its most peculiar and characteristic sort of performance, and to seek its office in that one of its functions which no other organ can possibly exert. Surely the same maxim holds good in our present quest. The essence of religious experiences, the thing by which we finally must judge them, must be that element or quality in them which we can meet nowhere else. And such a quality will be of course most prominent and easy to notice in those religious experiences which are most one-sided, exaggerated, and intense.

Now when we compare these intenser experiences with the experiences of tamer minds, so cool and reasonable that we are tempted to call them philosophical rather than religious, we find a character that is perfectly distinct. That character, it seems to me, should be regarded as the practically important *differentia* of religion for our purpose; and just what it is can easily be brought out by comparing the mind of an abstractly conceived Christian with that of a moralist similarly conceived.

A life is manly, stoical, moral, or philosophical, we say, in proportion as it is less swayed by paltry personal considerations and more by objective ends that call for energy, even though that energy bring personal loss and pain. This is the good side of war, in so far as it calls for "volunteers." And for morality life is a war, and the service of the highest is a sort of cosmic patriotism which also calls for volunteers. Even a sick man, unable to be militant outwardly, can carry on the moral warfare. He can willfully turn his attention away from his own future, whether in this world or the next. He can train himself to indifference to his present drawbacks and immerse himself in whatever objective interests still remain accessible. He can follow public news, and sympathize with other people's affairs. He can cultivate cheerful manners, and be silent about his miseries. He can contemplate whatever ideal aspects of existence his philosophy is able to present to him, and practice whatever duties, such as patience, resignation, trust, his ethical system requires. Such a man lives on his loftiest, largest plane. He is a high-hearted freeman and no pining slave.

---

16. [William] Benham's translation: Book III, chapters xv, lix. Compare Mary Moody Emerson: "Let me be a blot on this fair world, the obscurest, the loneliest sufferer, with one proviso—that I know it is His agency. I will love Him though He shed frost and darkness on every way of mine." [See also] R. W. Emerson, *Lectures and Biographical Sketches*, p. 188. [Ed. note: James is quoting from a devotional book generally thought to have been written by the Roman Catholic monk, Thomas à Kempis (c. 1380–1471).]

And yet he lacks something which the Christian *par excellence*, the mystic and ascetic saint, for example, has in abundant measure, and which makes of him a human being of an altogether different denomination.

The Christian also spurns the pinched and mumping sick-room attitude, and the lives of saints are full of a kind of callousness to diseased conditions of body which probably no other human records show. But whereas the merely moralistic spurning takes an effort of volition, the Christian spurning is the result of the excitement of a higher kind of emotion, in the presence of which no exertion of volition is required. The moralist must hold his breath and keep his muscles tense; and so long as this athletic attitude is possible all goes well—morality suffices. But the athletic attitude tends ever to break down, and it inevitably does break down even in the most stalwart when the organism begins to decay, or when morbid fears invade the mind. To suggest personal will and effort to one all sicklied o'er with the sense of irremediable impotence is to suggest the most impossible of things. What he craves is to be consoled in his very powerlessness, to feel that the spirit of the universe recognizes and secures him, all decaying and failing as he is. Well, we are all such helpless failures in the last resort. The sanest and best of us are of one clay with lunatics and prison inmates, and death, finally runs the robustest of us down. And whenever we feel this, such a sense of the vanity and provisionality of our voluntary career comes over us that all our morality appears but as a plaster hiding a sore it can never cure, and all our well-doing as the hollowest substitute for that well-*being* that our lives ought to be grounded in, but, alas! are not.

And here religion comes to our rescue and takes our fate into her hands. There is a state of mind, known to religious men, but to no others, in which the will to assert ourselves and hold our own has been displaced by a willingness to close our mouths and be as nothing in the floods and waterspouts of God. In this state of mind, what we most dreaded has become the habitation of our safety, and the hour of our moral death has turned into our spiritual birthday. The time for tension in our soul is over, and that of happy relaxation, of calm deep breathing, of an eternal present, with no discordant future to be anxious about, has arrived. Fear is not held in abeyance as it is by mere morality, it is positively expunged and washed away.

We shall see abundant examples of this happy state of mind in later lectures of this course. We shall see how infinitely passionate a thing religion at its highest flights can be. Like love, like wrath, like hope, ambition, jealousy, like every other instinctive eagerness and impulse, it adds to life an enchantment which is not rationally or logically deducible from anything else. This enchantment, coming as a gift when it does come,—a gift of our organism, the physiologists will tell us, a gift of God's grace, the theologians say,—is either there or not there for us, and there are persons who can no more become possessed by it than they can fall in love with a given woman by mere word of command. Religious feeling is thus an absolute addition to the Subject's range of life. It gives him a new sphere of power. When the outward battle is lost, and the outer world disowns him, it redeems and vivifies an interior world which otherwise would be an empty waste.

If religion is to mean anything definite for us, it seems to me that we ought to take it as meaning this added dimension of emotion, this enthusiastic temper of espousal, in regions where morality strictly so called can at best but bow its head and acquiesce. It ought to mean nothing short of this new reach of freedom for us, with the struggle over, the keynote of the universe sounding in our ears, and everlasting possession spread before our eyes.[17]

This sort of happiness in the absolute and everlasting is what we find nowhere but in religion. It is parted off from all mere animal happiness, all mere enjoyment of the present, by that element of solemnity of which I have already made so much account. Solemnity is a hard thing to define abstractly, but certain of its marks are patent enough. A solemn state of mind is never crude or simple—it seems to contain a certain measure of its own opposite in solution. A solemn joy preserves a sort of bitter in its sweetness; a solemn sorrow is one to which we intimately consent. But there are writers who, realizing that happiness of a supreme sort is the prerogative of religion, forget this complication, and call all happiness, as such, religious. Mr. Havelock Ellis, for example, identifies religion with the entire field of the soul's liberation from oppressive moods. "The simplest functions of physiological life," he writes,

> may be its ministers. Everyone who is at all acquainted with the Persian mystics[18] knows how wine may be regarded as an instrument of religion. Indeed, in all countries and in all ages, some form of physical enlargement—singing, dancing, drinking, sexual excitement—has been intimately associated with worship. Even the momentary expansion of the soul in laughter is, to however slight an extent, a religious exercise.... Whenever an impulse from the world strikes against the organism, and the resultant is not discomfort or pain, not even the muscular contraction of strenuous manhood, but a joyous expansion or aspiration of the whole soul—there is religion. It is the infinite for which we hunger, and we ride gladly on every little wave that promises to bear us towards it.[19]

But such a straight identification of religion with any and every form of happiness leaves the essential peculiarity of religious happiness out. The more commonplace happinesses which we get are "reliefs," occasioned by our momentary escapes from evils either experienced or threatened. But in its most characteristic embodiments, religious happiness is no mere feeling of escape. It cares no longer to escape. It consents to the evil outwardly as a form of sacrifice—inwardly it knows it to be permanently overcome. If you ask *how* religion thus falls on the thorns and faces death, and in the very act annuls annihilation, I cannot explain the matter, for it is religion's secret, and to understand it you must yourself have been a religious man of the extremer type. In our future examples, even of the

---

17. Once more, there are plenty of men, constitutionally sombre [sic] men, in whose religious life this rapturousness is lacking. They are religious in the wider sense; yet in this acutest of all senses they are not so, and it is religion in the acutest sense that I wish, without disputing about words, to study first, so as to get at its typical *differentia*.

18. [Ed. note] More than likely, the author is referring to that so-called mystical branch of Islam known as Sufism.

19. *The New Spirit*, 232. [Ed. note: This book, a collection of literary essays, was published in 1890. The quotation can be found on page 275 of the 1900 edition, published in New York by Boni and Liverright.]

simplest and healthiest-minded type of religious consciousness, we shall find this complex sacrificial constitution, in which a higher happiness holds a lower unhappiness in check. In the Louvre there is a picture, by Guido Reni, of St. Michael with his foot on Satan's neck. The richness of the picture is in large part due to the fiend's figure being there. The richness of its allegorical meaning also is due to his being there—that is, the world is all the richer for having a devil in it, *so long as we keep our foot upon his neck*. In the religious consciousness, that is just the position in which the fiend, the negative or tragic principle, is found; and for that very reason the religious consciousness is so rich from the emotional point of view.[20] We shall see how in certain men and women it takes on a monstrously ascetic form. There are saints who have literally fed on the negative principle, on humiliation and privation, and the thought of suffering and death,—their souls growing in happiness just in proportion as their outward state grew more intolerable. No other emotion than religious emotion can bring a man to this peculiar pass. And it is for that reason that when we ask our question about the value of religion for human life, I think we ought to look for the answer among these violenter examples rather than among those of a more moderate hue.

Having the phenomenon of our study in its acutest possible form to start with, we can shade down as much as we please later. And if in these cases, repulsive as they are to our ordinary worldly way of judging, we find ourselves compelled to acknowledge religion's value and treat it with respect, it will have proved in some way its value for life at large. By subtracting and toning down extravagances we may thereupon proceed to trace the boundaries of its legitimate sway.

To be sure, it makes our task difficult to have to deal so much with eccentricities and extremes. "How *can* religion on the whole be the most important of all human functions," you may ask, "if every several manifestation of it in turn have to be corrected and sobered down and pruned away?" Such a thesis seems a paradox impossible to sustain reasonably,—yet I believe that something like it will have to be our final contention. That personal attitude which the individual finds himself impelled to take up towards what he apprehends to be the divine—and you will remember that this was our definition—will prove to be both a helpless and a sacrificial attitude. That is, we shall have to confess to at least some amount of dependence on sheer mercy, and to practice some amount of renunciation, great or small, to save our souls alive. The constitution of the world we live in requires it:

Entbehren sollst du! sollst entbehren! Das ist der ewige Gesang
Der jedem an die Ohren klingt, Den, unser ganzes Leben lang
Uns heiser jede Stunde singt.[21]

---

20. I owe this allegorical illustration to my lamented colleague and friend, Charles Carroll Everett.

21. [Ed. note] James is quoting from Act One, Scene Four, of Johann Wolfgang von Goethe's early nineteenth-century tragedy, "Faust." The text translates as:

"Thou shalt renounce! Renounce shalt thou! That is the never-ending song
Which in the ears of all is ringing, Which always, through our whole life long,
Hour after hour is hoarsely singing."

For when all is said and done, we are in the end absolutely dependent on the universe; and into sacrifices and surrenders of some sort, deliberately looked at and accepted, we are drawn and pressed as into our only permanent positions of repose. Now in those states of mind which fall short of religion, the surrender is submitted to as an imposition of necessity, and the sacrifice is undergone at the very best without complaint. In the religious life, on the contrary, surrender and sacrifice are positively espoused: even unnecessary givings-up are added in order that the happiness may increase. *Religion thus makes easy and felicitous what in any case is necessary*; and if it be the only agency that can accomplish this result, its vital importance as a human faculty stands vindicated beyond dispute. It becomes an essential organ of our life, performing a function which no other portion of our nature can so successfully fulfill. From the merely biological point of view, so to call it, this is a conclusion to which, so far as I can now see, we shall inevitably be led, and led moreover by following the purely empirical method of demonstration which I sketched to you in the first lecture. Of the farther office of religion as a metaphysical revelation I will say nothing now.

But to foreshadow the terminus of one's investigations is one thing, and to arrive there safely is another. In the next lecture, abandoning the extreme generalities which have engrossed us hitherto, I propose that we begin our actual journey by addressing ourselves directly to the concrete facts.

5

CHARLES TAYLOR

"James: Varieties," from *Varieties of Religion Today: William James Revisited*

Canadian philosopher Charles Taylor has been a significant contemporary voice in the fields of political and social theory. Trained at Quebec's McGill University in history, and later at Oxford in philosophy, politics, and economics, Taylor represents what some have called a "postanalytic" perspective, inasmuch as he has questioned the utility of the highly individualistic and intellectualist tendencies that have come to define modern philosophical thought.

Taylor's work, focusing primarily on the relationship between secularization, modernity, and religion, has questioned trends such as naturalism (the assumption that only natural, tangible phenomena may be analytically studied) as well as the classic secularization models (which argue that as societies develop and modernize, they grow more publicly secular, with religion pushed to a more "private" sphere). Instead, in a move very much like William James's "pragmatism" and "radical empiricism," Taylor has promoted a view of religion and its study that looks to the utility of religious belief in improving social problems such as war and poverty, as well as arguing for the rigorous study of "spirituality" as an important component of human existence. Taylor's work fills an important niche in this present volume as it offers a model of scholarship that many religion scholars today find attractive.

Taylor has received numerous prestigious awards for his work, among these the 2007 Templeton Prize. In addition to his publication of *Varieties of Religion Today: William James Revisited* (2002), from which the following essay is excerpted, Taylor is the author of several books, which include, among others, *Sources of the Self: The Making of the Modern Identity* (1989), *Multiculturalism and the "Politics of Recognition"* (1992), *Modern Social Imaginaries* (2004), and *A Secular Age* (2007).

The following essay is the first chapter from his 2002 publication, *Varieties of Religion Today*. Here Taylor attempts to revive a conversation first started almost 100 years earlier by William James himself. Taylor's argument is that the utility of the Jamesian thesis is still alive, but it demands modification past what James's more narrow vision could have allowed; in other words, Taylor hopes to improve on, re-evaluate, and update what he sees as an otherwise timeless work. In a style consistent with his other writings on the importance of community, Taylor's arguments critique James's understanding of religion as a primarily individual experience.

One will find that, much like Raymond Williams and Robert Desjarlais, Taylor provides a historical argument that situates James's theological and intellectual positions. Arguably, however, unlike Williams and Desjarlais, Taylor's primary intent is not to ask questions about the nature of experience and the social conditions that create it, nor to entertain hypotheses that reduce religion to other social phenomena (a position called *reductionism*). In light of his affinity for James, one must thus consider whether and how the questions that Taylor asks are qualitatively different from his predecessor. The critical question here is not *whether* Taylor modifies James, but how he does so. Are these differences primarily cosmetic, or does Taylor overturn the core assumptions that James made about religious experience, and the category of "experience" more broadly?

"JAMES: VARIETIES," FROM *VARIETIES OF RELIGION TODAY*

It's almost a hundred years since William James delivered his celebrated Gifford Lectures in Edinburgh on *The Varieties of Religious Experience*. I want in these pages to look again at this remarkable book, reflecting on what it has to say to us at the turn of a new century.

In fact it turns out to have a lot to say. It is astonishing how little dated it is. Some of the details may be strange, but you easily think of examples in our world that fit the themes James is developing. You can even find yourself forgetting that these lectures were delivered a hundred years ago.

Which is not to say that there aren't questions one can raise about the way in which James conceives his subject. On the contrary; but this is not so much because of the difference between his time and ours; rather, these questions arise out of different ways of understanding religion that confronted each other then, and still do. To put it slightly more polemically: one could argue that James has certain blind spots in his view of religion. But these blind spots are widespread in the modern world. They are just as operative in our age as in his. I want first to discuss these limitations in James's concept of religious experience. Then I will try to engage what moved him in this whole domain, which is the issue of the "twice-born," the center of religious experience that you feel throbbing not only in the lives that James writes about, but also in his own life. Finally I make a few reflections on religion today in relation to James's discussion.

WHAT IS RELIGIOUS EXPERIENCE?

People have pointed out the relative narrowness of the Jamesian perspective before. James sees religion primarily as something that individuals experience. He makes a distinction between living religious experience, which is that of the individual, and religious life, which is derivative because it is taken over from a community or church. For James, "your ordinary religious believer, who follows the conventional observances of his country" has a religion that "has been made for him by others…. It would profit us little to study this second-hand religious life. We must make search rather for the original experiences which were the pattern-setters to all this mass of suggested feeling and imitated conduct. These experiences we can find only in individuals for whom religion exists not as a dull habit, but as an acute fever rather. But such individuals are 'geniuses' in the religious line" (James 1982, 6).

We see here the Jamesian view of religious life, its origins and continuance: there are people who have an original, powerful religious experience, which then gets communicated through some kind of institution; it gets handed on to others, and they tend to live it in a kind of second-hand way. In the transmission, the force and intensity of the original tends to get lost, until all that remains is "dull habit."

Later on, also toward the beginning of the book, James attempts to define religion as "the feelings, acts and experiences of individual men in their solitude, so far as they apprehend themselves to stand in relation to whatever they may consider the divine" (1982, 31). This is what is primary; it is out of religion in this sense that "theologies, philosophies and ecclesiastical organizations may secondarily grow." So churches play at best a secondary role, in transmitting and communicating the original inspiration.

I say "at best," because their effect can also be highly negative, stifling and distorting personal faith. James is not enamored of churches:

> The word "religion" as ordinarily used, is equivocal. A survey of history shows us that, as a rule, religious geniuses attract disciples, and produce groups of sympathizers. When these groups get strong enough to "organize" themselves, they become ecclesiastical institutions with corporate ambitions of their own. The spirit of politics and the lust of dogmatic rule are then apt to enter and to contaminate the originally innocent thing; so that when we hear the word "religion" nowadays, we think inevitably of some "church" or other; and to some persons the word "church" suggests so much hypocrisy and tyranny and meanness and tenacity of superstition that in a wholesale undiscerning way they glory in saying that they are "down" on religion altogether. (James 1982, 334–5)

No wonder that "first-hand religious experience ... has always appeared as a heretical sort of innovation." So that "when a religion has become an orthodoxy, its days of inwardness are over; the spring is dry; the faithful live at second-hand exclusively and stone the prophets in their turn. The new church ... can be henceforth counted as a staunch ally in every attempt to stifle the spontaneous religious spirit, and to stop all the later bubblings of the fountain from which in purer days it drew its own supply of inspiration" (1982, 337).

People who are against "religion," therefore, are often mistaken in their target. "The basenesses so commonly charged to religion's account are thus, almost all of them, not chargeable to religion proper, but rather to religion's wicked practical partner, the spirit of corporate dominion. And the bigotries are most of them in their turn chargeable to religion's wicked intellectual partner, the spirit of dogmatic dominion."

So the *real* locus of religion is in individual experience, and not in corporate life. That is one facet of the Jamesian thesis. But the other is that the real locus is in *experience*, that is, in feeling, as against the formulations by which people define, justify, rationalize their feelings (operations that are, of course, frequently undertaken by churches).

These two are clearly connected in James's mind. Feelings occur, he holds, in individuals; and in turn "individuality is founded in feeling" (1982, 501). The importance of feeling explains "why I have been so individualistic throughout these lectures." Now "compared with this world of living individualized feelings, the world of generalized objects which the intellect contemplates is without solidity or life" (1982, 502). Part of what gives feelings their primacy is that they determine conduct. One's feelings make a difference to one's action, a crucial point to a "pragmatist." But don't ideas as well? James thinks they don't, or not all to the same degree. Feelings generally determine conduct, without being inflected by the rationalizations. We can find a great variety of cases in which feeling and conduct are the same, while theories differ.

> The theories which Religion generates, being thus variable, are secondary; and if you wish to grasp her essence, you must look to the feelings and the conduct as being the more constant elements. It is between these two elements that the short circuit exists on which she carries on her principal business, while the ideas and symbols and other institutions form loop-lines which may be perfections and improvements, and may even some day all be united into one harmonious system, but which are not to be regarded as organs with an indispensable function, necessary at all times for religion to go on.   (1982, 504)

Now one can certainly criticize this take on religion. But before doing so, I should like to try to place it; that is, trace its origins and its place in our history and culture. It should be clear that this take is very much at home in modern culture.

We can trace its origins through a series of developments in our history. First, the emphasis on religion as personal is consonant with a major direction of change through the last several centuries in Latin Christendom. From the high Middle Ages, we can see a steadily increasing emphasis on a religion of personal commitment and devotion over forms centered on collective ritual. We can see this both in devotional movements and associations, like the Brethren of the Common Life in the fifteenth century,[1] and in the demands made by church hierarchies and leaders on their members. An early example of the latter is the decision of the Lateran Council in 1215 to require all the faithful to confess to a priest and be shriven, so as to receive communion at least once a year.[2]

---

1. [Ed. note] A Roman Catholic devotional community, composed mostly of laypeople, founded by Geert [Gerard] De Groot (1340–84) in the Netherlands in the mid-fourteenth century, which emphasized lay study of the Bible and personal piety.
2. [Ed. note] Sometimes called the Great Council, it was called by Pope Innocent III (1160/1–1216) and resulted in the bishops approving seventy decrees, among which were: the condemnation of various heretical teachings; the establishment of a chain of command among the Church's various leaders; a limit placed on the establishment of new religious orders; a requirement for Jews and Muslims to distinguish themselves from Christians by means different clothing; rules for the fifth Crusade in the "Holy Land" (in 1217); and a requirement for every Christian of age to confess their sins to their parish priest at least once a year (to "be shriven" is to have confessed one's sins, received absolution, and performed the required penitence).

From that point on, the pressure to adopt a more personal, committed, inward form of religion continued, through the preaching of the mendicant friars[3] and others, through the devotional movements mentioned above, reaching a new stage with the Reformation. The point of declaring that salvation comes through faith was radically to devalue ritual and external practice in favor of inward adherence to Christ as Savior. It was not just that external ritual was of no effect, but that relying on it was tantamount to a presumption that we could control God. The Reformation also tended to delegitimate the distinction between fully committed believers and other, less devoted ones. As against a view of the church in which people operating at many different "speeds" coexisted, with religious "virtuosi" to use Max Weber's term,[4] on one end, and ordinary intermittent practitioners on the other, all Christians were expected to be fully committed.

But this movement toward the personal, committed, inward didn't exist only in the Protestant churches. There was a parallel development in the Counter-Reformation,[5] with the spread of different devotional movements, and the attempts to regulate the lives of the laity according to more and more stringent models of practice. The clergy were reformed, their training was upgraded; they were expected in turn to reach out and demand a higher level of personal practice from their flocks. A striking figure illustrates this whole movement: in the history of Catholic France, the moment at which the level of practice, as measured by baptisms and Easter communions, reaches its highest has been estimated to fall around 1870 (Tombs 1996, 135).[6] This was well after the anticlericalism of the [French] Revolution and its attempts at dechristianization, and after a definite movement toward unbelief had set in among the educated classes. In spite of this incipient loss, the apogee of practice came this late because it stood at the end of a long process in which ordinary believers had been preached at, organized, sometimes bullied, into patterns of practice that reflected more personal commitment.

They had been pressed, we might be tempted to say, into "taking their religion seriously"; and this expression reflects how much James's take on religion, at least in one facet, is in line with our modern understanding. To take my religion seriously is to take it personally; more devotionally, inwardly, more committedly. Just taking part in external rituals, those that don't require the kind of personal engagement which, say, auricular

---

3. [Ed. note] These are members of Roman Catholic religious orders who took a vow of individual and collective poverty (thereby preventing ownership of property) and who therefore relied on laypeople for financial support.

4. [Ed. note] Max Weber (1864–1920), noted sociologist of religion, is remembered for, among other things, his proposed link between Protestant doctrine, the Protestant work ethic, and the rise of the economic system known as capitalism.

5. [Ed. note] Counter-Revolution is the name given to a roughly hundred-year period of Roman Catholic reactions to what became known as the Protestant Reformation; to Catholic historians, the so-called Protestant Reformation, which began among Catholics intent on reforming the Church, was itself part of a longer period of Catholic Reformation throughout the sixteenth and seventeenth centuries that did not necessarily have to result in a separate wing of Christianity.

6. Tombs places the high-water mark at 1880; Cholvy and Hillaire (1985, 317) set it earlier, around 1860. I have split the difference.

confession, with its self-examination and promises of amendment, entails, is devalued on this understanding. This isn't what religion is really about.

This kind of understanding has deep roots, of course, in our religious tradition. When the psalmist, speaking for God, tells us to set aside our offerings of bulls and sheep and to offer instead a contrite heart (e.g., Psalm 51)[7], we are already on the road to our contemporary notion of personal religion. But there were many stages along the way, and not every culture has pressed as single-mindedly toward this ultimate point as that of the Latin Christendom to which we are heirs in the West. There are other religious traditions in which devotional movements are important and admired, such as Hinduism with its modes of *bhakti*,[8] but in which this devaluing of the life of collective ritual hasn't taken place. And there were earlier phases of our history in which the relation between those who were more personally devout and committed, and those whose main participation was in collective ritual, was thought of in terms of complementarity rather than ranked as more and less real; in which these two facets were understood to complete each other, be it in the life of an individual or in the religious life of the community. Moreover, there are certainly parts of the Catholic world where this is true today; only they tend to be distant from the North Atlantic regions, where the movement toward committed inwardness has gone the farthest.

In these regions, James's stress on personal religion, even his insistence that this is what religion *really* is, as against collective practice, can seem entirely understandable, even axiomatic, to lots of people.

Indeed, this is so central to Western modernity that a variant of this take is shared by highly secular people. It may take the form of their devaluing religion, because they think it is inseparable from mindless or unreflective external conformity; in other words, because they think that a really inward commitment would have to free us from religion. That is exactly what James fears and is trying to argue against in the passage quoted above where he warns us against defining "religion" in terms of "church," and thereby dismissing it too quickly, and missing the value of the real thing.

In fact, a striking feature of the Western march toward secularity is that it has been interwoven from the start with this drive toward personal religion, as has frequently been remarked (see McManners 1993, 277–8). The connections are multiple. It is not just that the falling off of religious belief and practice has forced a greater degree of reflection and commitment on those who remain. This has perhaps been evident in more recent times. It is much more that the drive to personal religion has itself been part of the impetus toward different facets of secularization. It was this drive, for instance, which powerfully contributed to the disenchantment of the world of spirits and higher forces in which our

---

7. [Ed. note] Verses 15–19 of Psalm 51 (in the New Revised Version of the Bible) read: "O Lord, open my lips, and my mouth will declare your praise. For you have no delight in sacrifice; if I were to give a burnt offering, you would not be pleased. The sacrifice acceptable to God is a broken spirit; a broken and contrite heart, O God, you will not despise. Do good to Zion in your good pleasure; rebuild the walls of Jerusalem, then you will delight in right sacrifices, in burnt offerings and whole burnt offerings; then bulls will be offered on your altar."

8. [Ed. note] *Bhakti yoga* is the Hindu practice or discipline of personal devotion to a god or goddess.

ancestors lived. The Reformation and Counter-Reformation repressed magical practices, and then those facets of traditional Christian sacramental ritual that they began to deem magical; for Calvinists this even included the Mass. Later, at the time of the early American republic, a separation of church and state was brought about, mainly to give space for, and avoid the contamination of, personal religion, which itself had been given a further impetus through the Great Awakening.

Later again, the same stress on inwardness and serious commitment gave strength to the view that one should break with a religion in some of whose tenets one had difficulty believing. There is an "ethics of belief" (see Clifford 1947), and it should drive us into religious unbelief if we find that the evidence points that way. Moreover, many of the secular moralities that have taken the place of religion place the same stress on inner commitment. We have only to think of the hold of various forms of Kantianism on secular ethics.[9]

In this sense, James's take on religion is well adapted to a confrontation between religion and secular views. It can seem the ground on which this confrontation can take place which is most favorable to religion: it operates within common assumptions about the importance of personal commitment, and within these it presents religion in the most favorable light by defining it in terms of intense experience that can galvanize conduct. This is not an accident. James's discussion of religious experience was not unconnected with his own profound commitments in this area, however the stance of psychological observer he assumes in this book might mislead us. In a sense, it articulates his own resistance to the agnostic intellectual culture of his day.[10] I shall return to this below.

James's position thus emerges from the main sweep of Latin Christendom over recent centuries. But we still have to place it more exactly than that, because it clearly belongs to some rather than others of the sub-branches that this development has thrown up. I want to relate it here to some of these crucial branching points.

There are modes of devotion in which we try to come closer to God, or center our lives on him, where we proceed in a fashion that trusts and builds on our own inner élan [or enthusiasm or passionate spirit], our own desire to approach God. We see examples, on the Catholic side, in some of the major figures in what Henri Bremond has called "*l'humanisme dévot*" [devout humanism] in the French seventeenth century such as St. François de Sales (see Clifford 1947); or in Jesuit spirituality which follows the inner guidance of consolation and desolation. On the Protestant side, we have the Cambridge

---

9. [Ed. note] The German philosopher Immanuel Kant published two influential works on ethics in the late eighteenth century. For Kant, the morality of an action is determined not by its results but by what directs or motivates it (e.g., attempting to do one's duty). He coined the "categorical imperative," which is his still famous rule that judges the morality of actions in relation to their ability to be universalized: "Act only according to that maxim by which you can at the same time will that it should become a universal law." Kant is famous for arguing that lying is universally wrong—without exceptions, and no matter what the positive or negative consequences.

10. [Ed. note] Coined in the nineteenth century, "agnostic" is an English version of an ancient Greek word for the special or privileged knowledge of the insider or initiate (*gnosis*). In distinction from one who denies the existence of a god (that is, atheism), to be an agnostic is to recognize that one does not possess the sort of knowledge needed even to decide the question.

Platonists,[11] for instance, or [John] Wesley (who himself was influenced by French Catholic spirituality).

This can be contrasted with a religious practice that stresses the demands made by God on his "unprofitable servants," which consists in following the Law or God's commands, as these are prescribed in the tradition or Revelation, without necessarily relying for guidance on one's own inner sense of these things. It should be clear that this kind of practice can be as personal, committed, and "inward" as the devotional one, and it has been very prominent in the development of modern personal religion.

Of course, nothing prevents these two from combining in one religious life. One might even claim that they ought ideally to complement each other. I myself certainly lean in this direction, if I may step for a minute beyond the role of neutral commentator. But the fact is that they have frequently been polarized, and opposed to each other. Thus, in the remarkable spiritual flourishing of the French seventeenth century, devout humanism was strongly opposed by thinkers of the Jansenist persuasion, like [Antoine] Arnault and [Pierre] Nicole.[12] One can understand why; the hyper-Augustinian sense of our own sinfulness, even depravity, which was central to Jansenus' message, made it seem not only dangerous but presumptuous to trust the élan toward God that one (believes one) finds within. And famously, the later years of the century saw the epic battle between [Jacques-Bénigne] Bossuet and [François] Fenelon on this very issue: dare one aspire to an "*amour pur*" [pure love] for God, or must one be actuated by fear of him?

We can perhaps see something of the same polarization in various periods of Islamic history, including today. There is a facet of Islamic practice that emphasizes full compliance with the *shar'ia*,[13] and another that has been carried, for instance, by traditions of Sufism, and that build on the longing of the soul for unity with God, as in Rumi's famous image of the reed flute.[14] These have often been united, but there have also been times in which

---

11. [Ed. note] The Cambridge Platonists were a group of seventeenth-century philosophers (many of whom also had theological training) affiliated with Cambridge University who worked in the philosophical tradition of, among others, Plato. Their work was concerned with such topics as free will, rational proofs for the existence of God, rational proofs for the immortality of the soul, and developing a system of ethics.

12. [Ed. note] Founded on the teachings of Cornelius Jansen, Bishop of Ypres, Belgium, Jansenism was an early seventeenth-century school of Roman Catholic philosophy and theology based on the writings of Augustine of Hippo (354–430 CE) emphasizing the belief in original sin, the human need for the grace of God (as opposed to achieving salvation by doing good deeds), predestination, and more thoughtful and thus less frequent ritual of Communion. It was repeatedly condemned by Rome as a heresy.

13. [Ed. note] *Shar'ia* is the Arabic term for the Muslim legal tradition that is based on such sources as the Qur'an, the tradition of authoritative sayings attributed to the Prophet Muhammad (such sayings are known as hadiths), and *fatwas* (legal rulings of Muslim scholars).

14. [Ed. note] Jalal Al-Din Muhammad Rumi (1207–73) was a Persian scholar and poet whose writings emphasized the need for the believer to attain an intimate unity with Allah, and who is associated with Islamic mystical traditions, such as Sufism. His poem, "The Song of the Reed" (in Sir William Jones's 1772 translation from the Arabic) concludes as follows:

> Blest is the soul, that swims in seas of love,
> And long the love sustain'd by food above.
> With forms imperfectly can perfection dwell?
> Here pause, my song; and thou, vain world, farewell.

the first stream has turned with suspicion on the second. The hostility to Sufism among some contemporary Islamist movements is a case in point.[15]

If we see this contrast as an important branching point between two streams, then plainly James stands in that of devout humanism. But we need to situate him more precisely within this line. He plainly belongs to that strand of it which is ready to challenge the traditionally mediated revelation in the name of one's inner inspiration. His model is more George Fox the Quaker than it is St. François de Sales. Indeed, he quotes Fox at length in the continuation of the passage I cited above (James 1982, 335–6).

We can situate him further in another branching: he sides with the religion of the heart over that of the head. This was plain in the passage I quoted above about the irrelevance of theories to real religious life. He stands in the succession of that late seventeenth- and eighteenth-century revolt against intellectualism in religion, following the Pietists and John Wesley in Christianity, the Hassidim in Judaism,[16] which sees the fullness of religious commitment as lying in powerful emotions and their expression, rather than in the nuances of doctrine or the perfections of scholarship.

Now this whole stream of devout humanism, in its anarchic and emotive branches, passed through a number of transpositions en route to James in the late nineteenth century. One of these was Romanticism, wherein the inspired initiator of a new inward spirituality is thought of as the "genius"—a term that figured in my earlier quote about the "pattern-setters" of religion (James 1982, 6). And along with this comes the notion that the genius cannot really be fully followed by ordinary people. The full intensity of the experience is always to some extent blunted as the pattern of spirituality comes to be adopted by large groups. The intense heat of the original feeling cools; what was "acute fever" becomes "dull habit."

We are reminded of the contemporary theological teaching of [Adolf von] Harnack in Germany, who depicted the white-hot charisma of the New Testament period as cooling into routine under the constraints of institutionalization. This whole understanding of moral/spiritual life, in which routinization of inspiration is understood as a quasi-inevitable fate, like entropy in the physical universe, was secularized and diffused by [Max] Weber, who even borrowed the New Testament term "charisma" from Harnack. Charismatic interventions in history suffer unavoidably from "banalization" ([German] *Veralltäglichung*, usually translated "routinization"). Weber even uses entropy as a master image here. Charisma is the specifically "revolutionary creative power of history," but all existing charismatic force is somewhere on its way "from the original storm to a slow death by suffocation" (Weber 1922, 759, 762).

---

15. The way in which *shar'ia* compliance articulates with a strong, personal, committed religious life is well illustrated in the study discussed by Clifford Geertz in his "William James" lecture (Geertz 2000; see especially 179 ff.). I have greatly benefited from Geertz's lecture in my discussion of James here.

16. [Ed. note] Hasidism, derived from a Hebrew word for "pious" and "loving kindness," was originally an eighteenth-century, eastern European movement within Judaism commonly understood as more personal and devotional, in opposition to the more rational and systematized aspects of the tradition associated with detailed rabbinic scholarship on scriptures and commentaries.

This picture of the interplay of inspiration and banalization, so widespread in the post-Romantic but secular world, also shapes the outlook of William James. In what ways does this situation within these different branchings limit the scope of James's study? How are the phenomena of religion distorted or narrowed through being conceived in terms of religious "experience"?

Well, obviously we can't expect too much fit with religious life that is far away from the modern North Atlantic norms, which put such an emphasis on personal religion. But it would be churlish, even absurd, to hold against him that his discussion didn't relate very closely to the practice of Hindus in contemporary India. That wasn't his main focus, which was really about religion as we know it on our culture (although there is the occasional reference outside, to, e.g., the Buddha and al-Ghazzali[17]), a limitation that was quite understandable a century ago. In order to focus the discussion, I intend to follow James and concentrate on the North Atlantic world (although I, too, find it hard to resist the occasional glance sideways to other regions).

But one might counterattack and say that after all, he's talking about religious *experience*; he's not claiming anything about all the other forms that figure on the other branches I mentioned above, the ones he is not situated within. This answer, however, won't wash, because the issue is very much whether, in taking his stand where he does, he doesn't severely distort the other branches. And indeed, it is difficult to imagine not doing so. I have situated James in various branchings of our religious culture, and these branchings were the sites of vigorous polemic. A Fox, a Wesley didn't only take one branch; they condemned the other. Condemnations may of course be totally justified, but more often than not they are attended with some distortion; the question is, to what extent the ones that James falls heir to give him a mangled and partial view of some of the important phenomena of modern religious life.

Nothing is farther from my intention than to indulge in point-scoring here. The aim is not to show that James's sympathies were narrow. Indeed, exactly the opposite is the case. One of the things that make his book so remarkable is the wide sympathy coupled with unparalleled phenomenological insight, which mark James as the exceptional figure that he is. That's why we go on reading this book, and will go on finding ideas of extraordinary value in it well after its centenary has passed. As to the unfortunate fact that James is neglected by contemporary academic philosophers, with a few honorable exceptions, this may just show that, alas, wide sympathy and powers of phenomenological description are not qualities for which the discipline has much place at present.

But in spite of all this, it seems to me that James got certain things wrong, or saw some important phenomena less undistortively than others. And any assessment of his work has to come to grips with this. The more so, in that just because of the close fit between James's take on religion and certain aspects of modern culture, one might easily run away with the idea that what James describes as religious experience is the only form religion can

---

17. [Ed. note] Abu Hamid Muhammad ibn Muhammad al-Ghazzali (1058–1111) was a noted Muslim scholar, legal theorist, and writer, with whom today is associated the movement away from the influence of ancient Greek philosophers on early Muslim thought. Later in his life, he was influenced by Sufi forms of Islam.

assume today. As we shall see below especially in the third chapter,[18] there are important developments that might make this appear so, but it is not so.

So what did James get wrong, or at least less right? One good place to start is with something that he sees himself: he stands within a Protestant tradition of understanding. So one thing he has trouble getting his mind around is Catholicism. His wide sympathies fail him, for instance, when it comes to St. Theresa of Avila.[19] She is one of his sources, and he quotes her at length (James 1982, 408–10), but at another point he says in some exasperation that "in the main her idea of religion seems to have been that of an endless amatory flirtation—if one may say so without irreverence—between the devotee and the deity" (1982, 347–8).

More important, he has trouble getting beyond a certain individualism. Churches are necessary, he clearly concedes. How else can the set of insights around a certain intense experience be handed on? How else can others be inducted into them? How else can believers be organized to take the action that flows from their faith? Of course, something is inevitably lost as religion thus becomes "second-hand," but the alternative would be no transmission at all.

What doesn't figure here is the way what one might call the religious connection, the link between the believer and the divine (or whatever), may be essentially mediated by corporate, ecclesial life. Thus let us imagine taking up the other branch to which I contrasted devout humanism, so that we think of religion (also) as living out the demands made by God, or the ways we are called upon to follow by some higher source. Let us imagine further that these ways are in some respect inherently social: say that we are called upon to live together in brotherly love, and to radiate outward such love as a community. Then the locus of the relation with God is (also) through the community and not simply in the individual. But this is the way that the life of the Christian church has been conceived, among many Protestants as well as Catholics; and also the way Israel and the Islamic *umma*[20] have been conceived. Moreover, this is far from being a thing of the past; this is still the way in which many today understand their religious life. What James can't seem to accommodate is the phenomenon of collective religious life, which is not just the result of (individual) religious connections, but which in some way constitutes or is that connection. In other words, he hasn't got place for a collective connection through a common way of being.

There is also another kind of collective connection, which is even farther off his map, perhaps because it is quintessentially "Catholic." This is the connection that consists in the fact that the church is a sacramental communion; some of the force is carried in an expression like "mystical body." From one point of view this is just a facet of the connection

---

18. [Ed. note] In chapter 3 of *Varieties of Religion Today*, Taylor offers his version of the secularization thesis, according to which state or civil religion has in a sense come to fill the central cultural space once occupied by, for example, the Catholic church in medieval Europe.

19. [Ed. note] St. Theresa of Avila (1515–82) was a Spanish Carmelite nun and author who attempts to recover a more traditional form of devotional practice and played a prominent role in the Counter-Reformation. She was considered to have mystical visions and was eventually canonized in 1622 (making her a saint).

20. [Ed. note] *Umma* is the Arabic term used to name the worldwide community of Muslims.

through the church's common way of being. But it raises more explicitly the idea of God's life interpenetrating ours, and of this interpenetration being made fuller, more intense and immediate through our own practices. These practices cover the whole range, including those we might call ethical, or more generally the practices of charity; but the connection gains a certain intensity in the signs instituted to manifest it, which are called sacraments.

It goes without saying that this sacramental connection is also essentially collective; in fact it participates in the collective nature of the other kind of connection, which turns on a common way of life.

These kinds of things don't find a place in James's conceptual grid, and this fact partly accounts for the highly negative view about churches. Not that they aren't also full of the two "spirits of dominion" he cites. This is especially true of the Catholic church in Western Christendom, whose life in recent centuries has frequently been marred by a drive to dominate. But if a church is also a locus of collective connection, then one will not be able to think of it so exclusively in the negative terms that James displays.

A parallel point could be made about James's exclusion of theology from the center of religious life. This is particularly difficult for Christianity to accommodate. Not that there hasn't frequently been over-theologization, in the sense of an insistence on fine distinctions, even to the point of splitting churches on these issues, where a greater sense of what is essential, less ego invested in one's formulations, and a more abundant charity, might have averted schism. But the devotional, practical, and (if any) sacramental way of life needs some minimum articulation of what it is all about: some propositional formulations are unavoidable—about God, creation, Christ, and the like. Just as the life can't be separated from its collective expression, so it can't be isolated from a minimum of express formulation. The faith, the hope, are *in* something.

But here we push against the bounds of another criticism of James. Up to now I've been pleading that there are important, widespread religious forms that cannot be undistortively understood within his concept of religious experience. This is in a sense an empirical point. But one might make the more radical conceptual or transcendental point, that the very idea of an experience that is in no way formulated is impossible. The familiar arguments of [Georg Wilhelm Friedrich] Hegel (say, in the *Phenomenology of Spirit*, chapter 1), or of [Ludwig] Wittgenstein (say, in the *Philosophical Investigations*, I, section 261) come to mind. The experience can have no content at all if you can't say anything about it.

Of course, James was well cognizant of Hegel, albeit resistant to being recruited into the neo-Hegelianism of his day. He would have seen the point of this objection, and carried on with the reply that having some description is not the same as being theorized, and particularly not the same as being authoritatively theorized by some official *magisterium* that can lean on you for the heterodoxy of your experience.

The point is well taken, but it ought to force us towards a more adequate account of the implicit distinction here between ordinary unavoidable description and theorizing. Where does one draw the line? More to the point: do certain "experiences"—St. Theresa's, for instance—require rather more in the way of propositional background than others? If there are some that require quite a lot, what becomes in such cases of the supposed short circuit whereby feeling bypasses theory on its way to influencing conduct?

A similar set of considerations might be deployed to question the sense in which one can really have an individual experience. All experiences require some vocabulary, and these are inevitably in large part handed to us in the first place by our society, whatever transformations we may ring on them later. The ideas, the understanding with which we live our lives, shape directly what we could call religious experience; and these languages, these vocabularies, are never those simply of an individual. [21]

Does this make James's main thesis, about real religion being individual experience, unstatable? Not at all. We can make the point in the terms I mentioned above, where the question reposes on whether the religious connection is individual or collective. But once we fully appreciate the social nature of language, it does open another series of questions for James. There are (what are in one sense) individual experiences that are immensely enhanced by the sense that they are shared. I am sitting at home watching the local hockey team win the Stanley Cup. I rejoice in this. But the sense of my joy here is framed by my understanding that thousands of fans all over the city, some gathered at the rinkside, others also in their living rooms, are sharing in this moment of exultation. There are certain emotions you can have in solidarity that you can't have alone; the experience mutates into something else by the fact that it is shared. How much of what James thinks of as individual experience is socially enhanced or affected in this way? We could imagine a sect in which the individual's relation to God is everything; and yet people are brought into contact with God through revival meetings. They come to conversion at that climactic moment of decision when the preacher calls on people to come forward and declare their faith. This can be a white-hot experience, but in what sense is it individual? There are a number of questions here that need to be resolved. [22]

All that I have said above is meant to try to situate James's focus in the map of modern religious phenomena. He doesn't cover the whole field, but his vision is proportionately more intense of the realities he does fix his gaze on....

---

21. Thus Robert Wuthnow (1998), in discussing the increasing reports people give of meeting angels, and other similar experiences in recent years, notes that these tend to correlate with a religious upbringing in which realities of this kind had a place. (See his chapter 5, especially 125–6.)

22. My discussion here has been much helped by Nicholas Lash's (1986) critique of James.

PART III

THE UNIVERSALITY OF EXPERIENCE

6

JOACHIM WACH

"Universals in Religion," from *Types of Religious Experience: Christian and Non-Christian*

Known as one of the founders of the "Chicago School" in Religious Studies, which defined the field's central path of scholarship during the last half of the twentieth century, Joachim Wach (1898–1955) was a German-born scholar of religion whose primary contribution to the field was the promotion of a method called *Religionswissenschaft* (literally, "the science of religion"). This method claimed that religion has an important socio-historical component that should be studied apart from theological or reductionistic explanations. Although the "scientific" study of religion has come to mean something different in contemporary scholarship—namely, questioning certain assumptions about the *sui generis,* or unique and irreducible, nature of religion often descriptive of older models of religion like Wach's—his work in the mid-twentieth century represented an attempt to move away from overtly normative demands and toward what was then considered a more empirical endeavor.

Wach taught at the University of Leipzig from 1924 to 1935 when he was driven from his university post by a then-growing Nazi influence. He emigrated to the United States, teaching at Brown University until 1945, and ended his career at the University of Chicago, where he also spent the last ten years of his life. Over the course of his career, Wach published numerous works, all of which were underpinned by the *Religionswissenschaft* method. These include *Sociology of Religion* (1944); *The Comparative Study of Religions* (1961); *Types of Religious Experience: Christian and Non-Christian* (1965); and *Understanding and Believing: Essays by Joachim Wach* (1968).

The central assumptions underscoring *Religionswissenschaft* are fundamentally phenomenological. Phenomenological approaches to religion claim to bracket, or set aside, the issue of the truth of a particular religion, instead studying, systematizing, and categorizing religion's more physical or visible aspects. As such, phenomenologists do not claim to assess whether or not a religion is true, but only how it is manifested within society, and how it compares with other religions. In line with these phenomenological assumptions, Wach became known for his insistence that the goal of the scholar of religion is to *understand* (in German, *Verstehen*) religion, and in so arguing he paved the way for a large number of scholars who assume the possibility of scholarly objectivity as well as the scholar's capacity to identify with and/or understand the religious phenomena that they record.

The notion of *Verstehen* depends, in great part, on a belief in the universal and irreducible nature of religious experience; the capacity to fully understand the experiences of another comes about only by assuming that they implicitly share something in common. Wach was greatly influenced by theologian Rudolph Otto's definition of religion, which argued that religion was most fundamentally an experience of "the holy." The empirical, scientific study of this experience was thus, to Wach, dependent on cataloguing and classifying the similarities and differences between experiences of "the holy" that he and later scholars (most notably, famed scholar Mircea Eliade, who assumed Wach's position at Chicago after his death) believed that all religions shared.

While at one time the *Religionswissenschaft* method was seen as one of the most neutral methods of approaching religious phenomena, later scholars have argued that any perspective that assumes a sacred essence permeating human consciousness is neither self-evident nor natural; many have demonstrated how, in fact, such a perspective is historically constructed, as later essays in this volume will assert.

This essay, entitled "Universals in Religion," sets forth some of Wach's central assumptions about religion and methods appropriate for its study. He argues that religious experience should be understood in its theoretical, practical, and sociological expressions, and that, as the title expresses, one can uncover certain "universals" in religion through these methods. There is perhaps no better piece to spark conversation about issues now endemic to the field, which include claims of *Verstehen* and the insider/outside problem (the ongoing debate about how an insider's perspective should compare to a scholar's perspective, and whether the scholar is capable of "capturing" the insider's world), the significance of Protestant influence on the field as a whole, and what "empirical" has come to mean, thereby also unsettling what gets to count as "data."

"UNIVERSALS IN RELIGION," FROM *TYPES OF RELIGIOUS EXPERIENCE*

The careful research of many a generation of scholars, the travel reports, not only of adventurers, missionaries and explorers, but of many a person you and I count among our personal acquaintances, have brought home to well-nigh all of us a realization of the variety of religious ideas and practices that exist in the world.[1] The result of this realization

---

1. [Ed. note] It is important to recognize the direct link between the age of European expansion and colonialism, on the one hand, and the gains in knowledge that led to the development of new academic disciplines and tools for studying cultures, on the other (case in point: the development of Comparative Religion in the late nineteenth century). Although one can rather casually name "travel reports" of "adventurers," "missionaries," and "explorers," as a source for descriptions of the novel practices of other peoples, it is likely crucial to understand that the ability and motive for traveling afar was, in many cases, hardly innocent but, instead, linked to specific cultural, economic, and political interests that had much to do with expansion and domination. As such, Wach's opening line—although likely not intended to communicate this point—makes clear the sometimes unseen relationship between knowledge and power (a linkage much associated with the work of the late French intellectual, Michel Foucault).

has been bewilderment and confusion in many hearts and minds. Roughly three different types of reaction to the situation can be discerned: (i) skepticism, that is, the refusal to see in all these religious ideas and usages more than the expression of ignorance and folly, in other words a cultural and/or religious "lag"; (ii) relativism, that is, a disposition to dispense with the problem of truth in favor of a non-committal registration of all there is and has been, an attitude which has found much favor in the latter-day circles of scholars and intellectuals; and finally (iii) the desire to investigate the variety of what goes under the names of religion and religions in order to determine by comparison and phenomenological analysis if anything like a structure can be discovered in all these forms of expression, to what kind of experiences this variegated expression can be traced, and finally, what kind of reality or realities may correspond to the experiences in question. It is the last of the three types of reaction to the predicament characterized above which seems to us the only promising and fruitful one, and we propose to follow it in what we have to say here.

The first difficulty we encounter in trying to bring some order into the bewildering mass of material that geography, anthropology, sociology, archaeology, philology, history, and the history of religions have placed at our disposal, is the need for criteria which would enable us to distinguish between what is religious and what is not. Now you will not expect me to discuss the well-nigh endless series of definitions of religion which have been proposed by the great and the not-so-great during recent decades. We shall also find it impossible to use as our yardstick one of the classical historical formulations evolved in one of the great religious communities itself, say in the Christian. For we should soon discover that it is not possible to identify religion with what we have come to know as Christian or Jewish or Hindu, even if we forget for the moment that it would be far from easy to agree on which of the available formulations we want to use. Some of us might feel, at first thought, that it is after all not so difficult to determine what may be called religious and what is not religious; they would point to the neat divisions which we are accustomed to find in our textbooks, dealing with the lives of individuals, societies and cultures, past and present, in which separate chapters deal with man's political views and activities,[2] his economic situation, his interest in the arts, and his religious orientation, or with the social organization, the economics, the legal institutions, the arts and sciences, the moral life, and the religion of a given tribe, people or nation. But, on second thoughts, the unsatisfactory character of such parceling becomes evident; and that not only in the repetitions and omissions which this procedure entails. No wonder then that some investigators—and we find among them distinguished anthropologists, philosophers, and theologians—have come to the conclusion that religion is not anything distinct and *sui generis*,[3] but is a name

---

2. [Ed. note] Throughout this fifty-year-old essay, Wach employs the onetime common practice of using the gender-specific "man" to signify all human beings. Although this practice has been critiqued, over the past few decades, as evidence of a specific form of politics (whereby a part is universalized as representative of the whole—after all, the equally gender-specific signifier "woman" is rarely employed as a universal signifier capable of naming all human beings, regardless their gender), the essay's use of "man" is retained throughout.

3. [Ed. note] This Latin term, meaning self-caused, is commonly used to signify things that are thought not to derive from, or to be caused to originate by, anything outside themselves. As such, it is used to

given to the sum of man's aspirations, to the whole of the civilization of a people. If we reject this view, it is not because we want to separate sharply between religion on the one hand and on the other all that makes up an individual's or a society's other experiences and activities. But we are of the opinion that, in order to be able to assess the interrelation and interpenetration of the various interests, attitudes, and activities of man, we have to examine very carefully the nature of his propensities, drives, impulses, actions, and reactions. William James has rightly said: "The essence of religious experiences, the thing by which we must finally judge them, must be that element or quality in them which we can meet nowhere else" (James 1902).[4] We disagree with those who are prone to identify religion with just one segment of man's inner existence: feeling, willing, or cogitating. In order to lay down our criteria, we cannot be satisfied to examine only the conceptually articulated perceptions or only the emotions and affections and the respective expressions in which they have become manifest. We propose rather the following *four formal criteria* for a definition of what might be called religious experience:

1. Religious experience is a response to what is experienced as ultimate reality; that is, in religious experiences we react not to any single or finite phenomenon, material or otherwise, but to what we realize as undergirding and conditioning all that constitutes our world of experiences. We agree with Paul Tillich[5] when he says that "the presence of the demand of 'ultimacy' in the structure of our existence is the basis of religious experience" (Tillich 1947, 23). Before him William James said in his book on *The Varieties of Religious Experience* (James 1902, 58)—a passage quoted in Paul Johnson's *Psychology of Religion* (Johnson 1945, 36): "It is as if there were in the human consciousness a sense of reality, a feeling of objective presence, a perception of what we may call 'something there,' more deep and more general than any of the special and particular 'senses' by which the current psychology supposes existent realities to be originally revealed."[6] Or as the author of a recent textbook on

---

describe something understood to be unique and one-of-a-kind. When it comes to the study of religion, the phrase is often used to contest those who argue that religion is caused by other historical elements, such as it being a response to prior psychological or economic factors. These later scholars are generally known as "reductionists" because of their interest to "reduce" (as in the practice in the sciences, whereby features from one level of description are reduced to another, such as biological data being explained by using theories derived from physics) religion to some more elemental, non-religious feature of culture.

4. [Ed. note] Although it is not clear which edition of James's book Wach used for this quotation, the quotation comes from Lecture 2, "Circumscription of the Topic," from *The Varieties of Religious Experience*, reproduced earlier in this volume.

5. [Ed. note] Paul Tillich (1886–1965), German Protestant theologian who attained fame later in his career while teaching in the US, in part for his interest in cross-cultural work and the development of a theology of world religions. The phrase "ultimate concern" is much associated with his work, given Tillich's influential definition of religion as "faith in an ultimate concern."

6. Emile Durkheim agrees with James that "religious beliefs rest upon a specific experience whose demonstrative value is, in one sense, not one bit inferior to that of scientific experiments, though different from them" (Durkheim 1947, 417). He adds, and rightly, that it does not follow from the fact that a "religious experience exists and has a certain foundation, that the reality which is its foundation conforms objectively to the idea which believers have of it."

Psychology of Religion formulates it: "Religious experience is response to stimuli that represent an active reality viewed as divine, or as creative of values" (Johnson 1945, 47).[7]

This response has the tendency to persist, once communion with the source of life and values is established, and man is restless to reassure himself of its continuance.

2. Religious experience is a total response of the total being to what is apprehended as ultimate reality. That is, we are involved not exclusively with our mind, our affections, or our will, but as integral persons (this point is well brought out by Canon B. H. Streeter [1932, 157 ff.]).

3. Religious experience is the most intense experience of which man is capable. That is not to say that all expression of religious experience testifies to this intensity but that, potentially, genuine religious experience is of this nature, as is instanced in conflicts between different basic drives or motivations. Religious loyalty, if it is religious loyalty, wins over all other loyalties. The modern term "existential" designates the profound concern and the utter seriousness of this experience.

4. Religious experience is practical, that is to say it involves an imperative, a commitment which impels man to act. This activistic note distinguishes it from aesthetic experience, of which it shares the intensity, and joins it with moral experience. Moral judgment, however, does not necessarily represent a reaction to ultimate reality.

It should be borne in mind that one, two, or three of these criteria would not suffice to reassure us that we are dealing with genuine religious experience. All four would have to be present. If they are, we should have no difficulty in distinguishing between religious and non-religious experiences. However, there are *pseudo-religious* and *semi-religious* experiences. The former are non-religious and known to be such to the person or persons who pretend to them by using forms of expression peculiar to religion. The latter may show the presence of the second, third and fourth characteristics, but refer not to ultimate but to some aspect of "finite" reality. The intense and possibly sacrificial devotion with which somebody may "worship" a loved person, his race, his social group, or his state are instances of semi-religious loyalties. Because they are directed toward finite values, they are idolatrous rather than religious.

Now it is our contention, and this is the *first* proposition in regard to our topic, that religious experience, as we have just attempted to define it by means of these four criteria, is universal. The empirical proof of this statement can be found in the testimonies of explorers and investigators. "There are no peoples, however primitive, without religion and magic," is the opening sentence of one of [Bronislaw] Malinowski's well-known essays (1948, 1). In practically all cases where a rash negative conclusion has been reached, more careful research has corrected the initial error.

A *second* proposition is this: religious experience tends towards *expression*. This tendency is universal. Only in and through its expression does any of our experiences exist

---

7. Moore (1938, 86 ff., 95 ff.), criticizes Rudolf Otto's assumption of the cognitive nature of the numinous feeling. We distinguish between apprehension and intellectual expression.

for others, does any religious experience exist for us, the students of the history of religion. The religious experience of another person can never become the object of direct observation. Some important hermeneutical consequences result from the recognition of this fact.

Now for the *third* step in our search for universals in religion. A comparative study of the *forms* of the expression of religious experience, the world over, shows an amazing similarity in structure. We should like to summarize the result of such comparative studies by the statement: all expression of religious experience falls under the three headings of *theoretical expression, practical expression,* and *sociological expression.*[8] Everywhere and at all times man has felt the need to articulate his religious experience in three ways: conceptually; by action, or practically; and in covenanting, or sociologically. There is no religion deserving of the name in which any one of these three elements is totally lacking, though the degree and, of course, the tempo of this development may vary. Notwithstanding numerous attempts at establishing priority for one of these three modes of expression, we feel that it would be futile to argue that myth precedes cult or that both precede fellowship: history teaches us that the dynamics of religious life is made up of the interpenetration of these three aspects.

Before we can discuss in any greater detail the structure of these fields of expression of religious experience and the common elements to be found within an apparently endless variety of forms, we have to consider briefly some general factors which help to determine their development. Man finds himself always situationally conditioned: whatever he experiences, he experiences in *time* and *space.* Even if, in his religious experience, he seems to transcend these limitations—a feeling to which the mystics of all religions have given vivid and often paradoxical articulation ([such as the Christian mystic, Meister] Eckhart [who wrote]: "Time is what keeps the light from reaching us. There is no greater obstacle to God than Time"; see also Huxley 1945, chapter 12)—he cannot but give expression to what he has seen, felt, etc., ... by means of *analogy* from what is known and familiar to him.[9] The way of negation, of analogy and of eminence is used in all religious language. That we have to remember when we review the concepts of sacred time and of sacred space which are the framework within which religious thought and religious acts enfold themselves. Holy times and holy places are universal notions; no myth or doctrine, no cult or religious association is found without them (van der Leeuw 1938, 655–7; Eliade 1949, chapters 10,

---

8. Cf. [Compare with] the methodological prolegomena in Wach (1947), part 1; cf. there many references and bibliography for statements in the text above.

9. There is the analogy of the senses (sight, hearing, smell, touch; what is experienced is described as "light," voices are heard, sweet odors are smelt), then the analogy of physical phenomena (procreating, eating), that of the various activities of man (warfare, peaceful pursuits [agriculture; pastoral life; other professions]), traveling (pilgrimage), and of human relationships (kin, social, marital relations). Professor Bevan has especially studied the symbolic use of time and space notions. Urban again has stressed the analogies of the sun—"the Sun with its powerful rays, its warmth and light, its life-giving qualities, becomes a natural symbol for the creating and eliciting power" (Urban 1939, 589)—and sex—"sex, love, its heights and its depths, its horrible darkness and its blinding light is never wholly alien to the creative love of which Plato, no less than Christian theologians and philosophers, discourse" (Urban 1939, 591). Ewer (1933) analyzed the analogies of the senses in mystical symbolic language. Underhill (1930, chapter 6) has concentrated upon the symbolic notions of pilgrimage (for divine transcendence), of love and of transmutation.

11). Closely related to these categories within which religious apprehension expresses itself is the notion of a *cosmic* (that is natural, ritual and social) *order* upon which life, individual and collective, depends. The well-known Chinese concept of *Tao*, the Hindu *rta*, the Iranian *asha*, the Greek *dike*, designate the order upon which man and society depend for their existence (see Franke 1928; Wach 1947, 49; Rhys Davids 1917, 18, 279 ff.; Caillois 1939, 9 ff.; Eliade 1949, chapters 10, 11). In the religions of the American Indians, the Africans and Oceanians the directions, the seasons, the celestial bodies, colors, social organization, all follow this orientation, the cosmic law which the physical, mental and spiritual life of all beings has to obey.[10] Nature and its rhythm, culture and its activities, and polity and its structure are but aspects of this order. It is the foundation for all "ethics."

Religious experience, we saw, may be characterized as the total response of man's total being to what he experiences as ultimate reality. In it he confronts a *power* greater than any power which he controls by his own wit or strength. I should like to stress *two* points here. This encounter is not a question of intellectual inference or speculative reasoning, of which there are few traces in many of the lower so-called primitive religions.[11] That is to say, religion is emphatically not a kind of underdeveloped "science" or "philosophy." This misinterpretation, still widely current, is an unfortunate legacy from the rationalistically minded era of the Enlightenment.[12] The experience which we call religion is rather an awareness of apprehension, not lacking a cognitive aspect but not defined by it, a reaction to something that is sensed or apprehended as powerful. Rudolf Otto has spoken of a *sensus numinis* (sense of awe),[13] and this term seems to me a very apt designation. We

---

10. "The symbolism of the World Quarters, of the Above, and of the Below, is nowhere more elaborately developed among American Indians than with the Pueblos. Analogies are drawn not merely with colors, with plants and animals, and with cult objects and religious ideas, but with human society in all the ramifications of its organization, making of mankind not only the theatric centre of the cosmos, but a kind of elaborate image of its form" (Alexander 1937, Vol. 10, 185).

11. "He [the savage] encounters the divine stimulus here, there and anywhere within the contents of an experience in which percepts play a far more important part than concepts" (Marrett 1932, 144. Cf. also Frankfort *et al.* 1946, 130 ff.). [Ed. note: The evolutionary assumptions prominent among nineteenth-century scholars are still evident in this mid-twentieth-century essay, as evidenced in the use of such categories as "savage" and "primitive." Developmental assumptions lie behind the use of these categories, as well as the assumption (evident later in Wach's essay) that premodern peoples were somehow more in-touch with their experiences of "the sacred."]

12. [Ed. note] A common assumption among those nineteenth-century scholars known as "Intellectualists" (e.g., E. B. Tylor [1832–1917]) was that those narratives known as myths were, in fact, attempts on the part of evolutionarily early human beings to explain regularities they experienced in the natural world, something accomplished far better with the later development called science. They assumed, therefore, that despite differing in terms of their stage of evolutionary development and thus their intellectual sophistication, all human beings were rational, interested in explaining why things take place as they do.

13. [Ed. note] Rudolf Otto (1869–1937) was an influential German Protestant theologian whose interest in cross-cultural religious expressions is evident in his 1917 theological work, *Das Heilige*, translated from the German into English as the still-in-print *The Idea of the Holy*. Otto coined the Latin term "the numinous" to name that which he believed all religious adherents experienced; the numinous coincided with what he also termed the *mysterium tremendum et fascinans*: the tremendous awe-inspiring mystery that both compels and repels. In response to the emphasis on studying religion's rational aspects (such as creeds and doctrines), Otto focused on the non-rational (that is, emotive) elements of religious experience.

must reject all theories of religion which conceive of it as the fulfillment which imaginative or crafty individuals have supplied for a subjective, that is illusory, need. True, many a testimony to religious experience lets the latter appear as the result of a search, a struggle, but more often this experience has come as a bolt from the blue, with a spontaneity which contradicts the theory of need. Hence we prefer to say that there is a propensity, a *nisus* [to strive or endeavor] or *sensus numinis* which is activated in the religious experience proper.[14] The aspect of power which the comparative study of religion has recently vindicated as a central notion in the religions of widely different peoples and societies, indicates the "point of contact" between the reality which is confronted in religious experience and life in the everyday world: the "immanence of the transcendent." Religions differ in their notions as to the how, where, and when of the manifestations of power in the phenomenal world. But the acknowledgment that this power manifests itself in experienceable form is universal. To the degree that it appears diffused, we speak of *power-centers* such as are known in all primitive, higher and fully developed cults (see van der Leeuw 1938; Eliade 1949). The Swedish historian of religion, Martin Nilsson (1949, 91), has recently stressed the adjective character of terms for power such as *mana, orenda,* etc.[15] Not the phenomenon, object or person in which this power manifests itself, but a power that *transcends* it, is the object of man's awe. It is of great importance to understand that this power is apprehended as an elementary force which transcends moral or aesthetic qualifications. As such it is "mysterious." It was one of the great insights of the author of *The Idea of the Holy,* Rudolf Otto, that he caught the double notion of the *mysterium magnum* in the twin ideas of its terrifying and its alluring aspect. These two aspects are known to the theologians of all religions as Divine Wrath and Divine Love or Grace. Though their natural roles and relationships are differently conceived in different faiths, these two aspects of power are universally recognized. But we can still go one step further in our analysis of universal features in religious experience. It is possible to discern a double consequence of man's apprehension of numinous power at all times and everywhere: he either bows to it in submission, or he reaches out in an attempt to manipulate and control the mysterious forces of which he has become aware. The first, the *religious* way, leads up to the highest religious act, that of adoration; the second, the way of *magic*, sets him on the road to conquer and to appropriate as much of the power as will yield to his command. These two developments are not to be thought of in terms of a chronological and evolutionary sequence: on the one hand the magical is always with us, and on the other the presence of genuinely religious response to the numinous even in the primitive cults cannot be denied. Hence both are universal. It is only the *intention* inherent in it which distinguishes the religious from the

---

14. Thus the criticism which Moore (1938, 91 ff., 103 ff.) levels rightly at Rudolf Otto's concept of "feeling" does not apply to our theory.

15. [Ed. note] *Mana*, a term obtained by early anthropologists from Polynesian cultures, was used by nineteenth-century scholars as a technical term for the power they believed early humans thought to reside in people, animals, or objects; R. R. Marrett (1866–1943) proposed that a belief in *mana* was the earliest stage in the development of modern religion. The related term, *orenda*, which is derived from Native American peoples (notably, the Iroquois), denotes a mystical potency within things, their life force.

magical act. The very complicated question of the origins, the nature of the development of "science" (in the broader as well as the narrower sense of the natural sciences), and of its relation to both magic and religion, can be answered when we are more fully conversant with the nature of knowledge,[16] with the psychological motivations for wanting to know (Malinowski 1948, 72 ff., 76, 93 ff.).[17]

Perhaps the sociology of knowledge will help us at some time in the future. On the cognitive factor in the experience which we call religious we shall have a word to say presently.

After these brief remarks, which were meant to put in relief some universally valid features of religious *experience*, we will now turn to the examination of universals in the forms of *expression* of this experience (for the general framework see Wach 1947, part 1, chapter 2). We have said that the very fact that this experience tends to expression constitutes in itself a universal. We shall enlarge this statement now by asking: What *motivates* expression? There is first what I should like to call the demonstrative type of expression with which we are familiar from all kinds of experiences other than religious. The shout of joy or pain, witnessing to a profound emotion, is paralleled by the ejaculatory expression of awe or devotion. Then there is the communicative motif: we like to share our experiences with others, and we can do so only by means of sounds, words, or acts. Finally the missionary purpose has to be considered. We want to attract others, a purpose not alien to other types of experience, but constitutive of the religious. Finding these motives making for expression universally valid, we may ask further: What of the *modes* in which the expression of religious experience is cast?

Here we face the difficult question of the interrelationship of what we have called the intellectual, the practical, and the sociological expressions of religious experience (Kluckhohn 1942, 45 ff.; cf. Ratschow 1947). [Edwyn] Bevan, [Ernst] Cassirer, [Wilbur Marshall] Urban, Susanne Langer and others have studied the problem of symbolism and analyzed the structure of logical, aesthetic, and religious symbols (Bevan 1938; Cassirer 1923; Urban 1939, esp. chapter 12; Langer 1942, 10, n. 2; Eliade 1949, chapter 13; Wach 1947, 19; Danielou 1950, 423 ff.). The *symbol* is the primary means of expressing the content of any experience which we call religious. The use of symbolic expression is universal. By symbols a meaning is conveyed the nature of which may be conceptually explained, which may be acted upon, and which may serve as an integrating factor in creating religious fellowship. An example of a simple symbol is the *churinga* of the Australians (the bull-roarer, standing for the presence of totemic ancestors), on a higher level the *shintai* (sword, mirror, stone) of the Japanese, or finally, in the great world religions, the Buddhist wheel and the Christian cross.[18] In each case theoretical explanations, cultural use, and

---

16. Cf. the excellent chapter "Curiosity" in Marrett (1932, chapter 8). Cf. also Childe (1950).

17. Malinowski's solution [in his essay, "Myth in Primitive Society"]—the sociological theory of myth, in his own words—does not satisfy because of his preoccupation with the pragmatic aspect of both religious and magical activities. He neglects the problems of meaning, structure, and motivation. A more promising approach seems to be [offered by] Ernesto de Martino (1948, 11) who is concerned with the nature of the reality to which magic thought and acts refer.

18. [Ed. note] As with earlier scholars who were interested in *mana*, some elements of other cultures drew particular scholarly attention: the *churinga*: stone or wooden symbols of Australian aborigines; bull-roarer:

sociological effect contribute to unfold and explain the meaning of the symbol.[19] Stages in the development of these modes of expression can be traced: the African Bushmen, awed by the presence of the numinous at a given place, utter a numinous sound in which they express the vivid emotion that grips them, while throwing a few grains into a hole in the hallowed ground, an act which at the same time expresses and reinforces the communion which exists between fellow-worshippers. A second example: in the Egypt of the ancient kingdom the worshippers of a deity are gathered in a hut before the crude therio- or anthropomorphic images which stand as a symbol of the numinous presence.[20] The myth in which the nature and the significance of this manifestation of the divine is illustrated imaginatively, is alive in the minds of those present. A third example: the original intuition or basic religious experience of the founder of Islam is enfolded in the systematic doctrine of Islam, acted out in acts of devotion and charity, and is the foundation upon which the *umma* or congregation of the faithful rests. All this goes to show the universal presence of the three modes of expression of religious experience and their intimate interrelationship.

We now have to discuss the *means* by which religious experience is theoretically, practically, and sociologically expressed. Here too our expectation is to find elements present everywhere.[21] We begin with the *intellectual* expression. Religious experience, as confrontation of ultimate reality, entails a cognitive element. When Mohammed received his initial revelation, when the Buddha awoke to the realization of the impermanence of the phenomenal world, when Laotse became aware of the nature of the unalterable Tao,[22] this original intuition ("*Ur-intuition*")[23] in each case implied an apprehension of ultimate reality, of the relation of the visible to the invisible, of the nature of the universe and of man's nature and destiny which invited further conceptual articulation. We do not know to which intuitions the primitive cults owe their existence, but we can infer that generations of seers and priests helped to evolve the mythical concepts in which the numinous

---

found in Australia, among other places, a small carved piece of wood, often elliptical, attached to a length of chord, which, when twirled in circles, emits vibrating sounds that can be heard at some distance; *shintai*: the name given to objects in which kami, or ancestors/life force, are thought to reside in Japanese Shinto; Buddhist wheel: having eight spokes, the imagery of a turning wheel is often used to teach the Noble Eightfold Path, as well as to illustrate the movement of *samsara*, the cycle of births and rebirths; Christian cross: because crucifixion upon a cross was the form of execution for non-citizens of Rome, Jesus of Nazareth died in this fashion and the means of his death became the widely accepted symbol for Christians.

19. "Images are taken from the narrower and more intelligible relations and used as expressions for more universal and ideal relations which, because of this pervasiveness and ideality, cannot be directly expressed" (Urban 1939, 580, 586).

20. [Ed. note] From Greek terms, meaning that which has either an animal or human shape or form attributed to it. An example of the former would be finding animal shapes in the constellations and an example of the latter would be saying, "The sea was angry that day."

21. Rich inventories of the wealth of expressions of religious experiences are to be found in van der Leeuw (1938), of which a revised French translation appeared recently: *La religion dans son essence et ses manifestations. Phenomenologie de la religion* (Paris: Payot, 1948); and in Eliade (1949).

22. [Ed. note] Taoism is the name today given to a body of ancient Chinese teachings attributed to Lao-Tse (604–531 BCE). The Tao, or Path/Way, is believed to be an active force that animates the universe.

23. [Ed. note] *Ur-* is a German prefix, meaning first, original, primordial, or prototypical.

experiences of these peoples have come to expression. For *myth* is the *first form* of intellectual explanation of religious apprehensions. "It is," says Langer, "in the great realm of myth that human conceptions of reality become articulated" (1942, 169). "These stories," says Malinowski, "live not by idle interest, not as fictions or even as true narratives; but are to the natives a statement of a primeval, greater, and more relevant reality by which the present life, fate and activities of man are determined. Here the imaginative element prevails over the abstract" (1948, 86; see also Urban 1939, 571, 576 ff.). Contrary to the assumption of the Positivist school—[Auguste] Comte's theory of the stages[24]—this form of expression is universal; it is not bound to any one stage of development, as the use of mythical language in all the great religions indicates. Myth asks the perennial question Why? Why are we here? Where do we come from? Why do we act in the way we do? Why do we die?—questions which the awakened intellectual curiosity of man is apt to ask and to answer in imaginative, that is symbolic, language. The reason for the persistence of this form of expression of religious experience is to be found in the nature of this experience itself.[25] It ultimately transcends rationalization, as the religious thinkers of all times and places well know (Urban 1939, 598). The *second form* of the intellectual explanation of religious apprehension we call *doctrine*. It grows out of the attempt to unify and systematize variant concepts. Doctrine also is a ubiquitous, that is a universal element. We meet with considerable development or systematization of myth in the priestly schools of Polynesia, in Western Africa, in the Maya and Aztec centers of learning, and we find this process continued in ancient Egypt, in Sumeria, in Israel, in Asia Minor, in India, in ancient Greece and Rome, among the Celts and the Teutonic tribes. In all the major world religions a doctrinal development which includes reactions and protests can be traced. More often than not we meet with short confessions of faith, some of which have developed into creeds.[26]

From the examination of the formal side of the intellectual expression of religious experience, we turn to an analysis of its *content*. The great recurrent themes, treated in the myths as well as in the doctrines of all faiths, are (i) the nature and character of supreme reality: the deity of God; evil; the origin, nature and destiny of (ii) the world and (iii) of man (personality; sin; hope). In articulated theological doctrine these topics are treated in the disciplines known as theology, cosmology, and anthropology and eschatology. "The questions," says Tillich, "implied in human existence, determine the meaning and the theological interpretation of the answers as they appear in the classical religious concepts" (1947, 25). In several of the great civilizations in the history of the world, in Greece, in Persia, in India, in China, theological speculation has developed into philosophy of

---

24. [Ed. note] The French scholar Comte (1798–1857) is credited with being one of the founders of modern sociology; he championed what became known as Positivism: the science of studying the relations between observable data rather than speculating on ultimate causes or truth (to be distinguished from the later philosophical development known as Logical Positivism). Comte argued that society successfully moved through three stages: the theological, the metaphysical, and the positive—implying a gradual movement from mythological to scientific thinking.

25. Cf. the penetrating analysis in Leenhardt (1979, esp. chapter 12).

26. Cf., as an example, the development in early Christianity, suggestively traced by Cullmann (1949).

religion and philosophical thought as such, especially metaphysics.[27] Yet not only philosophy but science in practically all its major branches stems from this source. However important the thinking out of the implications of religious apprehension may be, it should never be identified with the total expression of religious experience. We agree here with Wieman when he says: "Events rich in value and events transformative of human existence run deeper than ideas and doctrines and are mightier" (1946, 217). The history of religious *thought* is only *one* though an essential and ubiquitous part of the history of religions. There are actually other than purely intellectual yet equally universally present means of expression of religious experience. "Man incited by God," says the author of the best book on worship, "dimly or sharply conscious of the obscure presence of God, responds to him best not by a single movement of the mind, but by a rich and complex action in which his whole nature is concerned, and which has at its full development the character of a work of art" (Underhill 1936, 23). "Ritual like art is," according to S. Langer, "essentially the active termination of a symbolic transformation of experience" (1942, 45).

The phenomenology[28] of the religious act shows a great variety of ways of acting which we shall, for our purpose, arrange typologically. It has been claimed that all life, as it is lived and acted, could be regarded as expressing that relationship that is experienced in the awareness of the numen. The great anthropologist R. R. Marrett put it in this way: "Being inwardly assured of its primacy as the ultimate source of vital and psychic energy, spirit has no need to fear the close intimacy with the natural functions that go with life as pursued on the material plane (1933, 18). Acts which in our view are remote from the religious sphere, such as eating, playing, mating, are cultural acts in many primitive and higher religions (1933, chapters 2, 4). In distinction from the general, there are specific cultural acts which we shall call *rites*. They have a special dedicatory character. In and through them the presence of the numen is acknowledged.[29] The contact with creative sources of life innervates and stimulates man to action. "Ritual," says Langer, "is a transformation of the experiences that no other medium can adequately express. It is not prescribed for a practical purpose, even not social solidarity" (1942, 39). The range of *media* employed in the cultural act is very wide: it runs the whole gamut from simple and spontaneous utterances and sounds, tones, words, gestures, and movements to highly standardized practices such as liturgy, sacrifice, sacred dance, divination, procession, pilgrimage. However, in order to determine if an act is genuinely religious or not, we have to examine the *intention* with which it is performed. A bow may be a token of respect, a conventional way of saluting one's acquaintances, and yet it may be, if it is executed in the presence of the numen, an

---

27. [Ed. note] Metaphysics is a term derived from Greek, meaning literally "after physics," designating the branch of philosophy that studies first principles and ultimate causes. It was originally the name given to an untitled text of Aristotle's that dealt with such topics as first principles, which was commonly catalogued "after" a manuscript entitled "Physics."

28. [Ed. note] Adapted from the phenomenological method in European philosophy, in the study of religion phenomenology designates a descriptive and comparative method that seeks to study phenomena, or "that which presents itself" to the senses, in an effort to understand or re-experience the meanings of the persons or groups under study.

29. For the divine "archetypes" of the cult: cf. Eliade 1949, 44 ff., and Pittenger 1949, chapter 1.

expression of religious awe. The kiss, another general sign, is a token of affection or just of greeting; yet it may become the shibboleth [or password] of a spiritual brotherhood and part of a ritual pattern. Prayer, on the other hand, is an exclusive act of recollection by which man establishes and cultivates his communion with the source of power. It is a universal form of worship, as the rich phenomenology of prayer which [Friedrich] Heiler has presented convincingly demonstrates. The Australian and the Bantu Negro, the Plains Indian and the Ainu [in ancient Japan], the Chinese and the Hindu, the Jew and the Christian pray. Universal also are the various types of prayer: silent and vocal, private and collective, spontaneous and standardized.

Life in the universe, in the social unit and in the individual, cannot go on, so it is felt by the religious, if it is not nourished, encouraged, and stimulated by rites which keep it attuned to cosmic or divine powers. *Rites of Passage* ([also the title of a book on the topic by Arnold] van Gennep) are practiced universally.[30] They consecrate the crises and marginal situations in individual and collective life. Prenatal preparations, ceremonies surrounding birth, name-giving, initiation at puberty, marriage, sickness, and burial rites are performed the world over to ward off the dangers lurking in the passage from one stage of life to another and to secure the indispensable contact with the divine source of life. "Ceremonial life," says R. R. Marrett, "is the outstanding feature of all primitive cultures" (1933, 12). It characterizes—with one great exception namely, modern Western civilization—all cultures. Not only the extraordinary or crucial events in life but also the regular activities of work and play cannot and must not be carried on unless the accompanying rites render them adequate and effective.[31] The making of tools, the building of houses, the construction of boats, the tilling of the soil, hunting and fishing, the making of war, in primitive and higher civilization call for incantation, divination, and dedication. Malinowski has discussed Melanesian garden ceremonies, [Melville J.] Herskovits [has discussed West African] Dahomean cooperative construction rites, [Talcott] Parsons described the agricultural ritual in the Pueblo settlements. Aztecs and Chinese, Greeks and Romans, Sumerians and Hindus observed the requirements of cosmic orientation in planning their settlements as carefully as the African Yoruba or the nomad North American Omaha. A devout Moslem will not start on any important or even trivial enterprise without placing it, through an "*inshallah*," in a deeper context.[32] It is the great vision of all *homines religiosi* [or religious humans] everywhere that all life is the expression of

---

30. [Ed. note] Rites of passage are those rituals that help to mark, and in marking help to transition a person between, changes in social identity and status, for example rituals of initiation, marriage, and death. See Gennep's 1909 book, *Les rites de passage* (English translation 2004).

31. "The attitude which is the worshipper's response to the insight given by the sacred symbol, is an emotional pattern, which governs all individual lives. It cannot be recognized through any clearer medium than that of formalized gesture; yet in this cryptic form it is recognized, and yields a strong sense of tribal or congregational unity, of rightness and security. A rite regularly performed is the constant reiteration of sentiments toward 'first and last things'; it is not a free expression of emotions, but a disciplined rehearsal of 'right attitudes'" (Langer 1942, 124).

32. [Ed. note] *Insha'allah* is an Arabic term for "Allah willing," as in the just as common English phrase, "God willing."

worship, that every act and deed witnesses to the continuous communion of man with God. The prophets, saints and mystics of the highest religions join in this vision with the humble folks whom we honor with the name of "Primitive" societies. Perhaps it would not be wrong to say that at no time and nowhere has this vision become actuality. Even if we do not quite agree with P[aul] Radin, who suggests in his book on *Primitive Religion* that the only men who really can be said to "have religion" and to practice it have been what he calls the religious formulators, yet we realize that the natural frailty of human nature—man's sinful nature as the Christian would say—prevents him as a rule from enjoying the realization of the Divine presence continually and from expressing it, as it were, uninterruptedly by his deeds and acts (1938, chapter 2). Even in the lives of saints and prophets, their great efforts to sustain this highest level of man's calling have not always been successful. Sluggishness, dullness, disobedience, temptation always work together to cause man to lapse. As he emancipates himself from the power that sustains him, his activities become centrifugal; they become, as we call it, "secularized." Yes, the very acts which were designed to witness to the highest communion lose their meaning, become, if they are still performed, empty, fossilized. It is the function of the prophet to revitalize the old forms or to devise new ways by which man can express in acts and deeds his religious experience. Reformation is a universal phenomenon required by the dialectics of religious life (cf. Wach 1947, chapter 5, section 10 "Reaction: Protest"; Tillich 1948, 4).

The world over we find that in different religions certain acts are regarded and recommended as especially efficacious in establishing and strengthening the communion between man and the numen which is the goal of all worship. Such are acts of self-discipline or self-denial or the performance of special duties; acts of *devotion* and acts of *charity*. Some may be expected of everyone, and some be defined as *opera supererogationis* [acts that are morally good but not required; beyond the call of duty]. I should be inclined to think that acts of devotion and service to one's fellow men are universally valid practical expressions of religious experience. It is the exception rather than the rule that in our modern Western civilization worship of one's God and care for one's brother could become separated and one played against the other. If we can be proud at having left behind the cruder practices of an extreme asceticism, there is less reason for rejoicing that so many of us moderns have at the same time, because we see no motivation for it, abandoned all and every act of self-denial.

With the notion that in certain acts of devotion the religious life may culminate or appear epitomized, the concept of the *sacramental* act developed. This has its roots in primitive religion and has come to fruition in the Hellenistic mystery cults, in Zoroastrianism, in Hinduism and Mahayana Buddhism, in Gnosticism and Manichaeism, and above all in Christianity. Aptly has [Evelyn] Underhill defined a sacrament as "the use of visible things and deeds not merely to signify but to convey invisible realities" (1936, chapter 3). Originally (Underhill 1936, 45) the sacramental acts were only special instances of the wider notion (46) according to which the effective and transforming grace of the numinous presence flows into souls (47), especially prepared by acts of dedication; but in the history of our own religion these sacramental foci have become isolated (48) and cut out from the context of the life which they are meant to consecrate.

It behooves us finally to mention one more universal feature of the practical expression of religious experience. All human action will be *conditioned* by the physical *material* in which and with which alone it can work. The word needs no vehicle, the tone may be enforced by the use of instruments, the performance of service hallowed by wearing a special vestment. There are the simple and the complex instruments used for the purpose of creating a numinous atmosphere, the emblems and "images" which stand for the presence of the unseen, be it the Pueblo feather-sticks, the Plains medicine bundle, the Japanese *shintai*, the Hindu *pratika* [symbolic images used in worship], the Hebrew ark [of the covenant], the Greek *agalma* [statues used in cultic ceremonies], or the [Greek] Orthodox ikon. Tone, word, color, stone, wood, and metal are universal media by means of which man has tried to give expression to the profoundest experience of which he is capable. He has become a *secondary creator*. The dangers which must accompany this development have given rise to protests of which the Hebrew prophets, the founder of Islam, and the Christian, Hindu and Buddhist reformers are impressive examples. Some of these protests are directed against the perfunctory or mechanical way in which such acts are all too often performed—[compare this with] the Old Testament prophets and Jesus—others, of a more radical nature, reject all outward forms of expression, as do the spiritualists and some, though not all, mystics. They feel that in spirit and in truth alone can true worship exist, whereas the motto of others is St. Augustine's "*Per visibilia ad invisibilia.*"[33] For both extremes—idolatry and evaporation of the *sensus numinis*—the history of religions affords many an example, but, as W[illiam] Temple has rightly said: "The goal is to fuse action and worship into the continuous life of worshipful service; in the holy city which came down from God out of heaven the seer beheld no place of worship because the divine presence pervaded all his life (Revelation 21.22)" (Temple, 1935, 494).

There is finally, besides the intellectual and the practical, a *third* way in which religious experience expresses itself: the sociological. Here too we meet with a universal trait. We discussed previously the various motives which make for the expression of any kind of experience. True, there is in the confrontation of man with ultimate reality something solitary—the "flight of the Alone to the Alone."[34] The solitary visionary is encountered at all stages of religious development from the lonely American Indian in quest of a Guardian Spirit to Søren Kierkegaard and William James (1902, 30 ff.), but the desire to communicate, to share, is a powerful motif in association and communication between men.[35] Here

---

33. [Ed. note] From Latin, this phrase means "Through the visible to the invisible," and implies that one can infer knowledge of God from observation of, or participation in, the natural world. Its phrasing is derived from the writings of Paul as well as from Augustine of Hippo's *Confessions*.

34. This is a popular translation of the last line of Plotinus's Enneads (6.9.11). Thanks to Melanie Williams for bringing this to my attention.

35. Durkheim has stressed this point (1947, 47), that religion is "something eminently social." But he has not always taken care to qualify this statement, as when he says (10), "They [religious representations and rites] are rich in social elements." The opposite one-sidedness we find in the work of a well-known contemporary of Durkheim, in James's classic *The Varieties of Religious Experience*, where the emphasis on the individual dominates. We agree with Durkheim, however, when he states: "In so far as he belongs to society, the individual transcends himself, both when he thinks and when he acts" (1947, 16 ff.). Cf. Wach (1947, 27 ff.).

the problem of [the] communication of religious experience poses itself. We moderns are all too prone to look on it as a technical question to which improved techniques of manipulation will supply the answer (Bryson 1948). The history of religion teaches us otherwise. Wherever a true call is felt, a genuine religious experience is had, the means of communicating it miraculously seem to be at hand. Only in a secondary sense did the prophets and teachers feel that the establishment of contact and of fellowship was in their power. Where men were living in a communion with the great reality, they understood each other.

It would be rash to add religious fellowship to other existing forms of association without qualifications. A religious group is not another type of club. If in religious experience man confronts ultimate reality, it is towards this reality that all communion that is to be called religious must be oriented. "No personal impression," says Otto in his book, *The Kingdom of God and the Son of Man* , "is as strong as the impression of the numinous or so well fitted to bind together a circle of those who receive the impression" (1938, 164). The *first* characteristic which distinguishes the cult-group from all other associations is that it is orientated primarily towards that reality which is apprehended in religious experience. *Secondarily*, it is constituted by the relations existing among its members. These two principles, which should guide the work of the sociologist of religion, denote two universal features characteristic of the sociological expression of religious experience (Wach, 1945, 428). We can test their validity by examining any cult group in primitive, higher, or the highest civilization. What determines the attitude of the members of a secret or mystery society in Polynesia, Africa, or of American Indians but the awareness of power and power centers? What makes the fraternal spirit prevailing in mystery societies, of which we find so many examples in the history of ancient Greece, Rome, and the Near East? The numinous experience reflected in the concept of salvation and acted in the sacred drama! If the atmosphere of the Christian brotherhood is *agape* [Greek: unconditional love] can this attitude be meaningful unless it be buttressed by apprehension of the love of God as it is revealed in the life and death of Jesus Christ? All religious communities, furthermore, have specific *notae*, [or] marks by which they desire to be identified (certain visionary experiences, faith, beliefs, a certain esoteric knowledge, an attitude or behavior).

Universally valid also are the *means* by which the religious community is integrated, namely, a common faith, a common cult,[36] and a common order. Symbols, myths, doctrines, professions of faith, rites and practices, constitute and preserve the identity and integrity of the fellowship. Moreover, every cult-group possesses a structure. Though we find great variety with regard to the degree of differentiation, some differences according to the natural criteria of sex and age, of charismata and skills, knowledge, healing power, etc., make for a diversity of functions. Even in the most egalitarian group reverence is paid to age and experience, to the gift of prophecy or teaching.

---

36. [Ed. note] Although it today has a normative sense and is commonly used to name groups perceived to be deviant and therefore dangerous, originally "cult," which derives from Latin, named the behavioral or ritual component attached to any social group, as in "the mystery cults" of ancient Greece or "the Cult of the Virgin Mary."

We agree with Temple that the apparent conflict between *experience* and *authority*, of which we hear so much from our contemporaries, is actually a tension of two indispensable, ubiquitous elements (see *Nature, Man, and God*, lecture XIII). For the *individual*, Temple says rightly, authority (be it in tribal custom or revelation), is first. He grows and develops within a world in which he finds tradition surrounding him on every side; in the *race*, experience is prior to authority, as can be easily proved. The structure of every religious group implies an *order*. Within this order there is room for freedom and spontaneity as well as for discipline. The history of religions is replete with examples of what happened to religious communities in which one of these two notions was sacrificed for the other.

Leadership is universal, though the sources of its authority and its functions are differently conceived in different cult-groups. Max Weber has convincingly shown that it may be exerted on personal or institutional authority (charisma), the prophet and the priest illustrating these two types of religious leadership (Weber 1947).

Here, then, are some universals in religion: man relating himself in the experience which we call religious to ultimate reality. This experience, which is had within the limitations of time and space, tends to be expressed theoretically, practically, and sociologically. The forms of this expression, though conditioned by the environment within which it originated, show similarities in structure; there are universal themes in religious thought, the universal is always embedded in the particular. Though the differences and conflicts arise from particular loyalties, these cannot simply be left out (as the Enlightenment would have it). They are the arteries through which the lifeblood of religious experience flows. But they have constantly to be checked and purified.

That the particular has not come into its own in this lecture is undeniable, but our topic for today was universals in religion. True, we have had to concentrate here on the formal elements which characterize religious experience and its articulation, but this might be also a way of contributing to the important problem of general and special revelation which is vividly discussed in contemporary theology (cf. the controversy between [Karl] Barth and [Emile] Brunner).[37] Though we have not indicated here how we conceive of the relation between the universal and the particular way in which God has made himself known to man, we have, we feel, demonstrated that there is a ground upon which we can stand in believing that God has at no time and nowhere left himself without witness. We believe, with Temple, that "natural religion ends in a hunger for what would transform it into something other than itself: a specific revelation" (Temple 1935, lecture XX;[38] see also Otto 1938, book 4; Wach 1947, chapter 8).

---

37. The sharp, public disagreement between these two early to mid-twentieth-century Protestant theologians revolved around their opposite views concerning the relationship (or lack of) between philosophy and theology, or the relationship between human reason and divine revelation. Barth, who prioritized God's revelation, disagreed strongly with Brunner's thoughts on the ability of human reason to infer information on God's will (what has traditionally been known as natural theology).

38. [Ed. Note] Wach mistakenly cites lecture LXX; the quote here is from the summary of lecture XX in the table of contents, on page xxxii.

7

DIANA ECK

"Bozeman to Banaras: Questions from the Passage to India," from
Encountering God: A Spiritual Journal from Bozeman to Banaras

A well-known contemporary scholar of comparative religion, Diana Eck's name has, in recent years, become synonymous with the study of American religious pluralism. In addition to her posts as Professor of Comparative Religion and Indian Studies and member of the Faculty of Divinity at Harvard, Eck is also the founder and director of the Pluralism Project, a Harvard-based research project that documents and examines the growing phenomenon of religious pluralism and the social impact of this diversity on American and other multi-religious cultures.

Raised in Montana as a Methodist and trained at Harvard, Eck's engagement with religious diversity began during her undergraduate travels to India. As the following essay details, the background for much of her work is rooted in an interest in reconciling her Christian faith with other religious perspectives. A strong proponent of interfaith dialogue, Eck has promoted a theological pluralism that advocates engagement and embrace of other religions, arguing that one can maintain one's own religious faith while simultaneously appreciating the differences between, the value in, and the great insights available from other religious systems. Ultimately, she argues, Christians can learn from an approach that pushes beyond the classic exclusivist ("no religion but my own is true"), or even inclusivist ("all religions worship the same God, although mine does it best") positions toward a pluralism that invites and celebrates difference. In her more recent work on the diversity of American religious culture, entitled *A New Religious America: How a "Christian Country" Became the World's Most Religiously Diverse Nation* (2001), she offers a model of civic pluralism very similar to this theological one. Civic pluralism, she contends, can be approached through paths of "exclusion," "assimilation," or "pluralism," with pluralism being offered as the best choice. Some of Eck's other noteworthy works include *Banaras, City of Light* (1982), *Darsan: Seeing the Divine Image in India* (1981), and *Encountering God: A Spiritual Journey from Bozeman to Banaras* (1993).

While Eck's scholarship has been widely read by both scholarly and popular audiences, her approach to religious pluralism does not remain uncontroversial. Many have called portrayal of American religious pluralism unidimensional and an unrealistically positive account of how people of different religious faiths actually get along. Others have criticized the clearly normative bias she has towards liberal Protestant understandings of morality and tolerance, as seen in her contention that engagement with different religious systems (one way that she defines "pluralism") is a prerequisite of mature religious faith. But perhaps the most persistent scholarly critique against her work questions the enduring sentiment that all religions share the same core, and that religion is fundamentally good, thus relegating religious violence or oppression into instances of religion's "perversion" or "distortion," as Eck labels it in this reading.

Entitled "Bozeman to Banaras: Questions from the Passage to India," this essay is the first chapter of Eck's aforementioned book, *Encountering God: A Spiritual Journey from Bozeman to Banaras*. Although in many ways a more personal account of how Eck reconciles religious pluralism with her own Christian belief, the framework established here is indicative of a general mindset undergirding her other works, which inform many academic understandings of religion. One could point to similarities in how Joachim Wach and Eck phenomenologically define religion, as seen in their shared sense that the historical differences between religions are secondary manifestations of a primary, underlying reality. One will see in this brief excerpt that the normative conditions established by Eck for approaching religious diversity are extremely popular today.

"BOZEMAN TO BANARAS: QUESTIONS FROM THE PASSAGE TO INDIA," FROM *ENCOUNTERING GOD*

I grew up in Bozeman, Montana, in the Gallatin Valley, one of the most beautiful mountain valleys in the Rockies. The Gallatin River cuts through a spectacular canyon to the south, then flows like a stream of crystal through the fertile farmlands of the valley. I had three horses stabled on our land by the Gallatin and spent hours every week riding along the river. By the time I was twenty, I had made my way "back East," as we called it, to Smith College, and then much further east to India, to the Hindu sacred city of Banaras, set on the banks of another river, the Ganges.[1] Banaras was the first real city I ever lived in. It was a city in the time of the Buddha, twenty-six hundred years ago, and the guidebooks called it "older than history." Bozeman had been settled for scarcely one hundred years.

As a twenty-year-old, I found Banaras to be about as far from Bozeman as any place on earth. The smoke of the cremation pyres rose night and day from the "burning ghats" along the river. The Ganges is a much bigger river than the Gallatin; it is a powerful river that seemed to flow with authority and peace as it slid along the ghats, the great stone steps of the city, where Hindus bathed by the thousands at dawn. Today these two places, Bozeman and Banaras, both convey the spiritual meaning of the word *home* to me. And these two rivers, the Gallatin and the Ganges, both flow with living waters I would call holy. Worlds apart, they carry currents of life and meaning whose confluence is in me,

---

1. [Ed. note] Among the most frequently visited pilgrimage sites in India, Banaras is in the northeast (near Nepal), along the Ganges River, which is itself considered a sacred site (due to its association with the god Shiva). Banaras is a favored site at which Hindus arrive to bathe ritually in the river. In a number of cases, devout Hindus arrive in Banaras to die and be cremated on funeral pyres along the river's wide, staircase-like banks, or ghats.

deep in my own spiritual life. All of us have such rivers deep within us, bearing the waters of joining streams.

This book is an exploration of the encounter of Bozeman and Banaras, a religious encounter that raises at the very deepest levels the question of difference, the inescapable question of our world today. The issues of race and culture, language and gender, take us into the question of difference in complex and multiple ways, but deeper still, I believe, are the issues of worldview, of religion, and of religious difference. For me, the question has its particular angularities, as it must for each of us. What does it mean, now, to be a Christian, having come to see with my own eyes the religious life of Hindu, Buddhist, and Muslim friends with whom I have lived in professional and personal relationships for many years? How has my own Christian faith been challenged and reformulated by taking seriously what I have learned in this encounter?

I begin this exploration with my own experience, not because my experience is so special but because it illustrates the kinds of personal, social, and theological encounters that are increasingly the reality of our common world. Today people of every faith meet one another, develop deep personal or professional friendships, perhaps even marry one another. Our experience with people of other faiths may be difficult or rewarding, or both. In any case, our "interfaith dialogue" does not usually begin with philosophy or theory, but with experience and relationships. Individually and collectively, our experience has now begun to challenge traditional religious thinking and to contribute decisively to the reformulation of our theologies.

For many people religion is a rigid concept, somewhat like a stone that is passed from generation to generation. We don't add to it, change it, or challenge it; we just pass it along. But even the most cursory study of the history of religions would undermine such a view. Religious traditions are far more like rivers than stones. Like the Ganges or the Gallatin, they are flowing and changing. Sometimes they dry up in arid land; sometimes they radically change course and move out to water new territory. All of us contribute to the river of our traditions. We do not know how we will change the river or be changed as we experience its currents. My task here is to articulate the questions that I know are not mine alone. As John A. T. Robinson put it in another context, that of rising secularism, some thirty years ago, "All I can do is to try to be honest—honest to God and about God—and to follow the argument wherever it leads" (Robinson 1962, 28).[2]

When W. W. Alderson first saw the Gallatin Valley in July of 1864, just two months after Montana became a US territory, he wrote:

> The valley and the stream looked so pleasant and inviting that we concluded to layover and look around....The grass was tall everywhere, and as it was just heading out, the valley looked like an immense field of grain waving gracefully before the

---

2. [Ed. note] Robinson (1919–83), an Anglican Bishop in England, wrote *Honest to God* in the early 1960s and it sparked a number of controversial theological debates. The little book challenged tradition and orthodoxy in an attempt to make Christianity more relevant for a scientific age.

gentle breeze....We had come to dig for gold and make a fortune in a year or two, but...the fever abating, we concluded to locate right here and engage in farming.

(quoted in Niebel 1966)

Today Bozeman is a thriving city with shopping malls and sprawling suburbs, but in my childhood it was a small college town of twelve thousand, a grid of tree-lined streets with Main Street running right down the middle. It was named for John Bozeman, a pioneer trail guide who, along with Alderson and two other members of the Bozeman Claim Association, had laid out the town in August of 1864. As a Girl Scout I earned a merit badge by writing the history of Bozeman's pioneer heritage: the sagebrush and gophers, the wooden sidewalks and muddy streets, the first cabins built in the summer of 1864, the Laclede Hotel on the site where the Montgomery Ward was later built. By the 1890s there was a train depot, an opera house with a ladies' parlor, and Cy Mount's Palace Saloon, with its gambling rooms lined with fine and intricately inlaid wood. And there were fine brick houses, one of which, I found, had retained its red color because the bricks had been soaked in stale beer before they were laid. There was one black man in town, Sam Lewis, who ran the barber shop. And there was an alleyway between Main and Mendenhall that was called Chinatown, with a laundry business and a restaurant.

The church I grew up in, the First Methodist Church on South Willson, was the oldest Methodist church building in the state. The foundation stone had been laid in 1873 by the first minister, the Reverend T. C. Iliff, in the days when Bozeman was still a frontier town with dirt streets and Saturday night shootouts. Mary Iliff, in her memoirs of life on the frontier as a young minister's wife, recalled her utter astonishment when she was presented with six Sioux scalps by a Nez Perce[3] medicine man named Amos, in gratitude for a kindness she had shown in boiling a sack of eggs for him. With trembling hands she thanked him for his gift (Lind 1992, 153–5).

T. C. Iliff, along with W. W. Van Orsdel, whom we knew as the legendary Brother Van, were the charismatic circuit riders who set the stage for Montana Methodism—preaching and singing with such charisma they were called the Heavenly Twins. Brother Van had answered an appeal in the *Christian Advocate* [newspaper] of St. Louis at a time when there were only ninety-five Methodists in all of Montana: "Are there not half a dozen young men in our theological schools who are ready to band together and, taking their lives in their hands, emigrate to this new country and assist in giving the privilege of the gospel to its people?" (Dorothy Eck, cited in Niebel 1966, 7). Brother Van and T. C. Iliff rode horseback from town to town, tending to their congregations. Iliff eventually became the field secretary for the Methodist church and the namesake of the Iliff School of Theology in Denver. Brother Van worked for forty-seven years as a Montana preacher and was said to be the "best-loved man in Montana" when he died. The anthem of Montana Methodism was and still is "Brother Van's Song," a beautiful, rousing hymn about the faith of those who plant and sow not knowing if they will live to see the harvest. The refrain soars with

---

3. [Ed. note] Lewis and Clark's expedition (1804–06) mistranslated this western Native American tribe's name by the French term, meaning "pierced nose." Today, the group's members prefer the term "Nimi'ipuu."

the words "The tears of the sower and the songs of the reaper shall mingle together in joy, by and by." It is a song of frontier farmers, who regularly lived with the risk of losing their crops, and frontier preachers who labored in faith not knowing if the harvest would come.

Montana is a big state with a strong sense of identity. From the windows of our house just at the edge of that grid of tree-lined streets, I could look out over a field of cattle to Bear Mountain. I learned the names of all the mountains that circle the valley—the Bridger Range, the Spanish Peaks, the Madison Range, the Tobacco Roots. And the rivers, too— the Gallatin, the Madison, and the Jefferson, all given their names by Lewis and Clark, who came through the valley in 1805 and 1806 with their Shoshone guide, Sacajewea. At Three Forks, just thirty miles up the valley from Bozeman, the three rivers join to form the Missouri. It is spectacular landscape, its size and vastness somehow made comprehensible by the act of naming and the mastery of those names. I gradually learned the names of mountains and rivers all over the state, for as teenagers my friends and I thought nothing of driving four hundred miles for a weekend basketball tournament or a Methodist youth rally. I learned another Montana reality as well: that this vast landscape included lands set apart as reservations for the native peoples who had lived here and whose homeland this was long before John Bozeman or any of the settlers had come—the Crow and the Northern Cheyenne in the southeast, the Blackfoot in the north, the Flathead and the Kootenay in the west. There were invisible borders and multiple cultures.

Our Methodist church camps were summer meeting places where I got my first taste of a wide and vibrant sense of the church. Various churches built their own cabins in Luccock Park, the camp in the hills above the Paradise Valley near Livingston. Those log cabins, named for our towns "Bozeman," "Livingston," "Billings," and "Big Timber," nestled like miniatures below the towering mountains we called Faith, Hope, and Charity. There in our summer camps we teenagers in the Methodist Youth Fellowship, the MYF, enacted the rites of bonding and commitment that are so formative in the adolescent experience of religion: confessing our secrets and dreams, singing round the campfire at night, sitting in silence and prayer as the fire began to die down, holding crossed hands in a circle of commitment around the glowing embers. When I became the state MYF president, I also went to the Flathead Lake camp, nearly four hundred miles away in the northwest part of the state. There the cabins were called "Kalispell," "Missoula," and "Great Falls," and there we sat on logs in the outdoor chapel at Inspiration Point for what we called "morning watch," looking out at daybreak past the wooden cross, over Flathead Lake toward the Mission Range.

I did a lot of building as a teenager in the Montana MYF—roofing, mixing cement, pounding and pulling nails. There were work camps every summer. We built a dining hall at Luccock Park under the supervision of my father, an architect and builder. We built a church at a little settlement called Babb on the Blackfoot Reservation in the grassy, windy prairie land east of Glacier National Park. We lived for a month in two spacious tepees, talking late into the night, sleeping in sleeping bags around the fire, and rising early for morning watch on the hilltop just above our campsite. We took an old school bus to Mexico, again with my father and mother, and built a silo on a rural development farm near Patzcuaro. Our workdays included drilling holes for dynamite, blasting, and mixing cement for the master masons from the little village of Huecorio to use in raising the stone walls of what had to be the most elegant and durable silo in all of Mexico. There our days began with morning watch on the rooftop terrace, where the twenty of us studied the Bible and sang hymns looking out over the farmlands toward Lake Patzcuaro with its island village of Janitzio.

The most durable product of these teenage summers, at least for me, was a sturdy faith in God, a very portable sense of what constitutes the church, and a commitment to the work of the church in the world. I arrived at Smith College in the fall of 1963 straight from the March on Washington,[4] where I had been with the national MYF delegation. I joined these friends again during the spring vacation of my freshman year to lobby in Washington, DC, for the Civil Rights Bill. Civil rights and Vietnam War, racism and militarism, were the issues that shaped the whole context of college in the 1960s, during the years I was at Smith. They came together in complex ways. One of my first summer jobs was a short stint working for the Montana Board of Health on the Northern Cheyenne Reservation out of Lame Deer in southeastern Montana. I saw at first hand the racism of my own state, where I had rarely met an African American, but had also rarely seen the real conditions in which most of the Native American peoples lived. After two weeks in Lame Deer, I was invited to an all-night prayer meeting of the Native American church. As we settled into a circle around the fire in the tepee, my host told me that the service was to pray for the Cheyenne boys who were serving in Vietnam. There were six from the tiny town of Lame Deer alone. The night was unforgettable: rounds of peyote,[5] chanting, prayer, drumming. It was a form of worship I had never seen, among people who were virtual neighbors and yet virtual strangers to me in Montana, people whose sons and brothers were disproportionately drafted for service in Vietnam.

It was in this context of the Vietnam War that I first went to India. The move had only an indirect logic to it, a logic animated by the concern and yet the inadequacy so many American college students felt about the US war in Asia. As a sophomore in college, I was aimed toward the study of Latin America. But when I saw the announcement of the University of Wisconsin's College Year in India program posted on the bulletin board in Wright Hall during midyear exams, I was immediately drawn to the possibility. Nothing and no one in my past had prepared me for an encounter with that part of the world. I knew nothing of Asia. In fact, the Vietnam War seemed a tragic testimony to how little most of us in America knew about Asia. The boys from Lame Deer were there. A few friends from my high school were there. My friends from Amherst thought of nothing but how to avoid going there. So I applied to go to India. It was Asia. Close enough. Maybe

---

4. [Ed. note] The March on Washington for Jobs and Freedom, which attracted approximately a quarter of a million people, took place August 28, 1963. It was at this event that Martin Luther King delivered his now-famous "I Have a Dream" speech on the steps of the Lincoln Memorial.

5. [Ed. note] Peyote is a small round cactus, native to the southwestern US, containing mescaline, a psychoactive ingredient; the cactus is ingested (either eaten or drunk as part of a brew) as part of ritual ceremonies. Peyote is a controlled substance unless it is used as part of a religious ceremony, as in the practices of the Native American Church (incorporated in 1918), which blends Christian beliefs with traditional, pan-Native American beliefs and practices.

I would learn something. I took a spring term course taught by a visiting professor from Poona on the thought of two of India's most important twentieth-century thinkers, Gandhi and Aurobindo.[6] That summer—which was for some a Mississippi summer, for some a Vietnam summer—I spent in the language labs at the University of Wisconsin learning Hindi.

In September of 1965, with a new group of friends from the summer of language study in Madison, I arrived in India. There was not much in Bozeman or Northampton, or even in Patzcuaro, that could have prepared me for Banaras, a vibrant, congested city sitting high on the banks of the River Ganges. Its intensity was overwhelming. I had been in Banaras only a few days when I wrote home, "Wandering half-scared through the side-walk narrow streets near the Chowk market today was an exhausting experience, exhausting because it was as if I had walked through all of India, seen, felt, tasted, smelled it all in three hours. There were too many people, too many faces, too many cows, too many catacomb streets and dead ends, too little air. The utter concentration of life, work, misery, odor, and filth in this area of the city was staggering."

Despite my feelings of claustrophobia and bewilderment, I was immediately impressed by the religiousness of Banaras. There religion was surely *the* most important observable fact of daily life. The whole city seemed to revolve on a ritual axis. There were temples everywhere, large and small, inhabited by images of gods and goddesses whose names I did not know, whose multi-armed forms I could not even distinguish one from the other, and whose significance was totally beyond my grasp. The bathing ghats along the Ganges were the scene of morning rituals for pilgrims. We had not been there more than a day or two when we rose before dawn and took rickshaws to the riverfront to see the sights for which Banaras is so famous. Thousands of Hindus were there at Dasashwamedh Ghat, bobbing in the water, standing waist deep their hands folded in prayer, chanting to a crescendo of bells as the sun rose over the river. Perhaps the one piece of my Montana past that I brought with me to the comprehension of that first dawn on the Ganges was "morning watch." For two miles along the ghats, Hindus bathed in the Ganges and worshiped as the sun broke the horizon. The city pulsed with the life of faith as vibrant as any I had known, and as different.

That year I came to know, for the first time, people of faith from a tradition not my own. I did not know any Jews, let alone Hindus or Muslims, when I set off from Montana for Smith College. I knew little of the faith of others, but at that point in life I was quite clear about the center of my own Christian faith: love, justice, human dignity, and the steady sense of being linked in kinship to Christ and to the Christian community. It was a faith nourished, as all faith finally is, by people—energetic, loving, committed, visionary people.

---

6. [Ed. note] Mohandas K. Gandhi (1869–1948)—later known by the honorific title, Mahatma, meaning "great soul"—was an Indian-born lawyer, trained in England and who practiced early on in South Africa, and who became intimately associated with India's mid-twentieth century efforts (eventually successful) to attain independence from Britain. Sri Aurobindo (1872–1950) was the India-born and British-trained scholar who, early in his life, was also associated with India's efforts to gain independence. He eventually withdrew from political activity and became known widely as a spiritual master and writer.

The only people of that sort I knew—and I had the good fortune of knowing quite a few of them as a teenager—were Christians.

It was in Banaras that I experienced the first real challenge to my faith. Not surprisingly, it did not come in the form of ideas, even though I was enrolled in a course in Advaita Vedanta philosophy at the Banaras Hindu University.[7] It came in the form of people— Hindus whose lives were a powerful witness to their faith. I had conceived a completely naïve fieldwork project on "Hinduism and the Indian Intellectual." Knowing little about Hinduism myself, I concocted a set of questions about the gods, the meaning of *karma* [meaning action, ritual action, or the universal law of actions and reactions], the meaning of reincarnation, and so forth, and set out on my bicycle to meet scholars, poets, and professionals in Banaras and to ask what they believed. It was not a very good project, but I couldn't have found a more interesting introduction to India.

One of those I met was Achyut Patwardhan, a former freedom fighter who had spent his share of years in prison in the service of the nonviolent movement for India's independence. He was a man of simple, self-giving love. Like the civil rights leaders I had admired at home, he had put his life on the line in the service of justice. "You see suffering," he said to me, "and you don't debate about it or make yourself act. Those who love simply act, respond naturally with the spontaneous good that is human. Perhaps all you can do is take another person's hand. This, then, is sufficient." Patwardhan was, to me as a twenty-year-old, a man of God and a great spiritual friend at a time of my life when questions were tumbling through my mind. He was a man whose life was a witness to love and justice. He was very much like the people I had most loved and admired as a teenager. But he was not a Christian. He did not find an example and a companion in Christ, as I did. To my surprise, it did not seem to me that he somehow ought to be a Christian. What did this mean about some of the biblical claims of my own tradition?

In November I met J. Krishnamurti,[8] a man who did not fit any category at all. He was giving a series of daily talks at Rajghat in Banaras. Not only was he not a Christian, he was not a Hindu, not a Buddhist. That was just his point. "Truth is a pathless land," he said. "You cannot approach it by any path whatsoever, by any religion, by any sect." He did not say, Follow me. On the contrary, he said, "I desire those who seek to understand me to be free, not to follow me, not to make out of me a cage which will become a religion, a sect" (Foure 1964, 8–9). He did not care for the labels of any religion. Indeed, he observed the way in which we fearfully, anxiously, shape our whole lives by religious, political, cultural, and personal labels and names—all of which function as a buffer zone of security between ourselves and the experience of life.

---

7. [Ed. note] Advaita Vedanta is one among a variety of Indian philosophical schools of thought which argues, among other things, that self is equal to the totality of the universe. Today, Advaita Vedanta is widely seen as representative of orthodox Hinduism (that is, textbook descriptions of Hinduism often presume this philosophical position to be normative when, in fact, it is one among others).

8. [Ed. note] The India-born Jiddu Krishnamurti (1895–1986), lived in India, England, and the US. Early in his life he was identified by others as a spiritual savior but, after attracting a worldwide movement of disciples, he abandoned this role and became a famous philosopher and writer who taught that the distinction between observer and observed is illusory.

Krishnamurti posed my first real encounter with the "otherness" of a worldview. No one in my world had ever asked about the value of labeling, judging, discriminating, and categorizing experience or suggested that by doing so we distance ourselves from experience. We call it a beautiful sunrise on the Ganges and don't ever really see it because we have dispensed with it by giving it a name and label. Perhaps we write a poem about it to capture it in words or take a photograph of it and feel satisfied that we "got it." We name so-and-so as a friend or an enemy. The next time we encounter that person, the pigeonhole is ready. Are not our minds perpetually busy in these maneuvers? I must admit, at twenty it had never occurred to me to ask such questions. And what about religion? Is it really just a name? I had to ask myself about being a Christian. Did the name matter? Did the label provide me with a shelter or barrier to shield me from real encounter and questioning? What did I have invested in this name? Everywhere I turned I saw question marks.

It is possible, however, that Krishnamurti's ideas would have meant little to me had not Krishnamurti himself been so arresting. Never had I experienced the quality of presence— I suppose now I would say "spiritual presence"—that he brought into a room. It is what I then called his "existentialism," for want of a better word. He spoke without notes, simply, directly, and he continually named and challenged the nature of our attention to him. Were we taking down notes? Why? Were we hoping to seize what he had to say? Were we comparing his ideas to those of Teilhard de Chardin or Zen Buddhism?[9] Were we judging his thoughts with our likes and dislikes? Why couldn't we just listen? Is simple presence and attention so impossible? The questions Krishnamurti asked were not about the world and its injustices, they were questions about me and my habits of apprehending the world. Though I had read some of Paul Tillich's work the year before and had especially liked *The Shaking of the Foundations* (1955), this was the real shaking of the foundations for me.

Krishnamurti and Patwardhan were important to me precisely because they were what Christians might call "witnesses" to their faith; they somehow embodied their faith in their lives. In retrospect, it is somewhat embarrassing to articulate this as a discovery, but as a twenty-year-old it came as news to me: Christians did not have a corner on love, wisdom, and justice. Christians were not the only ones nourished by faith and empowered by their faith to work to change the world. I knew nothing of the Hindu devotional traditions of *bhakti* then, but I met people—like Krishnamurti and Patwardhan—whose very lives were a message of God-grounded love. These people, unbeknownst to them, pushed me into a life of work and inquiry, spiritual and intellectual. I became a student of comparative religion and focused my work on Hinduism and the traditions of India. And as a Christian I began to realize that to speak of Christ and the meaning of incarnation might just mean being radically open to the possibility that God really encounters us in the lives of people of other faiths.

---

9. [Ed. note] Pierre Teilhard de Chardin (1881–1955) was a French Roman Catholic scholar and writer who is known today for his work on the convergence of science and religion, specifically the link between Christian theology and theories of biological evolution. Zen—a branch of Buddhism that developed in Japan from Chinese roots, and which emphasizes the individual's quest to experience satori, or fleeting enlightenment—acquires its name from "zazen," meaning sitting meditation.

That first year in Banaras changed the course of my life. I have been back and forth to India a dozen times now. I did doctoral work in comparative religion and wrote my thesis and then my first book on the city of Banaras [1982]—which Hindus call Kashi, the City of Light. It is a study of what the city, the Ganges, and the gods mean to Hindus. When I returned for research on my doctoral thesis, eight years after that first year in Banaras, I learned the names of all those gods, their stories, their powers. I visited as many of the city's thousand temples as any Hindu. I went up and down the ghats of the riverfront, learning their hidden shrines by heart. I circled the city on my bicycle and visited its protective guardians. I spoke to teachers and priests, scholars and pilgrims. Perhaps my teenage fieldwork along Main Street in the saloons and churches of old Bozeman had whetted my appetite for taking on one of the world's oldest and most complicated cities.

When I had finished the book on Banaras, I began a study of the Hindu temples and shrines that link the whole of India in interwoven networks of pilgrimage places. I traveled up and down the sacred rivers of India, visiting the headwaters of the Ganges in the Himalayas, the Narmada in the highlands of Madhya Pradesh [a province in north central India], the Godavari in the hills of Maharashtra [a province in western India], and the Kaveri [River] in the Coorg hills of the south. I went to major temples and wayside shrines and visited the four *dhams* [or among the four most respected temples in India], the divine abodes at the four corners of India—Badrinath in the northern Himalayas, Rameshvaram at the tip of southern India, Puri on the Bay of Bengal in the east, and Dvaraka on the Arabian Sea in the west. As a scholar and professor of religion, this kind of intellectual work is no small challenge—to glimpse the world of meaning in which people of another faith live their lives and die their deaths. But it is another question—equally important but very different—which I am pursuing here: What does all this mean to me, as a Christian?

THEOLOGY IN THE ENCOUNTER OF WORLDS

The meeting of Banaras and Bozeman, "East and West," can be duplicated in a hundred keys and a hundred languages. The encounter of worlds and worldviews is the shared experience of our times. We see it in the great movements of modern history, in colonialism and the rejection of colonialism, in the late twentieth-century "politics of identity"—ethnic, racial, and religious. We experience our own personal versions of this encounter, all of us, whether Christian, Hindu, Jewish, or Muslim; whether Buddhist, Apache, or Kikuyu [Kenya's largest tribal group]; whether religious, secular, or atheist. What do we make of the encounter with a different world, a different worldview? How will we think about the heterogeneity of our immediate world and our wider world? This is our question, our human question, at the end of the twentieth century.

My own versions of this question are: How can those of us who are Christians articulate our own faith fully aware of the depth and breadth of the faith of others? How do we affirm our own holy ground even as we sojourn in the holy lands of other faith traditions, even as we find ourselves to be more than sojourners, to be at home there? How is Christian faith, or a "Christian worldview," challenged and changed when we take seriously the fact that we are not alone as religious people, when we recognize as truly religious the traditions, the lives, and the pilgrimages of our neighbors of other faiths?

Not everyone has encountered the gods of India, but in the 1990s most people have encountered something of a religion not their own and have found questions welling up, expressed or unexpressed, about the meaning of this encounter for their own faith. For Christians, it might be a Passover seder[10] or a Sabbath meal shared with Jewish friends; it might be the Ramadan fasting of a Muslim colleague here in North America,[11] or time spent living or traveling in an Islamic society, where prayer is so visible and natural a part of daily life. Many Christians have taken up Buddhist or Hindu meditation practices, and have wondered about the relation of these disciplines of meditation to their own faith. Many have seen the film *Gandhi* or have read Gandhi's autobiography and felt the religious challenge of the Sermon on the Mount presented more clearly in the life of this twentieth-century Hindu than in that of any contemporary Christian. Many have sensed the holiness of the Dalai Lama[12] and asked what such holiness has to do with the things they call holy in their own tradition. Many have read the scriptures of other traditions of faith, like the *Bhagavad Gita*,[13] and have wondered what the insights they have gained might have to do with their own faith.

The questions that rise from experience to challenge the real meaning of our faith are basic theological questions. They are theological because they have to do with ultimate meaning, with the one we call God, with articulating our faith in a way that makes sense both of our tradition and the world in which we live. What is Banaras to a Christian? Who is Krishna? When Muslims pray to Allah do they pray to the God Christians know in Christ? Is there one God whom we all know by different names? Are there different gods? False gods? These are questions that academics and theologians find awkward to address, or want to address only by raising hermeneutical, or interpretive, considerations, backpedaling quickly away from the questions themselves. Yet to be honest as persons of faith who encounter the religious life of other faiths and are both challenged and enriched by that encounter requires that we ask such questions. They emerge out of the very heart of our experience. And they are not theoretical questions with no relevance to the lived-in

---

10. [Ed. note] Seder is the name for the ceremonial evening meal associated with Passover—a Jewish holiday celebrated in the first month of the Jewish calendar (in the early Spring each year), and which commemorates the time when it is believed God "passed over" the firstborn of Israel on the way to killing the firstborn of Egypt, in an effort to free the Hebrew slaves.

11. [Ed. note] As mandated by the Qur'an, a healthy, adult Muslim must fast during the daylight hours throughout the entire month of Ramadan, the ninth month of the Muslim calendar (which occurs each Fall). The fast is broken at the end of each day with a communal evening meal.

12. [Ed. note] The Dalai Lama is the religious and political leader of Tibet (and thus Tibetan Buddhism), believed to be a reincarnation of past leaders. Today, the Fourteenth Dalai Lama is known worldwide and, in 1989, was awarded the Nobel Peace Prize.

13. [Ed. note] Translated as "Song of the Lord," and often known simply as "the Gita," the *Bhagavad Gita* is part of an ancient tradition of epic literature in India, and derives from a much larger text known as the *Mahabharata*, which narrates the exploits of the mythic Bharata family. The Gita, which narrates events on the eve of a battle for control of the ancestral kingdom, highlights the teachings of the great god Vishnu, who—in disguise as the servant Krishna—instructs the great warrior Arjuna on the importance of doing one's duty and on the nature of reality.

world. Our answers fundamentally shape the way in which we think of the cultures and the peoples with whom we share that world.

Questions such as these are raised, of course, within each community of faith—by Jews, Christians, Muslims, Hindus, Buddhists, and others. How do Muslims think about Christians and Hindus? How are Buddhists challenged by the strong language of ethical monotheism as articulated by Jews, Christians, and Muslims? Today people of all faiths are more or less aware of one another, and those who articulate the meaning of faith for today must do so in the complicated context of religious plurality. I am keenly interested in what people of other faiths are saying as they work to interpret the world anew in the light of their experience, but they must speak for themselves. I speak only as a Christian, convinced that those of us who are Christians cannot close our eyes to the diverse world of human religiousness, affirming our faith as if others, with their claims and questions, did not exist. Jesus engaged fully and openly with the people of his world and his time, regardless of tradition, culture, ethnicity, or social status. Our Christian faith requires no less of us.

MORNING IN CHIANG MAI

It was nearly twenty years after those daybreak mornings at Inspiration Point on Flathead Lake, and more than ten years after my first glimpse of dawn on the Ganges, that I led a morning worship service in Chiang Mai, Thailand, and found that I had moved farther toward the frontiers of Christian faith than I had realized. As a lecturer at Harvard, I had been invited by the World Council of Churches[14] to a theological consultation on interfaith dialogue. People representing the whole spectrum of Christian views on mission and dialogue were there in Chiang Mai, a quiet city where the Buddhist tradition suffused daily life and where saffron-robed monks could be seen walking silently past our hotel in the morning, stopping at homes and shops to receive in their begging bowls the food given as alms by the laity.

I was asked to be responsible for morning worship on one of the eight days of the consultation. Since we had all come together to discuss theological issues in Christian relations to other faiths, I thought it would be appropriate to include a responsive reading from another religious tradition. I chose a passage from the fourth chapter of the *Bhagavad Gita*, where Lord Krishna teaches the struggling Arjuna that whenever righteousness decays and unrighteousness is on the rise, He, the Lord, comes into being in age after age. When we came to the responsive reading, I read my part and was astonished to find that perhaps only a third of those present seemed to be joining in the response. The rest sat in silence. I had not anticipated for a moment that it would be troublesome to this group of theologians to meditate upon the scripture of another tradition in this worship context, but I learned a great deal that day about my own tradition. I had unwittingly unleashed a

---

14. [Ed. note] WCC is an international organization of theologically liberal Christian churches—originally mostly in North America and Europe, but now worldwide—that works on issues of interreligious dialogue.

major controversy. What I had done was discussed—indeed hotly debated—right down to the issue of whether or not the incident should be mentioned in the report of the consultation, and if so, at what point.

The most extreme opponents to the responsive reading from the Gita were those who objected to what the passage had to say—it spoke of many divine incarnations and of rebirth. Furthermore, they objected to the fact that they had been asked to take these words upon their lips in a worship context. Others were opposed because, they said, responsive reading is not a form of study but of prayer, and they could not be asked to pray in the words of another tradition. Some appreciated including a Hindu scripture in Christian worship and saw it as a way of taking seriously the spiritual challenges of the *Bhagavad Gita*. I am sure, however, that the majority of those there—both those who took the controversial words of the Gita upon their lips and those who did not—were simply uncertain. What did the passage mean? What would it mean for a Christian to speak these words?

In 1938, when Christians of the International Missionary Council[15] gathered in Tambaram at Madras Christian College to discuss "The Christian Message in a Non-Christian World," D. G. Moses, an Indian Christian professor of philosophy at Nagpur University, rose in the midst of the debate and said, "Time was when each thought his own religion superior....But with the ever increasing means of communication and transportation and the growing study of comparative religion, the old attitude has been made impossible. We know too much of the religions of the world today to assume naïvely the unquestioned superiority of one's own faith" (Paton 1939, 64). For some, the point Professor Moses made was obvious. At the Tambaram conference were Asian Christians as well as Western missionaries who had spent their lives in Asia and who had come to know intimately and appreciatively the religious lives of devout Hindus, Muslims, or Confucians. For many others at Tambaram, however, to see Christianity as one tradition of faith among others equally ancient and resonant was to crack open the door of relativism.

What Moses expressed at Tambaram resounds even more profoundly in our world today. The tremendous growth in the study and understanding of religion, the translation of the sacred texts of Hindus, Buddhists, and Muslims, the deeper understanding of their traditions of faith, *has* made the old attitude impossible. Those of us who are Christians speak of the uniqueness and centrality of Christ, and yet at the same time we know that our Muslim brothers and sisters affirm the uniqueness and centrality, indeed the finality, of God's revelation in the Holy Qur'an. And we know that when Buddhists speak of insight into the nature of life, death, and suffering, they are not speaking of a narrow truth that is peculiar to Buddhists, but are making a claim to universal truth which they invite all of us to see for ourselves.

People of many religious traditions bear witness to the truth, the transcendence, the universality, the uniqueness, and the distinctive beauty of what they have known and seen.

---

15. [Ed. note] Headquartered in London and New York, the International Missionary Council (IMC), established in 1921, was an organization of fourteen interdenominational associations of Christian missionary societies. In 1939 it became affiliated with the World Council of Churches (WCC) and, in 1961, it was integrated within the WCC as its "Commission on World Mission and Evangelism."

To recognize this plurality of religious claims as a profoundly important fact of our world does not constitute a betrayal of one's own faith. It is simply a fact among the many facts that emerge from the historical and comparative study of religion. What we make of that fact from our different perspectives of faith is one of the most important challenges of our time. This challenge cannot be addressed by academic scholars of religion alone, for it is not solely a matter of understanding the religiousness of others, though that alone is an enormous task. It is a matter of interpreting our own religious world and faith in the light of that understanding. In other words, how does the understanding of others, which is the aim of the scholar of comparative religion, reshape our self-understanding? We know from human experience that the reformulation of our self-understanding happens constantly in interpersonal relations, but how does it happen in interfaith relations?

THE SKEPTICS, THE SEEKERS, THE SAVED

This book addresses theological questions, but it is not a book *about* theology, to make a fine distinction. There has been a flood of books about theology and religious pluralism in the past ten years. They are for the most part schematic books that line up Christian alternatives to this "problem" of pluralism. They are important books, but there is a once-removed quality to them. They are written primarily in the tribal language of theologians, for theologians, about theological problems. For the most part, the authors do not engage in rethinking their own faith, but rather theoretically ponder how one might do so if one were to try. But theological questions are not merely theoretical; they are the life and death questions of real people attempting to live with intellectual and personal honesty in a world too complex for simplistic answers. Here I have tried to write for ordinary people who do not think of themselves as theologians, but who struggle with real questions of faith in the world in which we live.

For some who will read these pages, Christianity is a problem. They may not understand how a person like me, a scholar and professor in a large secular research university, could be a Christian at all. They have perhaps long since given up on religion and find the public image of Christianity narrow, fanatical, or simply irrelevant. I don't blame them. I too sometimes find the public image of the Christian tradition disturbing and even repelling. While my own experience of the church, from Montana Methodism to the World Council of Churches, has been life-giving and has helped me to grow, I know that many people have very different experiences in churches that are stagnant, irrelevant to their lives, or even destructive. It is no wonder that they have turned away. No religion is without ugliness, perversion, and distortion, for religious traditions, especially religious institutions, are not dropped from heaven, but are our human creations as we struggle to respond to our sense of the Transcendent. Many of the people who have dropped out of churches in disgust or boredom are truly interested in religious questions and intrigued to discover that some people like myself, who call themselves Christians, wrestle with the implications of Hindu philosophy, practice "Buddhist" meditation, and think that Christianity is not over, but still in the process of becoming.

There are others for whom it is not Christianity, but the interaction with other religious traditions that poses the problem. These people are very much part of the river of the Christian tradition, but they are not sure what to make of the traditions of faith that have watered different lands and nurtured other civilizations. They do not have a feel for what it would be like to be anything but a Christian. Some are actively hostile to the presupposed truths of other religious traditions and insist that they are not truth at all, but falsehood; they would not speak the words of the *Bhagavad Gita* because they believe these words are simply untrue, blasphemy. They have very clearly articulated theologies; they know just what they believe and why. Most Christians do not live with such certainties, however. They may be cautious about other faiths, or they may be quite open and yet feel they do not know enough about any other faith to be engaged with its claims to truth.

One thing is certain. In thinking about other faiths, most churchgoing Christians have imprinted upon their minds a few lone fragments of scripture. There is John 14:6: "I am the way, and the truth and the life; no one comes to the Father but by me." There is Acts 4:12: "And there is salvation in no one else, for there is no other name under heaven given among men by which we must be saved." This is all the theological equipment they have to grapple with a new world of many faiths. And when they travel to India and see the mind-boggling variety of the Hindu tradition, or when they meet Muslims across the street in Leeds or Lexington, or when their colleague at the office heads for the Buddhist meditation center after work, or when their daughter dates and marries a wonderful young man who is Muslim or Jewish, these fragments of scripture are simply not enough to make sense of the world and their experience in it.

This book, then, is a theology with people in it. They are the people I have encountered in my studies of the history of religion, in my fieldwork in India, and in my travels throughout the world. I cannot think about Christianity and about my own faith without hearing their voices, so it makes sense to give them narrative space in my theological thinking. What questions do they ask of me? What questions do I ask of them? This mutual questioning and listening is what is meant by "interfaith dialogue." While dialogue may be pursued at carefully arranged meetings and consultations, like the many I have participated in through working with the World Council of Churches, the most compelling and important dialogue is that which arises in the communities and contexts of our daily lived experience, what some would call "the dialogue of life." Interfaith dialogue, whether the intentional and formal dialogue of the interfaith movement or the informal daily conversation at the street corner, is the very context out of which Christians must seek a new understanding of faith today.

FEMINISM, LIBERATION, AND PLURALISM

For me, this task is doubly complex because I hear not only the voices of Hindu or Buddhist friends and teachers as I write, but also the voices of women within my own tradition who have never been given much narrative space in the history and theology of Christianity. Indeed, the voices of women have not been fully heard in Hinduism, Buddhism, Islam, or Judaism either. Our voices have been suppressed in the texts and in the leadership of most of the world's religious traditions, though it is clear that women have done much to sustain the vibrance and vigor of these very traditions. So it is always with a profound sense of dissonance that I view the formalities of many world interfaith events, where the colorful male panoply of swamis, rabbis, bishops and metropolitans, monks and ministers line up together for a photograph of interfaith fellowship. They are portraits of a fading world, for women's hands and voices are reshaping all of our traditions.

The emergence of women's voices is worldwide—as priests and pastors in the Christian tradition, as rabbis and theologians in the Reform and Conservative Jewish tradition, as feminists in the Orthodox Jewish community, as Gandhian activists and scholars in India, as Muslim feminists insisting on their right to the radical justice and equality of the Qur'an. As the Buddhist tradition grows in new soil in the West, many of its finest teachers are women. As the Catholic church experiences the turmoil of our century, many of its leaders, ordained or not, are women. Even where women's voices are not yet fully heard, they sound the beginnings of real religious revolutions. In every tradition, these are revolutions happening before our very eyes.

Liberation theology, feminist theology, and pluralist theology are all major currents in the Christian tradition today. All three are about the redefinition of the *we* in theological thinking and the renegotiation of the *we* in our common political and cultural life. They are all attempts to reconstruct more inclusive and more relevant forms of Christian thinking and Christian engagement. Liberation theologians articulate the Gospel as understood by the poor, the marginalized, those who speak the word of truth outside the houses of privilege and comfort and who insist that our priorities be set, not by the interests of the mighty, but by the priorities of the poor. Feminist theologians give voice to the concerns of both women and men who insist on the presence and perspective of women in Christian leadership, teaching, and interpretation. Pluralist theologians insist that Christians must also listen to the voices of people of other faiths and not pretend that we can do our theological and ethical thinking in a vacuum, without engaging in energetic interreligious exchange.

Unfortunately, there has not as yet been much interrelation between these three currents of theological thinking. Many Christians who speak of the "preferential option for the poor"[16] seem not to recognize that most of the world's poor are not Christians who will speak the Gospel in a new prophetic voice—they are Muslim poor or Hindu poor. To hear their voices necessitates interreligious dialogue. Many of those who want to listen to the voices of Buddhists and Hindus pay scarcely any attention to the voices of women and reinforce in their interreligious dialogue the patriarchies of all the traditions; many who want to give voice to the perspectives of women within the Christian tradition don't think for a moment about Hindus and Buddhists. Everyone is busy on his or her own front. In a sense this is not a criticism, for feminist and womanist theologians, liberation theologians, and pluralist theologians have all, in their own ways, unleashed their respective revolutions

---

16. [Ed. note] "God's preferential option for the poor" is a phrase associated with mid- to later twentieth-century Liberation Theology which combined Central American Roman Catholic theology with Marxist economic critique.

in Christian thinking today. I believe, however, that we all must begin to think of these issues together, for I am convinced that they belong together as part of our effort to rebuild a sense of community that does not make difference divisive and exclusive.

When I first went to India in 1965, I had not heard the word *feminism* or connected gender issues with theological thinking. While I was in India, Betty Friedan came to the Smith College campus to speak about *The Feminine Mystique*. Mary Daly was probably still at her typewriter working on *The Church and the Second Sex*, which was published in 1968.[17] Her book *Beyond God the Father*, which so shaped the intellectual world of graduate studies in the seventies, was still years away. But there in India, living and studying in Banaras, I encountered a multitude of gods and goddesses imaged in poetry, song, and stone. In India, through the rich theological imagination of Hindus, my understanding of God the Father was challenged by the language of God the Mother, God the Dancer, God the Lover, and God the Androgyne [literally meaning man-woman]. In India I encountered the problem and the limits of my own religious language several years before I felt it surface through the currents of feminist writing in the Christian church. When I said, "Our Father...." —which I still do—there began to be footnotes at the bottom of my mind, mental reservations about just what Father means and does not mean. And the list has become longer through the years.

Dialogue in which we listen as well as speak may seem so commonsensical it is scarcely worth making a fuss over. And yet dialogue, whether between women and men, black and white, Christian and Hindu, has not been our common practice as an approach to bridging differences with understanding. Power and prestige make some voices louder, give some more airtime, and give the powerful the privilege of setting the terms for communication. We have had a long history of monologues. Much of the Christian missionary movement has been based on a one-way discourse of preaching and proclamation, with little thought to listening and little space for it. The Christian mission movement moved, for the most part, in the wake of European empires and in the company of the politically and economically powerful. The church did not have to listen—in India, in East Asia, in Africa, or in South America.

MUTUAL TRANSFORMATION

Today the language of dialogue has come to express the kind of two-way discourse that is essential to relationship, not domination. One might call it mutual witness: Christians have not only a witness to bear, but also a witness to hear. In the process of mutual testimony

---

17. [Ed. note] Betty Friedan is the author of the 1963 book, *The Feminine Mystique*, an early feminist book that documented the frustrated lives of mid-twentieth-century American women, many of whom had lives as housewives and who therefore obtained their identity through their husbands' careers and children's accomplishments. Mary Daly is a feminist Christian theologian who taught at Boston College for over thirty years. Her widely read writings are outspokenly critical of patriarchal traditions within the Church and society at large.

and mutual questioning, we not only come to understand one another, we come to understand ourselves more deeply as well. It leads to what John Cobb (1982) calls "mutual transformation." Dialogue does not mean that we will agree, but only that we will understand more clearly and that we will begin to replace ignorance, stereotype, even prejudice, with relationship. It is the language of mutuality, not of power.

During the years in Banaras I worked and studied with two teachers, both men in their eighties, whose equanimity and patience, love of learning, love of God, and love of the Ganga, the River Ganges, were luminous. They became family to me, and I to them. In my study of the Hindu tradition, I asked many questions of them. But I was not the only one with questions. They had questions, too. "Why do you pour yogurt on the gods?" I would ask, astonished. "Is it true that Christians in the West wear their shoes right into churches?" they would ask, equally astonished. When I asked about the worship of Shiva and Krishna, I was also asked about Christ.

I could hear them sizing me up, interpreting me in their own world of meaning. Who was this woman who had come from so far away, who asked so many questions about temples and gods, who studied Sanskrit and made so many mistakes? My friends in Bozeman may have wondered, as I have myself, how it was that a young woman who grew up in the high valleys and fresh air of the Rocky Mountains was so drawn to the city of Banaras, studying temples in its crowded alleyways and breathing the air of the cremation grounds. But this posed no problem to my teachers and friends in Banaras. "You must have been a Hindu in your last lifetime," said one. "You lived here in Banaras in a former life, which is why you have such a feeling for this city," said another. "You were part of our family, which is why you have come to be among us now," said another. One of my teachers, Kuber Nath Sukul, insisted, "You are my granddaughter, because your mother was born just about the time my only daughter died. Welcome home."

In our relationship, I surely was a witness to my own faith as a Christian. They knew I was a Christian, that I was a Protestant, and that even so I went to the little Catholic church that met in an apartment building called Vishnu Bhavan at the end of Lanka Street. But I was not the only one to bear witness to my faith. So did my teacher Ambika Datta Upadhyaya, whom I addressed with the reverential and affectionate title Pandit-ji, when he spoke with quiet confidence about the meaning of death, even his own death. So did his wife, whom I called Mata-ji, in her observances of fasting and prayer.[18] So did my friend Shanti and her family, poor as they were, with so many children and but one buffalo to count as wealth, when they offered me a tumbler of sweetened milk at each and every visit.

The give and take of dialogue among people of religious faith must inevitably raise questions for our own faith. These are the questions that should shape our theological thinking. When I read the *Bhagavad Gita*, I cannot isolate the understandings and questions that have emerged from that scripture in a separate file of my mind and go about my spiritual business as a Christian as if I had never read it. If I have been touched, challenged, or changed by the *Bhagavad Gita*, I must deal with that remarkable fact. If I find the Gita

---

18. [Ed. note] The two terms Pandit-ji and Mata-ji are honorific titles that roughly translate as Respected Teacher and Respected Mother. Thanks to Jack Llewellyn for comments on the meaning of these terms.

to be a comfort in moments of loss or grief or difficult ethical choices, which I do, I must make sense of that fact when I think about my Christian faith.

Just as I cannot isolate what I have learned from the *Bhagavad Gita*, so I cannot bracket the life I have shared with Hindus when I wrestle with what it means for me to be a Christian today. I cannot put aside the bonds of respect and affection that link me to these people, and place them, even gently, outside the Kingdom. A. G. Hogg, who was the principal of Madras Christian College at Tambaram for nearly three decades, put it very well when he spoke of discovering real faith among the Hindu students with whom he worked for so many years. In the presence of such faith, he wrote, we should feel not merely respect, but religious reverence. At the International Missionary Council in 1938, he asked rhetorically of his fellow missionaries,

> Is there any such thing as a religious faith which in quality or texture is definitely not Christian, but in the approach to which one ought to put the shoes off the feet, recognizing that one is on the holy ground of a two-sided commerce between God and man? In non-Christian faith may we meet with something that is not merely a seeking but in real measure a finding, and a finding by contact with which a Christian may be helped to make fresh discoveries in his own finding of God in Christ? (Paton 1939, 94–5)

Among Hogg's students at Madras Christian College was the young Radhakrishnan,[19] who was to become one of modern India's finest Hindu philosophers. It is no wonder the British educator felt the challenge of a genuine faith and a compelling, but very different, theological vision. There are many Christians who have had the experience described by Hogg, sensing in the presence of true faith, whether Hindu or Muslim or Buddhist, that we should take off our shoes, for the ground on which we are standing is holy ground. It is holy not only because it is sacred for the Hindu, Muslim, or Buddhist. It is holy ground where we ourselves may be challenged to deeper faith.

---

19. [Ed. note] Sarvepalli Radhakrishnan (1888–1975) was the India-born philosopher who eventually was appointed to lecture on Comparative Religion at Oxford University and who held senior political positions in various independent Indian governments.

PART IV

THE EXPLANATION OF EXPERIENCE

8

WAYNE PROUDFOOT

"A Classic Conversion Experience" and "Explaining Religious Experience," from *Religious Experience*

With Wayne Proudfoot's work on religious experience we see a rather dramatic departure from some of the previous essays in this volume that assume the universality, and particularly, the self-evident nature, of religious experience. Proudfoot is a scholar of the philosophy of religion at Columbia University whose work has focused on religious experience, pragmatism and the influence of William James, theories and methods in the study of religion, and modern Protestant thought. His publications include *William James and a Science of Religion: Reexperiencing the Varieties of Religious Experience* (2004); *Religious Experience* (1987); and *God and the Self: Three Types of Philosophy of Religion* (1976).

What has made Proudfoot's scholarship both popular and controversial has been his advocacy for reductionism. Reductionism refers to a way of accounting for a complex phenomenon by pointing to the constituent parts that comprise it; in the case of religious phenomena, a reductionist might look to economic, social, or psychological sources to better understand the source of the event or to account for its existence. This approach stands in opposition to non-reductionist models, which might argue that religion is *sui generis* (that is, a completely unique thing irreducible to other elements), or that the perspective and interpretive ability of the religious participant should be privileged above all others.

Proudfoot answers this debate through his distinction between descriptive reduction and explanatory reduction. He contends that the description of the experience or event had by the participant should remain just as the subject him/herself relates it, inasmuch as this description is valuable data for the scholar. Changing the exact description given by the participant through reductionistic means (what Proudfoot calls descriptive reduction) is problematic because it compromises an important piece of evidence—the participant's perception of an event or thing. Thus if a person has a "religious" experience, the scholar should make careful note of the qualities that this experience carries and the labels the participant uses to describe it.

Having established this, Proudfoot argues that another level of reductionism is now not only possible, but necessary. Whereas scholars should not engage in descriptive reductionism, the scholar is free, he argues, to invoke his or her own interpretation of events when it comes to *explaining* the described event, an act known as explanatory reduction. Thus he argues not for a reduction of the participant's description of an event, but for the possibility of a reduction of their explanation of the event.

The following includes two selections from Proudfoot's *Religious Experience*. In the first Proudfoot argues, similarly to Desjarlais above, that experience *follows from* rather than precedes the language used to "interpret" the experience; that is, the available language one uses to explain one's experience may in fact have produced the experience. In the second selection, Proudfoot establishes how tricky the relationship is between description and explanation, particularly when one is discussing religion. Proudfoot suggests that reductionist explanation has been dismissed because of its threat to religion, and that certain strategies that appear explanatory might be undertaken to protect long-standing beliefs about religion's uniqueness, including those that, through language, have a tendency to create the very phenomena about which they report. He concludes that one of the scholar's jobs is to consider the historical and cultural explanations that might cause a person to use religious labels over others in the process of description.

"A CLASSIC CONVERSION EXPERIENCE," FROM *RELIGIOUS EXPERIENCE*

Given the results of [Stanley] Schachter's experiments,[1] it seems quite plausible that at least some religious experiences are due to physiological changes for which the subject adopts a religious explanation. Bodily states that elicit evaluative needs are not limited to arousal of the sort produced by an adrenaline injection. Certain classical meditation states function to decrease heart rate and to dampen rather than arouse autonomic functions. Laboratory-induced sensory deprivation has resulted in subjects' reports that are often quite similar to classical descriptions of mystical experience. Any significant physiological change from equilibrium could have the effects Schachter ascribes to arousal and, if the person were uninformed with regard to the origin of the change, would give rise to the need for a label or explanation.

In his chapter on conversion in *The Varieties of Religious Experience*, James quotes at length from one Stephen Bradley's report of his conversion experience. Bradley had just returned from a revival service in which the preacher had been unusually forceful and in which the sermon was based on a text from Revelation. Bradley had been impressed, but he claimed that his feelings were unmoved.

---

1. [Ed. note] Earlier in the book, Proudfoot discusses Schachter's research experiments. Subjects were injected with adrenaline in order to create a state of arousal. The study showed that the state of arousal was insufficient to produce emotion—the same adrenaline dose could create happiness in a subject at a party, but anger if the subject were arguing with a spouse. Schachter used these experiments to prove that the subject's thoughts about the situation or context were necessary to create the experience of emotion— that is, such experiences of emotion do not take place independently of our cognitive understanding of our physiological states.

I will now relate my experience of the power of the Holy Spirit which took place on the same night. Had any person told me previous to this that I could have experienced the power of the Holy Spirit in the manner which I did, I could not have believed it, and should have thought the person deluded that told me so. I went directly home after the meeting, and when I got home I wondered what made me feel so stupid. I retired to rest soon after I got home, and felt indifferent to things of religion until I began to be exercised by the Holy Spirit, which began in about five minutes after, in the following manner:

At first, I began to feel my heart beat very quick all of a sudden, which made me at first think that perhaps something is going to ail me, though I was not alarmed, for I felt no pain. My heart increased in its beating, which soon convinced me that it was the Holy Spirit from the effect it had on me. I began to feel exceedingly happy and humble, and such a sense of unworthiness as I never felt before … My heart seemed as if it would burst, but it did not stop until I felt as if I was unutterably full of the love and grace of God. In the mean time while thus exercised, a thought arose in my mind, what can it mean? And all at once, as if to answer it, my memory became exceedingly clear, and it appeared to me just as if the New Testament was placed open before me, eighth chapter of Romans, and as light as if some candle lighted was held for me to read the 26th and 27th verses of that chapter, and I read these words: "The Spirit helpeth our infirmities with groanings which cannot be uttered." And all the time that my heart was a-beating, it made me groan like a person in distress, which was not very easy to stop, though I was in no pain at all, and my brother being in bed in another room came and opened the door, and asked me if I had got the toothache. I told him no, and that he might get to sleep …

I now feel as if I had discharged my duty by telling the truth, and hope by the blessing of God, it may do some good to all who shall read it. He has fulfilled his promise in sending the Holy Spirit down into our hearts, or mine at least, and I now defy all the Deists and Atheists in the world to shake my faith in Christ.

(James 1902, 790–93)

Bradley's testimony reads like a textbook example designed to illustrate Schachter's theory. He notices his heart rate suddenly increase. He looks to discover the cause of it and in the context of having just returned from the revival service, attributes it to the Holy Spirit. The palpitations are attributed to an external force, not to pain or an ailment, and thus present no need for alarm. But he must still make some sense of this force. A thought arises in his mind: What can it mean? He sees clearly a passage in Romans that confirms the attribution of his stirrings to the Holy Spirit. Eventually this leads Bradley to "defy all the Deists and Atheists in the world to shake [his] faith in Christ." What began as mysterious palpitations ends with attributional certainty.

Bradley, like so many prospective devotees before and since, could not understand his feelings in naturalistic terms. Religious symbols offered him an explanation that was compatible both with his experience and with his antecedent beliefs. He did not consider explanations involving Krishna, Zeus, or the Qur'an. The content of the scripture and the experience of being moved or physiologically aroused were confidently linked. These are the two components required by Schachter's theory. It seems likely that religious concepts and doctrines often provide labels for experiences of arousal which initially appear to be anomalous. Bradley's testimony is striking in part because of his conscious recognition of the physiological effects and explicit acknowledgment of a search for a hypothesis by which to account for them. More often the interpretation is simultaneous with the recognition of the symptoms, so that the subject reports an immediate perception of the palpitations as the work of the Holy Spirit. In settings in which religious experiences are sought or anticipated, the explanatory scheme is firmly in place prior to the experience. Revivalists understand this, as do gurus and spiritual directors.

The experience of Pentecost[2] among the disciples of Jesus may be amenable to a similar explanation. As Luke describes it, the disciples were gathered together shortly after Jesus' death. The setting was a religious one. Suddenly a sound came from heaven, and the disciples experienced voices speaking through them. Luke reports that "All were amazed and perplexed, saying to one another, 'what does this mean?'"(Acts 2:12–13, RSV). Some observers provided a naturalistic explanation, accusing the disciples of drunkenness. But Peter, noting the early hour, rejects this hypothesis and quotes from the words of the prophet Joel: "And in the last days it shall be, God declares, that I will pour out my spirit upon all flesh, and your sons and your daughters shall prophesy, and your young men shall see visions, and your old men shall dream dreams" (Acts 2:17). This interpretation carries the authority of the Hebrew prophets. It is provided in order to account for an arousing experience that was unsought and unexplained. Peter's interpretation relates the disciples' shared experiences to the tradition of Yahweh's[3] promise and to their conviction of its fulfillment in Jesus, a tradition and a conviction that had recently been threatened by Jesus' death and apparent defeat.

In the case of Stephen Bradley, our information is insufficient to enable us to account for his initial symptoms. Perhaps they were due to the excitement of the revival meeting, though he claims to have been unaffected at the time. In the case of the disciples, it is not surprising that their reunion after the death of their teacher, in the setting of a religious festival, should have been a moving one. In both cases the arousal was interpreted in religious terms and attributed to divine activity, and in both cases that attribution produced conviction and behavioral consequences.

The results of a controversial experiment in the psychology of religion may also be subject to reinterpretation in the light of Schachter's theory. [Walter] Pahnke (1970) attempted to induce experimentally a form of mystical experience with the aid of psilocybin. In the setting of a Good Friday service, theology students received either psilocybin or a mild control drug, nicotinic acid. The results show that the subjects receiving the

---

2. [Ed. note] According to the New Testament, several days after Jesus rose from the dead and ascended to heaven the Holy Spirit descended upon Jesus' apostles. The day this event was supposed to have occurred became known as the Day of Pentecost. Proudfoot takes this story as more or less literally true; it is worth noting that many contemporary New Testament scholars would argue that the story is highly fictionalized or even outright fabricated.

3. [Ed. note] Yahweh is the name of the god in the Jewish and Christian scriptures.

hallucinogen labeled their experiences in religious terms to a significantly greater extent than did those who received the placebo; and their reports of their experiences showed a significantly greater coincidence with nine characteristics previously gleaned from the reports of classical mystics. Pahnke's experimental design can be viewed in retrospect as parallel to that of Schachter, but with attention to a different dependent variable. Pahnke sought to maintain a constant cognitive context (the Good Friday service and the use of seminarians for subjects) and manipulated the arousal agent. [Walter] Clark (1970, 191) calls attention to the fact, omitted in the published accounts, that one of Pahnke's subjects seems to have been immune to the religious effects of the hallucinogen because of a firmly held naturalistic interpretation. This subject was skeptical from the outset, was randomly selected for the experimental condition, and did not report any of the characteristics of the religious experience. Although one subject is statistically unimportant, the case does provide some evidence for a Schachterian interpretation. The subject was unwilling or unable to adopt the attributions suggested by the context, and so the effects of the psychedelic drug were not experienced as mystical or religious. Pahnke's conclusion that mystical experience might be caused by some quality of the hallucinogen is then called into question. Perhaps psilocybin functions only as a rather powerful agent of arousal, differing only quantitatively from the arousal produced by the nicotinic acid. The attributional or interpretative component might then be the crucial factor in those experiences that were reported in terms reminiscent of classical mystics.

The history of religion is replete with religious labeling and explanation of anomalous bodily states and activities. Gerschom Scholem (1973, 125–38) has shown that the abnormal physical and mental condition with which the seventeenth-century Jewish mystical messiah Sabbatai Sevi was afflicted is well documented and was widely known before his association with [Jewish theologian] Nathan of Gaza. Nathan provided a religious explanation of Sabbatai's pathology, declaring him to be the messianic figure awaited by those who adhered to the Lurianic school of Kabbalah. This explanation was eagerly accepted by the prophet himself and by hundreds of thousands of followers.[4]

---

4. For the definitive account of Sabbatai Sevi and his movement, see Scholem (1973).

> For after the beginning of the mass movement in 1666, the believers no longer spoke of an "illness." This term disappears. In their view both phases of the disease were divine dispensations for which they employed theological terms, traditional ones as well as new coinages, corresponding exactly to the modern terms "depression" and "mania." The new vocabulary ... speaks of periods of "illumination" and of the "hiding of the face" respectively. The anguish of the melancholic sufferings, which all specialists agree are extremely severe though they have no physiological basis, is explained by Nathan in theological terms when in the summer of 1665 he writes about "the severe afflictions, too immense to be conceived, which R. Sabbatai Sevi suffered on behalf of the Jewish nation." (Scholem 1973, 130)

In speculating about the transformation of Jesus from local exorcist and charismatic wonder-worker to Messiah, Morton Smith writes:

> He of course tried to understand himself in terms made available by his own culture, and seems to have thought himself, at first, a prophet, later, the Messiah. He also thought that he had ascended into the heavens, entered the kingdom of God, and was therefore freed from the Mosaic law.
> (Smith, M. 1973, 140)

Any bodily changes or feelings may be accounted for in religious terms when the subject's past experience and present context make such an account plausible and compelling. The common element in religious experience is likely to be found, not in a particular physiological or even mental state, but in the beliefs held by the subject about the causes of that state.

"EXPLAINING RELIGIOUS EXPERIENCE," FROM *RELIGIOUS EXPERIENCE*

The term *experience* is ambiguous. When I inquire about what a person has experienced at a certain moment, my question is ambiguous between two meanings: (i) how it seemed to that person at that time; and (ii) the best explanation that can be given of the experience. This ambiguity is present in our ordinary talk about perception. I may have been frightened by the bear that I saw up ahead on the trail. My friend points out to me that it is not a bear but a log, and my fear subsides. What did I really see up ahead? By one interpretation of the word *see*, I saw a bear. That is the way I apprehended it, and that apprehension accounts for my fear and behavioral response. By another interpretation, what I really saw was a log, and I took it for a bear. I was wrong about what I experienced, and now that I can explain what happened I can correct my mistake.

This distinction is similar to, but differs from, [Roderick M.] Chisholm's distinction between the comparative and epistemic uses of "appear" words.[5] It differs because Chisholm suggests that the comparative use, the description of how it appears to the subject, is a report of an immediate experience that is independent of interpretation or other beliefs. No such unmediated experience is possible.[6] The distinction drawn here is between one interpretation, which presupposes a particular explanation of the experience, and another interpretation, also assuming an explanation, which is adopted by another person or by the same person at a later time. The perception of the object ahead as a bear was one explanation, and that was replaced by a better explanation when more information became available. That better explanation led to a reinterpretation of the experience.

It is important to note that both senses of *experience* assume explanations. It is not the case that explanation enters only into the second sense. The first, the description of his

---

5. [Ed. note] In a 1950 essay entitled "The Theory of Appearing," Chisholm (1916–1999) offered a critique of the status of "appears words," as in the claim that "the sky appears blue to me," which he called the fallacy of sense-datum inference. Simply put, he questioned whether the claim that the sky was blue necessarily implies that one can be confident inferring that the sky is in fact blue. To rephrase it, he argued that it was incorrect to assume a necessary link between reported experiences of a state of affairs and the actual status of the state of affairs themselves. Accordingly, "appears words" that are used in reports are not neutral words but, instead, are doing work inasmuch as they are linking a perception to a normative claim about the world at large.

6. [Ed. note] Often, those who advocate the distinct quality of religious experiences will argue that these experiences are "unmediated," that is, they do not rely upon, nor are shaped by, prior knowledge, language, tradition, or assumptions.

or her experience as assumed by the subject at the time of the experience, presupposes an explanation. If the distinguishing mark of the religious is that it is assumed to elude natural explanation, then the labeling of the experience as religious by the subject includes the belief that it cannot be exhaustively explained in naturalistic terms. The attempts of scholars as diverse as [Mircea] Eliade and [D. Z.] Phillips to preclude issues of explanation from entering into accounts of religious experience and belief are undercut by the recognition that explanatory commitments are assumed in the identification of an experience as religious.

The distinction we have drawn between descriptive and explanatory reduction[7] is tailored to meet this ambiguity. Descriptive reduction is inappropriate because the experience must be identified under a description that can be ascribed to the subject at the time of the experience. The experience must be described with reference to its intentional object. In the example given above, my fright was the result of noticing a bear ahead of me. The fact that the analyst must attempt to formulate a description of the experience which captures the way it was apprehended by the subject does not mean that no explanation is incorporated into the subject's description, nor does it mean that the analyst is not engaged in an inference toward the best explanation in his attempt to arrive at that formulation.

The identification of an experience under a description that can be ascribed to the subject is required before any explanation of the experience can be proposed. Every explanation assumes a description of that which is to be explained. One cannot explain phenomena as such but only phenomena under a description (Danto 1975, 218–32).[8] An event, action, emotion, or experience can be identified only under a certain description, and reference must be made to that description in any explanation that is offered. If the relevant description is not acknowledged, it will be tacitly assumed. The analyst's choice of the appropriate description of an experience or action is not entirely independent of the explanation he goes on to offer. If a practice is completely baffling to me under a certain description, and would be recognizable as a practice common to the culture in which it is ensconced if the description were altered slightly, then I will be tempted to alter it and to ascribe the discrepancy to defects in my observation or in the reports from which I am working. If the evidence for the original description is compelling, I must accept the anomaly and search further for an explanation; if it is weak, I may adjust the description in the interest of overall plausibility. This is the proper point at which to invoke [W. V. O.]

---

7. [Ed. note] Earlier in the book, Proudfoot argued for a distinction between descriptive reductionism and explanatory reductionism. The former is improper, he argues, because it fails to report accurately on what the participant describes as his or her perceptions and understandings. Having recorded these accurately, however, he argues (contrary to scholars of religion such as Eliade, a well-known critic of reductionism in the study of religion) that the scholar can attempt to account for the participant's claims by appealing to another language of explanation, such as psychology or biology. So long as these two steps are kept distinct—description and explanation—Proudfoot believes that reductionism ought to take place in the study of religion.

8. [Ed. note] This reference does not appear in Proudfoot's bibliography, and the editors have been unable to identify it.

Quine's principle of charity.[9] I want my total account, with its descriptive and explanatory components, to be the most plausible of the available alternatives. I adjust each until I reach a reflective equilibrium.

The recognition that religious experience is constituted by concepts and beliefs permits an optimism with respect to the descriptive task which would not otherwise be possible. There is no reason, in principle, to despair about the possibility of understanding the experience of persons and communities that are historically and culturally remote from the interpreter. The difficulty is not posed by an unbridgeable gap between an experience that can only be known by acquaintance and the concepts in which that experience is expressed. Because the concepts and beliefs are constitutive of the experience, careful study of the concepts available in a particular culture, the rules that govern them, and the practices that are informed by them will provide access to the variety of experiences available to persons in that culture. Though it may be difficult to reconstruct, the evidence required for understanding the experience is public evidence about linguistic forms and practices. We attempt to formulate a description of the experience from the perspective of the subject, but the evidence is, in principle, accessible to us.

This conception of religious experience also shows that the variety of that experience is much greater and richer than has been suggested by those who claim that a single experience of the numinous or sacred, or a few such types, underlie all the diverse reports in different traditions. Just as the experiences of *nirvana* and *devekuth*[10] differ because they are informed by different concepts and beliefs, so the often rather subtle doctrinal differences between religious communities, or subgroups of the same community, will give rise to different experiences. [Søren] Kierkegaard, [the Danish philosopher], was able to distinguish rather precisely several different forms of despair by examining the concepts that enter into those forms. A wide variety of conversion experiences or experiences of religious awe or wonder can be distinguished in the same manner. The catalogue of varieties can never be completed.

If explanation is as central to the study of religious experience as this account suggests, then why has it not been recognized as such? Why is the explanatory component so often disguised or ignored in favor of appeals to a sense or a consciousness that is contrasted with belief? There are two motivations for this procedure: phenomenological accuracy and a protective strategy adopted for apologetic purposes. The first arises from the fact that those who report religious experiences typically take them to be independent of and more fundamental than beliefs or theories. The sense of the infinite or the consciousness of finitude is not apprehended as a theoretical commitment but as an inchoate sense that provides a practical orientation. It seems to the subject to be inaccurate to classify it with inference, inquiry, and hypothesis. Since an understanding of

---

9. [Ed. note] The American mathematician and philosopher, Quine (1908–2000), proposed that, when attempting to assess the logical status of an argument, one should be generous and offer the strongest possible and thus most sympathetic interpretation of its meaning.

10. [Ed. note] *Nirvana* is the Sanskrit name given to the Buddhist experience of enlightenment; *devekuth* is the Hebrew term for a mystical union with God.

the experience requires that it be identified under a description that accords with that of the subject, it is tempting to assimilate it to the case of sensations, and to assume that sensations are independent of practices and beliefs. For these reasons, phenomenological accuracy appears to some to require that the experience be described so as to make it independent of beliefs.

The appeal to a sense or consciousness that is allegedly innocent of explanatory commitments has an apologetic advantage. If such an appeal could be made, it would be unaffected by any developments in science or other kinds of inquiry. It would, as Schleiermacher said, leave one's physics and psychology unaffected.[11] Religious belief and practice could be seen as derived from this independent experience, and the difficult questions that have been raised for religion by changes in our other beliefs could be circumvented. Rather than seeing the experience as constituted by the beliefs, one could view the beliefs as expressive of the experience. The direction of derivation would be reversed, and that would serve the task of apologetics. If it did not provide a way of justifying religious beliefs and practices, it would at least protect them from the criticism that they conflict with ordinary and scientific beliefs.

As we have seen, the protective strategy used by those who argue that religious experience is independent of concepts and beliefs is parallel to that adopted by those who claim it is permeated by concepts but independent of referential or explanatory commitments. In both cases, accounts of religious experience are restricted to those that would be endorsed by the person having the experience, and consequently the possibility of those accounts conflicting with the claims of the believer is precluded. Whether one describes an allegedly pre-linguistic affective experience or confines oneself to elucidating the grammar of a particular religious practice or experience, the result cannot possibly come into conflict with any beliefs or explanations from outside the religious perspective.

A consequence of such strategies is that language that appears to be descriptive may be intended to evoke or reproduce the experience that is purportedly described. Schleiermacher is explicit about his assumption that direct acquaintance is required for understanding the sense of the infinite; thus he sees the need to elicit that sense in his readers. Rhetorical language is carefully constructed, and the speech or essay becomes an edifying discourse, of which Schleiermacher's *On Religion* [originally published in 1799] is a prime example. He regards his evocative language as a catalyst that directs the reader's attention to a sense that is already present but has not been nurtured. In fact, however, the language may be not merely catalytic but constitutive of the experience. If the reader follows Schleiermacher's instruction to attend to the moment before the rise of consciousness and to recognize the unity intuited there, he or she may discover that unity.

---

11. [Ed. note] Among other texts he wrote, Schleiermacher (1768–1834), a Protestant theologian, is known for his book, *On Religion: Speeches to its Cultured Despisers* (1799), in which he argued that what we commonly call religion (its traditions, rituals, institutions, etc.) is in fact evidence of a prior feeling of having absolute dependence on another, and that other he called God. Because religion's roots were in emotion, he argued that one could be both rational and religious—a position he championed in opposition to Enlightenment criticisms of religion.

That discovery ought not, however, to be cited as evidence for the unity of the world or of the infinite. An experience that has been evoked by carefully chosen rhetoric and by assuming a cultural tradition informed by theism cannot be taken as evidence for a unity that is independent of our concepts and beliefs.

Descriptions of doubt, anxiety, or faith in existentialist literature are often employed in a similar way. Kierkegaard displays dazzling literary and analytic skills in the service of edification. His analyses are often designed to elicit experiences and affections in his reader. Just as the spiritual director and the skilled revivalist preacher know how to evoke certain emotions and attitudes, an author can employ rhetorical skills to elicit affections in a reader. That ability presupposes a considerable amount of analysis. Kierkegaard's writings contain very subtle analyses of despair, faith, and doubt. As [the ancient Greek philosopher] Aristotle knew, one can often learn more about emotions and attitudes from the orator or poet than from anyone else. Unlike Aristotle's *Rhetoric*, however, Schleiermacher's *On Religion* and most of Kierkegaard's pseudonymous works are written in a rhetorical style intended to elicit that which is being described. Much of the literature in the history and phenomenology of religion can also be viewed in this light. Such terms as *numinous*, *holy*, and *sacred* are presented as descriptive or analytical tools but in conjunction with warnings against reductionism,[12] they function to preclude explanation and evoke a sense of mystery or awe. They are used to persuade the reader that the distinguishing mark of the religious is some quality that eludes description and analysis in nonreligious terms. [Rudolf] Otto's use of *numinous* is an example of how one can employ the term to create a sense of mystery and present it as analysis. Such approaches to the study of religion are offered as neutral descriptions, but they assume not only a theory of religion but also religious theory.

We have distinguished the tasks of description and explanation and have argued that explanation is central both to religious experience and to its study. What kind of explanation, then, might we expect to construct for religious experience? An experience or an event can be explained only when it is identified under a description. And we have concluded that the distinguishing mark of religious experience is the subject's belief that the experience can only be accounted for in religious terms. It is this belief, and the subject's identification of his or her experience under a particular description, which makes it religious. If the concepts and beliefs under which the subject identifies his or her experience determine whether or not it is a religious experience, then we need to explain why the subject employs those particular concepts and beliefs. We must explain why the subject was confronted with this particular set of alternative ways of understanding his experience and why he employed the one he did. In general, what we want is a historical or cultural explanation.

---

12. [Ed. note] It is commonly argued, by some scholars of religion (represented best in this volume by Joachim Wach's essay), that, because religion is a distinct realm of human experience, to explain it as being the result of some other aspect of human history (such as resulting from psychological or economic factors) is to do an injustice to the original experience itself. Thus, such scholars argue against reducing the participant's disclosures; instead, or so it is argued, they must be understood on their own terms.

This holds both for discrete, datable religious experiences, of the sort on which [William] James concentrates, and for the identification of an underlying and pervasive religious moment in experience. Why did Stephen Bradley identify his accelerated heart rate as the work of the Holy Spirit? What caused Astor to regard what he saw as a miracle whereas Bingham[13] remained skeptical? Why did Schleiermacher apprehend the moment that precedes thought as a sense of the infinite and discern a feeling of absolute dependence which accompanies all consciousness of the polarity of self and world? For Bradley, we would need to know something about Methodist revivalism in early nineteenth-century New England, about the particular meeting he attended earlier in the evening, and about the events in his life up to that moment. To explain Astor's beliefs about what he saw it would be necessary to acquaint oneself with Roman Catholic teachings on miracles, the significance of the shrine at Lourdes, and the details of Astor's background. To explain Schleiermacher's sense of the infinite, his feeling of absolute dependence, and his apprehension of all events as miracles one would need to know more about his early years among the Moravians,[14] his study of [the seventeenth-century philosopher, Baruch] Spinoza, and the circle of friends in Berlin for whom he wrote *On Religion*. Each of these instances requires acquaintance with the Christian tradition and with the particular forms of that tradition which shaped the person and his experience.

For experiences sought in highly manipulative settings, as in meditative traditions where the training is carefully prescribed and a person is guided by a spiritual director in the interpretation of the states of mind and body achieved by the regimen, explanations of the sort suggested by Schachter's experiment seem clearly relevant. The novice learns to make attributions that accord with the tradition, and he engages self-consciously in manipulations to attain states that confirm those attributions. For seemingly more spontaneous but still relatively discrete and datable experiences in less contrived settings, one would still look to explain the experience by accounting for why the subject makes these particular attributions. Just as Schachter's experiment sheds light on the experience of emotions in natural settings, attention to the meditative traditions may provide insight into the allegedly natural, spontaneous examples of religious experience. The phenomenologist of religion has often claimed that elaborately contrived ritualistic settings are expressions of the pervasive sense of the sacred or the infinite in human experience, but it seems more likely that the supposedly natural and spontaneous experiences are derived from beliefs and practices in much the same way that an experience is produced in the

---

13. [Ed. note] In the chapter on "Mysticism" Proudfoot offers an example of two men—Astor and Bingham—witnessing someone astonishingly recover from an illness. Given their different preconceptions, they experience the event differently. Astor sees it as a miracle while Bingham "views it as an event that is anomalous with respect to the present state of medical knowledge but will doubtless one day be explained" (138). Proudfoot claims, "Their different beliefs about the appropriate kind of explanation lead them to identify the event differently" (138).

14. [Ed. note] The Moravians are a Reformation denomination that originated in the mid-fifteenth century in ancient Bohemia and Moravia (which is today part of the Czech Republic); personal piety, or one's experience of God's saving grace, was an emphasis of this group, in opposition to what they portrayed as the priority given in the Roman Catholic tradition to ritual, tradition, and the place of the institution.

more disciplined traditions of meditative practice. How did Schleiermacher and others come to think that the sense of the infinite or the sense of finitude was independent of and prior to the beliefs and practices of a culture shaped by theism? His identification of what he takes to be a universal moment in human experience seems clearly to reflect the concept of God as Creator and Governor derived from the Hebrew Bible and the traditions it formed. The consciousness Schleiermacher accurately describes may, upon investigation, turn out to be the product of prior religious beliefs and practices.

Inquiry may demonstrate that some sense or intuition that appears to be independent of beliefs and practices is actually an artefact that developed under particular historical circumstances. Elizabeth Anscombe (1958, 1–19) calls attention to the fact that some of the central concepts of modern moral philosophy, including the distinctively moral uses of *ought* and *right*, have no parallel in Aristotle or in other classical authors. Contemporary moral philosophers debate [eighteenth-century Scottish philosopher David] Hume's claim that one cannot derive ought from is,[15] or [George E.] Moore's discussion of the naturalistic fallacy,[16] as if they were trying to clarify concepts that are invariant across periods and cultures and that are crucial for moral experience everywhere. Why, then, does that sense of ought seem so alien to the moral reasoning we find in Aristotle? Anscombe points out that between Aristotle and [David] Hume our language and practice was shaped by theism, particularly by Christianity. She suggests that the modern concept of moral obligation is not an intuition that is independent of culture and belief, but that it derives from a law conception of ethics, and that that conception assumes belief in a divine lawgiver.

> Naturally it is not possible to have such a conception unless you believe in God as a lawgiver; like Jews, Stoics, and Christians. But if such a conception is dominant for many centuries, and then is given up, it is a natural result that the concepts of "obligation," of being bound or required as by a law, should remain though they had lost their root; and if the word "ought" has become invested in certain contexts with the sense of "obligation," it too will remain to be spoken with special emphasis and a special feeling in these contexts.   (Anscombe 1958, 6)

The concept of ought, and the related sense of obligation, have survived outside of the conceptual framework that produced them and made them intelligible.[17] The moral

---

15. [Ed. note] In the study of ethics, scholars distinguish between "ought" and "is"; the latter implies a description of a state of affairs (e.g., The door is closed), whereas the former implies a normative command concerning how a state of affairs must be (e.g., The door ought to be closed). When it comes to the development of ethical rules, it is claimed by some that the "ought" cannot be derived from the "is"—that is, just because a door happens to be currently closed does not necessitate that it must be closed.

16. [Ed. note] Moore (1873–1958) argued that it was a logical mistake to try to arrive at conclusions regarding "the good" based upon the properties we believe characterize good things. The mistake being made is to misunderstand goodness as merely being a property that a thing can possess (such as height or weight or color).

17. [Ed. note] A late nineteenth-century anthropologist would call something that outlived the context that originally made it meaningful and sensible a "survival."

sentiments Hume describes and maps so well are artefacts that were formed by earlier beliefs and practices.

It seems quite likely that the feeling of absolute dependence [as it was phrased by Schleiermacher] and Otto's sense of the numinous are legacies of belief in the God of the Hebrew Bible and Christian tradition and of the practices informed by that belief. These experiences now appear to be autonomous and independent of that belief and that tradition. At a time in which belief in a transcendent Creator and associated metaphysical doctrines have been rejected by many, the habits of interpretation informed by those beliefs remain firmly entrenched in cultural patterns of thought, action, and feeling. Belief in God as Creator once provided the justifying context for these affections and practices. Now the direction of justification is reversed, and attempts are made to defend the beliefs by appeal to the affective experiences and practices. The sense of finitude, the feeling of absolute dependence, the practice of worship, and the grammar that governs the use of the word God are appealed to in order to justify the traditional religious statements without which this sense, feeling, practice, and grammar would not be intelligible.

These are only some suggestions of the kind of explanation that might be offered of religious experience. While one might venture a hypothesis to account for Bradley's accelerated heart rate or the recovery that Astor witnessed, that approach will not yield an explanation of their experiences. What must be explained is why they understood what happened to them or what they witnessed in religious terms. This requires a mapping of the concepts and beliefs that were available to them, the commitments they brought to the experience, and the contextual conditions that might have supported their identification of their experiences in religious terms. Interest in explanations is not an alien element that is illegitimately introduced into the study of religious experience. Those who identify their experiences in religious terms are seeking the best explanations for what is happening to them. The analyst should work to understand those explanations and discover why they are adopted.

9

ANN TAVES

Excerpt from "Conclusion," from *Fits, Trances, and Visions: Experiencing Religion and Explaining Experience from Wesley to James*

A professor of American religion and Catholic studies at the University of California, Santa Barbara, Ann Taves's areas of expertise include the study of Catholicism, "tradition" as a category of analysis, and psychological and experiential models of religion, among others. As a scholar also concerned with methodological and theoretical issues in the study of religion, Taves has written and lectured extensively on historical understandings of religious experience and its resultant impact on Christian theology, the relationship between cognitive science and the study of religion, and theorizing involuntary experiences (such as spirit possession). Her book publications include *Religious Experience Reconsidered* (2009), *The Household of Faith: Roman Catholic Devotions in Mid-Nineteenth Century America* (1986) and *Fits, Trances and Visions: Experiencing Religion and Explaining Experience from Wesley to James* (1999), from which the following essay is excerpted.

Fits, Trances, and Visions is a historical study of some of the most dramatic and controversial ecstatic experiences in America throughout the eighteenth and nineteenth centuries, including trances, mesmerism, tongue-speaking, and faith-healing, among others. Understanding the significance that the term "experience" carries within the study of religion, Taves argues that one cannot understand religious experience—or any experience, for that matter—outside of the context in which that experience takes place. She privileges William James's view that attempting to view a phenomenon outside of its context is a lost analysis, for the extracted phenomenon is rendered dead inasmuch as it is robbed of the very components that made it socially meaningful.

By arguing that experiences cannot be analyzed outside of their social, cultural, and/or psychological frameworks, Taves is asserting—much like Proudfoot above—that there is no such thing as an unmediated experience; that is, even if such a thing as a pure experience exists, the human to whom it happened has no other modes of description than intrinsically social ones with which to account for such an occurrence. With this theoretical background in mind, Taves shows how various involuntary experiences in one period and setting could be read as religious phenomena, and then extracted and reworked in another as psychologically based. New contexts allowed for the refashioning of older experiences to recreate and re-establish the dominance of more contemporary intellectual, social, and psychological trends.

In light of Taves's work, one might ask whether a cultural context actually *creates* experience (that is, experience would be impossible without it), or whether culture is merely the *filter* through which a freestanding experience is interpreted. Introducing this line of inquiry is a Pandora's Box, of sorts, for as Taves has so aptly noted, acknowledging the processes by which religious experiences are created also demands scrutiny of the sense that religion, itself, is the product of a social creation. For if one sees experience as an independent event or memory which is filtered through a specific cultural lens, then one is making the argument that something of experience still exists before its social interpretation is applied. If, however, one argues that the actual sensory phenomena that are taken to be "religious experience" do not exist unless their possibilities are first created by these cultural outlets, then a much different argument on the nature of experience is forwarded. What are the implications for the study of religious experience—and perhaps, religion more generally—if either one of these positions is true? The political edge of this matter is taken up in the next essay by Robert Sharf.

EXCERPT FROM "CONCLUSION," FROM *FITS, TRANCES, AND VISIONS*

THE CATEGORY OF RELIGIOUS EXPERIENCE

"Religious experience" meant something very different in 1750 and in 1900 in the Anglo-American context. Within late eighteenth- and nineteenth-century evangelicalism, "religious experience" meant religious experience as understood in a particular tradition. The phrase "religious experience" often appeared in the titles of religious autobiographies. There were, for example, numerous accounts of the "life and religious experience" or the "religious experience and spiritual trials" of individuals, both ministers and laypeople. Almost all such accounts were by Protestant authors and a disproportionate number of the Protestants were Methodist.[1] In this usage, religious experience was presumptively authentic and particular. With the publication of *The Varieties of Religious Experience*, William James theoretically constituted "religious experience" as an object of study, defining it as a generic "something" that informed "religion-in-general" apart from any tradition in particular. He did so by abstracting that which he identified as religious experience (some of which had been identified as such in its original context) from the theological

---

1. The life and religious experience of Mme. Guyon is the only Catholic title. Among the Protestant authors, we find Methodists, Quakers, Baptists, United Brethren, and Adventists. "Religious experience" did not always appear in the titles of pious memoirs, but was one among several stock phrases that signaled such an account. *The Memoirs of the Life, Religious Experience, Ministerial Travels and Labours of Mrs. Zilpha Elaw, An American Female of Colour* captures the flavour of such titles. "Religious experience," here positioned between her "Life" and her "Ministerial Travels and Labours," referred to her experiences of conversion, sanctification, and call to the ministry. Although there are a few collections of religious experiences, they did not cross denominational lines.

contexts in which it had been embedded and linking these diverse experiences together by means of psychology.

In the historical context we have examined, the concepts of "enthusiasm," the "mesmeric state," and "the subconscious" were parallel constructs. Each [of these concepts] abstracted particular experiences from the contexts in which they had been embedded and linked them together by means of a psychological or proto-psychological theory. Indeed, as we have seen, the experimental psychology of the subconscious underlying the *Varieties* was continuous with the early psychology of animal magnetism. Whereas anti-enthusiastic theories attempted to explain false religion, James, in keeping with the mediating tradition more generally, attempted to explain what he took to characterize religion-in-general, without at the same time intending to explain it away. Although James's approach, unlike that of the anti-enthusiasts, was sympathetic to religion-in-general and seemingly sympathetic to traditional supernaturalism, it too dramatically reconstituted the experience of Protestant supernaturalists. The concept of religious experience as a generic something (i.e., in his case, a movement from an uneasiness to its solution) that informs religion-in-general reconstituted traditional Protestant supernaturalism just as radically as did the concept of enthusiasm or the concept of a mesmeric state.

One of the ironies revealed by this study is that each of the major discursive categories used to think theoretically about involuntary experience—enthusiasm, mesmeric states, and the subconscious—carried assumptions about religion. Defined as "false inspiration," enthusiasm was an outright theological concept, freighted with assumptions about true and false religion. Mesmeric states and the subconscious, which emerged as more or less scientific terms, were freighted with conceptions about the natural and supernatural, science and religion, and, in the case of the latter, the normal and the psychopathological. The freighted character of both the theological and scientific concepts points to the ways in which each of these concepts was embedded in its own traditions of discourse and practice. Theorizing about religion is often explicitly connected to the practice of religion in the context of theological schools, but we tend to assume that such theorizing is more objective or dispassionate in secular universities where it is formally disconnected from the practice of religion within particular traditions. Although the two situations may be different, we should not be lulled into thinking the latter situation is less complex or less likely to impose its presuppositions on particular forms of religion in practice.

This book was structured so that we might examine the interplay between theory and practice both from the perspective of those constructing the concepts and from the perspective of those whose experiences were being reconstituted in terms of the new construct. In doing so, I wanted to make several points. First, that it matters what we call things. As scholars, we are involved in constituting the "objects" we study whether we are insiders or outsiders to the traditions we are studying. Second, we constitute the objects of our study by means of comparison whether we make these comparisons explicit or not. Third, since we cannot write ourselves out of this process, it is important that we take responsibility for the comparisons we construct. James was quite conscious of this process, although most who employ the modern concept of "religious experience" are less so.

COMPARISON, COLONIZATION, AND TRANSFORMATION

The danger of not being aware [of the comparisons we construct] lies in the power of such concepts to reconstitute and in the process to subsume the experience of others into what becomes, in effect, a reified colonizing discourse.[2] When we acknowledge our concepts as constructs and acknowledge the comparisons that inform them, they lose much of their power to colonize. If, following Marilyn Waldman, we stipulate our comparative "catchments" tentatively and heuristically, our comparative questions create sites for dialogue. In such a context, our experiences, our ideas about experience, and our engagement with the experiences of others all take their place in the flow of experience, as it is constituted and reconstituted, over time. I think we must acknowledge that this last process is inevitable. By approaching the experiencing and explaining of religion historically, I have tried to make the larger point that the experience of religion cannot be separated from the communities of discourse and practice that gave rise to it *without becoming something else*.

This point appears to be contradicted by La Roy Sunderland's and Mrs. M'Reading's claim that her experience of being "caught up to Paradise" in the context of a religious service preached by Sunderland in 1824 was "just the same" as her experience while "entranced" in 1839. The mesmeric tradition presumed that a common mental state (*an experience as it were*)—whether designated as mesmeric, magnetic, somnambulistic, trance, or hypnotic—informed the whole gamut of what I have called involuntary experiences. While mesmeric *discourse* postulated a common mental state, I want to suggest that mesmeric *practice*, rather than evoking some common mental state, instead evoked bodily knowledges, including personal and cultural memories, and recast them in new forms that were secular or naturalistic. In claiming that the new forms were in fact "the same as" the traditional religious forms, mesmerists rewrote the past, discrediting traditional religious practices and limiting their ability to reproduce themselves other than as a circumscribed counter-culture.

What makes Sunderland's story intriguing is that it actually contains traces of the past, of the prior narrative, that he and Mrs. M'Reading were intent on rereading. Sunderland referred to Mrs. M'Reading as his convert. Referring to her experience when Sunderland preached in her church in 1824, Mrs. M'Reading said, "I was then [in 1824] 'caught up to Paradise,' as St. Paul was, and ... I saw Jesus and all the angels so happy." Although she does not say so explicitly, this was probably a description of her conversion experience. Sunderland describes himself or Mrs. M'Reading as inducing such experiences by means of pheno-magnetic practices, but I do not think the second experience could have happened the way it did without the first. While entranced, Mrs. M'Reading did not enter a generic mental state; rather, the new situation evoked bodily memories such that she

---

2. Ian Hacking (taking "trance" as an unproblematic term) writes that in "our ignorance about trance, and our wish to make it pathological ... we colonize our own past, destroying traces of the original inhabitants. That is, we read multiple personality into other uses of trance, those that appeared in earlier European societies, and find it very hard to see them as they were seen then, not as precursors of multiple personality disorder, inadequately diagnosed, but as cultural uses of trance with their own integrity" (1995, 146).

(in some sense) returned to a heaven that she had first experienced in the context of a Methodist preaching service. Without those bodily memories formed in that very particular context, Mrs. M'Reading would not have had that experience.

Although the new story described the two experiences as identical and implied that the experience she had originally understood to be religious could be elicited by secular means, I suspect that this was only so in a very limited sense. Sunderland's stories were not intended to demonstrate his power to produce religious experiences, but rather to demonstrate his ability to elicit or replicate experiences through secular means that were in his view falsely deemed religious. In eliciting the "same" religious experience in what was in effect a "sterile" environment, Sunderland produced a counter-narrative that discredited the tradition and undercut its ability to reproduce itself.

As in the case of "flashbacks" linked to trauma, "the same" experience occurred because a bodily memory was recalled or evoked. Nonetheless, once evoked by a mesmerist rather than a preacher the experience took on a different meaning. It was no longer an experience of conversion or sanctification or a visionary journey to heaven but a mental product of a mesmeric state induced by the mesmerist. While the bodily memory or "experience" was evoked in a new context, the inner form and content of that experience content was still derived from the older tradition. The new context in which the bodily memory or experience was evoked negated the older tradition by reconstituting the experience as mesmeric rather than visionary. The situation was parallel to what occurs when therapists evoke or work with flashbacks (i.e., the intense bodily memories) of victims of post-traumatic stress. The flashbacks in such cases are not literally "the same as" the original trauma, although this is not always apparent to the patient. Working with the flashback in the therapeutic context reconstitutes the flashback as a flashback and begins to make the bodily memory of the traumatic experience more manageable.

CONTRIBUTION TO A NATURALISTIC THEORY
OF INVOLUNTARY ACTS

Sunderland might have agreed with the argument I just made, given that his associationist understanding of trance provides one possible way of explaining why experiences cannot be abstracted from the discourses and practices that constitute them without creating a new experience. If trance, as he argued, cannot exist in practice without "associations," then severing the relationship between a "mental state" and its "associations," whether in theory or in practice, destroys the original experience and reconstitutes it as something else. The associations serve to cue the experience. Thus, he wrote: "Some will sink into a state of trance, by merely sitting in the chair where they have been entranced before; and the sight of any place where the mind has been peculiarly impressed, revives the same feelings, and we live over again the scenes which, otherwise, had remained entirely obliterated from recollection" (Sunderland 1868, 104–5, 107–8).[3] What Sunderland referred to

---

3. For more recent discussions of cueing, see Rouget (1985) and Marks (1974).

as peculiar impressions on the mind are analogous to what I, following Paul Connerton, have been referring to as bodily memories (1989, 72–3).[4] The cue (e.g., the place where the original experience occurred) revives the bodily memory (i.e., the peculiar impressions on the mind, including the associated feelings) such that, in Sunderland's words, "we live over again the scenes which, otherwise, had remained entirely obliterated from recollection" (as, for example, with flashbacks). In the story about Mrs. M'Reading, Sunderland's presence may have served as the associative cue that evoked her bodily memory of her earlier experience.

When Mrs. M'Reading lived over the experience of being "caught up to Paradise" in the mesmeric context, her experience was reconstituted as a mesmeric experiment rather than a heavenly journey. This new explanation of her experience probably replaced the older one and, thus, brought her visionary career to an end. If we bring Frederick Myers's notion of "chains of memory" to bear on this situation, we might envision some alternative scenarios. Had Mrs. M'Reading's bodily memory of being "caught up to Paradise" been evoked in the context of a Methodist or Millerite camp meeting, the outcome would probably have been very different. Rather than ending her visionary career, further experiences in that context would likely have extended or elaborated the "chain of memory" that she associated with Paradise. Although she only saw Jesus the first time she journeyed to heaven, they might have spoken the second time or he might have gazed at her intently (as he did Ellen Harmon). Had Mrs. M'Reading's experience been evoked in the context of a Spiritualist gathering some ten years later, she might not have assumed that animal magnetism and heavenly journeys were incompatible and her journey might have been taken as a sign of mediumistic abilities worthy of further development.

We can, in other words, imagine Mrs. M'Reading developing in a number of different directions. Had the bodily memory not been evoked at all, she might simply have remained a Methodist with a dramatic conversion experience. Evoked in a mesmeric context, she became a woman who was easily entranced, a good mesmeric "subject." Evoked in a Methodist or Millerite camp meeting, she might have become a visionary. Evoked a decade later in a Spiritualist circle, she might have become a medium. As a mesmeric subject, a visionary, or a medium, Mrs. M'Reading would have elaborated her bodily memories of the first experience, albeit in different ways. As a mesmeric subject, she reconstituted her memories as a secular experience. As a visionary, she might have elaborated them as a supernatural experience of a particular sort, (say) Millerite or Methodist. As a medium, she might have reconstituted them as both a natural and a religious experience of communicating with spirits. From the perspective of Myers's theory of secondary selves, Mrs. M'Reading would have been developing a secondary self through the elaboration of a chain of memories had she pursued any of these three courses. As a mesmeric subject, a Millerite visionary, or a Spiritualist medium, however, she would have held in each case a very different chain of memories....

---

4. This way of speaking as constituted and reconstructed in connection with chains of associated or disassociated memories avoids the dualisms associated with the contemporary debates over "recovered" and "false" memories.

127

THE INTERPLAY BETWEEN THEORY AND PRACTICE

[William] James's conceptual distinction between the science of religion (things made) and living religion (things in the making) corresponds to and furthers the distinctions between theory and religion-in-practice that inform the book. As James explains in more detail in *A Pluralistic Universe*, "when you have broken reality into concepts you never can reconstruct it in its wholeness.... But [he said] place yourself...inside of the living, moving, active thickness of the real, and all the abstractions and distinctions are given into your hand" (1977 [1909], 116). In short, James said, "What really exists is not things made but things in the making. Once made, they are dead, and an infinite number of alternative conceptual decompositions can be used in defining them" (117).

The closer we are to the experience in question the more we can see of the way it is embedded in and connected to other things. The more we abstract or disconnect "experience" from the *narrating of experience* in order that it may participate in more abstract discourses, the more it is fragmented or, as James says, "decomposed." First-person narratives allow us to focus on the narrating of experience and thus provide historians with our primary means of access to the experience-in-practice of an individual or community. Such narratives provide a means of reconstituting the links between experience and the bodily knowledges, cultural traditions, and social relations that went into making or composing the experience. Third-person narratives are a step removed, although they often contain and rework first-person narratives. Theories of experience, whether theological, spiritual, philosophical, sociological, or psychological, are the farthest removed and the most fragmented. Nonetheless, as we have seen, they inform the making and unmaking of experience at the level of narrative in varied and complicated ways.

Many phenomenologically oriented scholars of religion share James's comparative interest in the interplay between the general and the particular, that is, between theories of religion and living religions.... [H]owever, most historians or phenomenologists of religion limit their comparisons to religious phenomena. Few share James's interest in comparing religious and nonreligious phenomena. Such comparisons shift our attention from the study of religion *per se* to the *processes* by which religious and nonreligious phenomena are made and unmade. I think this is a more interesting and fruitful question. However, in pursuing it we lose a sense of religion (or not-religion) as a substantive thing. Indeed, once we latch on to this question, it becomes clear that the question of "what is religion" (which really asks what is authentic or true religion) is disputed within traditions and not just between them. One locus for these disputes about "what is religion" clusters around "experience." Because of the disputes, both among insiders and between insiders and outsiders, the study of religion opens out at this point into the study of everything.

PART V

THE UNRAVELING OF EXPERIENCE

10

ROBERT H. SHARF

"Experience," from *Critical Terms for Religious Studies*

Robert Sharf is a professor of Buddhist studies at the University of California, Berkeley. Having earned degrees in Chinese studies and Buddhist studies, Sharf's work focuses primarily on medieval Chinese Buddhism, as well as Japanese Buddhism, Buddhist art, and the study of ritual, theory, and method in the study of religion.

Sharf is the author of *Coming to Terms with Chinese Buddhism: A Reading of the Treasure Store Treatise* (2002) and co-editor of *Living Images: Japanese Buddhist Icons in Context* (2001). In both, Sharf questions certain scholarly understandings of Asian religions that have created "master narratives" through which Buddhism, in particular, has been popularly portrayed. Similar to his work in the following essay, Sharf argues in the aforementioned books for a re-evaluation of the many theories and models that have come to define the field of Buddhist studies.

This essay, simply titled "Experience," embarks upon an exploration of the political weight behind the rhetorical use of the term "experience" in religion, and offers an important insight into the relevance of context when examining experiential claims. Sharf begins by noting that "experience" is a category used widely as a point of contrast against things deemed "empirical" or "objective," and inasmuch as popular understandings of religion portray it as a phenomenon that contains a mystical, experiential, or subjective component, "experience" becomes an authoritative term. Part of the popularity of the category of experience, Sharf argues, is that it has legitimized various interests endemic to the field; as evidence of this, he points particularly to its utility in phenomenological circles (see essays in this volume by Joachim Wach and Diana Eck for examples of this approach).

Pulling from his own areas of expertise, Sharf furthers his argument on context by examining the conflation of experience and mysticism in Asian religion. First, he takes up the question of whether one can differentiate between a "core" experience and the cultural interpretations or conditions that cause that "core" to exist (known as the perennialist hypothesis), a similar discussion broached in the introduction to Ann Taves's work (see previous essay). Sharf finds this notion "philosophically suspect," asserting that no unmediated core—no raw experience—is possible since every experience is created *by* and *through* the medium of culture. In this sense, Sharf is a proponent of the idea that culture is not a secondary force acting upon an experience, but is the very agent *and* material from which experiences are formed. He uses this foundation to further his point that when one examines the context and construction of popular notions of Asian spirituality, one finds a relatively recent—and very Western-influenced—phenomenon.

Sharf ends this essay with multiple points of inquiry. Consider his contention that experience, as a category, is ultimately authoritative because it provides a sense of self in the midst of modernity's objectification and commodification of people. Consider also his argument that appeals to experience remain authoritative because they are relatively empty signifiers—that is, they always refer to some unknowable realm. Are these observations accurate, and if so, what might be the relationship between the two?

"EXPERIENCE," FROM *CRITICAL TERMS FOR RELIGIOUS STUDIES*

The exercise of thought cannot have any other outcome than the negation of individual perspectives.

(Georges Bataille)

1.

One might expect an essay on the term "experience" to begin with a definition, but immediately we confront a problem. To define something entails situating it in the public sphere, assuming an objective or third-person perspective *vis-à-vis* the term or concept at issue. The problem with the term "experience," particularly with respect to its use in the study of religion, is that it resists definition by design; as we will see, the term is often used rhetorically to thwart the authority of the "objective" or the "empirical," and to valorize instead the subjective, the personal, the private. This is in part why the meaning of the term may appear self-evident at first, yet becomes increasingly elusive as one tries to get a fix on it. (Gadamer places experience "among the least clarified concepts which we have," 1975, 310.)

In spite of (or perhaps owing to) the obscurity of the term, experience as a concept has come to play a pivotal role in the study of religion. The meaning of many religious symbols, scriptures, practices, and institutions is believed to reside in the experiences they elicit in the minds of practitioners. Moreover, a particular mode (or modes) of experience, characterized as "religious," "spiritual," "visionary," or "mystical," is thought to constitute the very essence of religion, such that the origin of a given tradition is often traced to the founder's initial transcendent encounter, moment of revelation, salvation, or enlightenment. This approach to religious phenomena is not confined to academic discourse alone; many lay adherents feel that the only *authentic* form of worship or scriptural study is one that leads to a personal experience of its "inner truth." Consequently, scholarship that does not attend to the experiential dimension of religious practice is dismissed by many as reductionistic.

Some scholars go further. Not content with limiting the range of the term "experience" to particular individuals, they go on to speak of the "collective experience" of an entire community or culture. Attention to the collective or "lived" experience of a religious community is touted as one way of overcoming cultural bias—our tendency to view the beliefs and actions of people different from ourselves as backward, foolish, or bizarre. If we can bracket our own presuppositions, temper our ingrained sense of cultural superiority, and resist the temptation to evaluate the truth claims of foreign traditions, we find that their *experience* of the world possesses its own rationality, its own coherence, its own truth. This approach, sometimes known as the phenomenology of religion, enjoins the "imaginative participation in the world of the actor" in order to arrive at "value free" and "evocative" descriptions (Smart 1973, 20–21).

This use of the concept "religious experience" is exceedingly broad, encompassing a vast array of feelings, moods, perceptions, dispositions, and states of consciousness. Some prefer to focus on a distinct type of religious experience known as "mystical experience," typically construed as a transitory but potentially transformative state of consciousness in which a subject purports to come into immediate contact with the divine, the sacred, the holy. We will return to the issue of mystical experience below. Here I would only note that the academic literature does not clearly delineate the relationship between religious experience and mystical experience. The reluctance, and in the end the inability, to clearly stipulate the meaning of such terms will be a recurring theme in the discussion below.

2.

It is not difficult to understand the allure of the rhetoric of experience in the modern period. Both Western theologians and secular scholars of religion found themselves facing, each in their own way, a host of challenges that, for the purposes of this essay, I will group under the two headings of *empiricism* and *cultural pluralism*.

By empiricism I refer to the notion that all truth claims must be subject, in theory if not in fact, to empirical or scientific verification. This was a potential problem for modern theologians, as many essential elements of theological reflection are simply not amenable to empirical observation or testing. By emphasizing the experiential dimension of religion—a dimension inaccessible to strictly objective modes of inquiry—the theologian could forestall scientific critique. Religious truth claims were not to be understood as pertaining to the objective or material world, which was the proper domain of science, but to the inner spiritual world, for which the scientific method was deemed inappropriate.

Unlike the theologian, the secular scholar was not necessarily invested in the truth claims of any particular religious tradition. However, scholars of religion do have a vested interest in the existence of irreducibly *religious* phenomena over which they can claim special authority. That is to say, other academic disciplines—history, anthropology, sociology, or psychology, for example—could (and sometimes did) claim to possess the requisite tools for the analysis of religion, a claim that threatened to put the religion specialist out of a job. By construing religion as pertaining to a distinct mode of "experience," the scholar of religion could argue that it ultimately eludes the grasp of other more empirically oriented disciplines.

The second challenge for both theologians and secular scholars was that of cultural pluralism. By the twentieth century it had become difficult for Christian theologians to simply ignore the existence of non-Christian traditions, much less to smugly assert Christian superiority. But to take other traditions seriously entailed the risk of rendering Christianity merely one of several competing systems of belief. In privileging religious experience theologians could argue that all religious traditions emerged from, and were attempts to give expression to, an apprehension of the divine or the ultimate. Differences in doctrine and forms of worship are to be expected due to vast differences in linguistic, social, and cultural conditions. What is key, however, is that as a response to a fundamentally human (and thus pan-cultural and ahistorical) sense of the transcendent, all religious traditions could lay *some* claim to truth. This allowed Christian theologians to affirm the validity of Christian revelation without necessarily impugning their non-Christian rivals.

Cultural pluralism was no less a problem for secular scholars of religion, who had to contend with the knowledge that the category "religion" was itself a cultural product. Many, if not most, non-Western traditions lacked an indigenous lexical equivalent for "religion" altogether, and attempts to define or stipulate the nature of religion were often tainted with Western presuppositions. Like the theologian, the scholar of religion found the very existence of his ostensible subject of expertise open to question. By appealing to non-tradition-specific notions such as the "sacred" or the "holy"—notions that blur the distinction between a universal human experience and the posited object of said experience—the scholar could legitimize the comparative study of religion even while acknowledging the specifically Western origins of the category itself. The scholar could then argue that if places such as India or Japan or pre-Columbian America lacked an indigenous term for religion it was not because they lacked religious experience. On the contrary, every aspect of their life was so suffused with a sense of the divine that they simply did not distinguish between the secular and the sacred.

3.

The ideological aspect of the appeal to experience—the use of the concept to legitimize vested social, institutional, and professional interests—is most evident when we turn to the study of mysticism. As mentioned above, mystical experience is generally construed as a direct encounter with the divine or the absolute, and as such some scholars claim that the "raw experience" itself is not affected by linguistic, cultural, or historical contingencies. Obviously, a given individual's understanding and articulation of such an experience will be conditioned by the tradition to which he or she belongs. Thus a Christian might talk about witnessing the Holy Spirit, a Hindu about absorption into Brahman, a Buddhist about the extinction of the self. But if one is able to see beyond the superficial, culturally determined differences between these accounts one discovers a single unvarying core. Or so goes the argument advanced by William James (1961/1902), Rudolf Otto (1958/1917), Aldous Huxley (1945), W. T. Stace (1960) and Robert Forman (1990), among others. Needless to say there are important differences in the views of these scholars, but all more-or-less agree that it is possible to distinguish between a core experience (or core experiences) proper, and the divergent culturally conditioned expressions of that core. Such a position led naturally to attempts to isolate the universal features of mystical experience through the analysis of "first-hand reports." William James, for example, proposed four such features, namely, noetic quality, ineffability, transiency, and passivity (1961); Rudolf Otto speaks more loosely of "creature feeling," awefulness, overpoweringness, energy, and fascination (1958). Others reject the essential features approach altogether in favor of a looser "family resemblance" model, and several scholars argue that not one but two or more primary experiences exist, distinguishing, for example, between "introvertive" and "extravertive" types (Stace 1960).

This understanding of mystical experience, sometimes known as the "perennial philosophy" (a term popularized by Huxley's book of that title), proved quite influential among scholars of religion. But how is one to make conceptual sense of such an experience? One popular explanation goes as follows: logically we can, and indeed must, distinguish the object of consciousness from the *knowing* of that object; otherwise, we would be indistinguishable from insentient robots or automatons that are able to respond to stimuli without being conscious of them. There is, in other words, a residue in all conscious experience that cannot be reduced to the content of consciousness alone. This knowing factor, variously referred to as pure consciousness, pre-reflective experience, the true self, the *cogito*, and so on, is the proper object of a mystic's self-knowledge. Mystical experience consists in the direct, though somewhat paradoxical, apperception of, or absorption into, the knowing subject itself. Since this experience of pure subjectivity is free of individuating ego, mystics are led to speak of being one with the world, or one with the absolute. (If some theistically oriented mystics avoid explicitly monistic language, it is due to the doctrinal constraints imposed by their respective dualistic traditions.)

This is, of course, a highly simplified account of the perennialist position, and its defenders do not speak with a single voice. Be that as it may, in the past few decades this approach to mysticism has come under concerted attack from a number of scholars, notably Gershom Scholem (1969), Steven Katz (1978; 1983; 1992), Wayne Proudfoot (1985) and Grace Jantzen (1995). The objections are manifold. To begin with, critics note that we do not have access to mystical experiences *per se*, but only to texts that purport to describe them, and the perennialists systematically misconstrue these texts due to their *a priori* commitment to the perennialist position. Read impartially, there is little internal evidence to indicate that these very disparate accounts are actually referring to one and the same experience.

Besides, the very notion that one can separate an unmediated experience from a culturally determined description of that experience is philosophically suspect. According to Katz, "neither mystical experience nor more ordinary forms of experience give any indication, or any grounds for believing, that they are unmediated" (1978, 26). In other words, mystical experience is wholly shaped by a mystic's cultural environment, personal history, doctrinal commitments, religious training, expectations, aspirations, and so on.

Yet another problem with the perennialist position emerged as scholars turned to the intellectual genealogy of the category "religious experience" itself. The concept turns out to be of relatively recent, and distinctively Western, provenance. Wayne Proudfoot traces the roots of the idea to the German theologian Friedrich Schleiermacher (1768–1834), who argued that religion cannot be reduced to a system of beliefs or morality. Religion proper, claimed Schleiermacher, is predicated on a feeling of the infinite—the "consciousness of absolute dependence" (see, for example, Schleiermacher 1928). According to Proudfoot, this emphasis on feeling was motivated by Schleiermacher's "interest in freeing religious doctrine and practice from dependence on metaphysical beliefs and ecclesiastical institutions" (1985, xiii; see also Jantzen 1995, 311–21). Schleiermacher's strategy proved fruitful: the notion of religious experience provided new grounds upon which to defend religion against secular and scientific critique. The "hermeneutic of experience" was soon adopted by a host of scholars interested in religion, the most influential being William James, and today many have a difficult time imagining *what else* religion might be about. Yet prior to Schleiermacher, insists Proudfoot, religion was simply not understood in such terms, and it is thus incumbent upon us to reject the perennialist hypothesis in so far as it anachronistically imposes the recent and ideologically laden notion of "religious experience" on our interpretations of premodern phenomena.

4.

The claim that religious experience is a relatively late and distinctively Western invention might strike the reader as dubious at best. Did not mystical experience play a central role in the religions of Asia since time immemorial? We read repeatedly that Asian mystics have charted the depths of the human psyche, explored a vast array of altered states of consciousness, and left behind detailed maps so that others may follow in their footsteps. Hinduism and Buddhism, to pick the two best-known examples, are often approached not as religions, philosophies, or social systems, but rather as "spiritual technologies" intended to induce a transformative experience of the absolute in the mind of the practitioner. Thus, while the emphasis on experience might be relatively new in the West, this is clearly not the case in the East. Or so one might suppose from the plethora of writings on the subject.

But not so fast. The notion that Asian religions are more experientially rooted than their Western counterparts is one of those truisms so widely and unquestioningly held that corroboration of any kind is deemed superfluous. But when we turn to premodern Asian sources the evidence is ambiguous at best. Take, for example, the many important Buddhist exegetical works that delineate the Buddhist *marga* or "path to liberation"—works such as "Stages on the Bodhisattva Path" (*Bodhisattvabhumi*), "The Stages of Practice" (*Bhavanakrama*), "Path of Purity" (*Visuddhimagga*), "The Great Calming and Contemplation" (*Mo-ho chih-kuan*), "The Great Book on the Stages of the Path" (*Lam rim chen mo*), and so on. These texts are frequently construed as descriptive accounts of meditative states based on the personal experiences of accomplished adepts. Yet rarely if ever do the authors of these compendiums claim to base their expositions on their own experience. On the contrary, the authority of exegetes such as Kamalasila, Buddhaghosa, and Chih-i, lay not in their access to exalted spiritual states, but in their mastery of, and rigorous adherence to, sacred scripture (Sharf 1995a). This situation is by no means unique to Buddhism: premodern Hinduism was similarly wary of claims to authority predicated on personal experience (Halbfass 1988). The notion that meditation is central to Asian religious praxis might seem to support the thesis that Asian traditions exalt personal experience. But here too we must be cautious: contemporary accounts of Asian meditation typically *presume* that they are oriented toward meditative experience, and thus such accounts must be used with considerable caution. Besides, while meditation may have been esteemed in theory, it did not occupy the dominant role in monastic and ascetic life that is sometimes supposed. (This point is often overlooked by scholars who fail to distinguish between prescriptive and descriptive accounts.) Even when practiced, it is by no means obvious that traditional forms of meditation were oriented toward the attainment of extraordinary "states of consciousness." Meditation was first and foremost a means of eliminating defilement, accumulating merit and supernatural power, invoking apotropaic deities, and so forth. This is not to deny that religious practitioners had "experiences" in the course of their training, just that such experiences were not considered the goal of practice, were not deemed doctrinally authoritative, and did not serve as the reference points for their understanding of the path (Sharf 1995a). Indeed, as we will see below, personal experience, no matter how extraordinary, *could not* serve as such a reference point precisely because of its ambiguous epistemological status and essentially indeterminate nature—a point appreciated by not a few medieval Buddhist exegetes.

The complementary notions that Asian religious traditions are predicated on mystical experience, and that meditation is a means to induce such experience, are so well ingrained that it might be useful to pause for a moment to consider their provenance. The valorization of experience in Asian thought can be traced to a handful of twentieth-century Asian religious leaders and apologists, all of whom were in sustained dialogue with their intellectual counterparts in the West. For example, the notion that personal experience constitutes the heart of the Hindu tradition originated with the prolific philosopher and statesman Sarvepalli Radhakrishnan (1888–1975). Like his European and American predecessors, Radhakrishnan argued that "if philosophy of religion is to become scientific, it must become empirical and found itself on religious experience" (1937, 84), and "it is not true religion unless it ceases to be a traditional view and becomes personal experience" (1937, 88). Thus in a single stroke Radhakrishnan could associate true religion with both personal experience and the empirical method. Radhakrishnan did not stop there, however, but went on to place the rhetoric of experience in the service of Hindu nationalism. He argued that if "experience is the soul of religion," then Hinduism is closest to that soul precisely because it is not historical, but based directly on the "inward life of spirit" (1937, 89, 90).

Radhakrishnan's intellectual debt to the West is no secret. Although he was educated in India, he was steeped in Western philosophical and religious thought from an early age, and his specific interest in experience can be traced directly to the works of William James (1842–1910), Francis Herbert Bradley (1846–1924), Henri Bergson (1859–1941), and Baron F. von Hügel (1852–1925), among others (Halbfass 1988, 398). Radhakrishnan held numerous academic posts in India and England, including the Spalding Professor of

Eastern Religions and Ethics at Oxford, and his writings are filled with appreciative references to a variety of American and European thinkers popular at the time, from Evelyn
Underhill (1850–1941) to Alfred North Whitehead (1861–1947). What is curious is not
that he should have placed his synthesis of Western and Indian philosophy in the service of
an overtly apologetic and nationalist project, but that given this project he is nevertheless
considered by many to be a credible "native source" on the subject of traditional Hinduism.

One can, perhaps, find antecedents of Radhakrishnan's hermeneutic in the writings
of Debendranath Tagore (1817–1905), an early leader of the Western-influenced Hindu
reform movement Brahmo Samaj, who held that the teachings of the Vedas may be affirmed
through one's own experience. However, Tagore, like his predecessor Rammohun Roy
(1772–1833), was intimately acquainted with Western thought in general, and Christian
critiques of Hinduism in particular. His exegetical writings, and his work for the Brahmo
Samaj, were directed toward the "purification" of Hinduism so as to stay the growing influence of Christian missionaries and their converts. In the end there is simply no evidence
of an indigenous Indian counterpart to the rhetoric of experience prior to the colonial
period (Halbfass 1988).

Western conceptions of "Asian spirituality" are equally indebted to the writings of
that indefatigable proselytizer of Zen Buddhism, D. T. Suzuki (1870–1966). According to
Suzuki, religious experience is not merely a central feature of Zen, it is the whole of Zen.
In his voluminous writings Suzuki advanced the notion that Zen eschews all doctrine,
all ritual, all institutions, and is thus, in the final analysis, not a religion at all. Zen is pure
experience itself, the experiential essence lying behind all authentic religious teachings.
Zen is associated, of course, with particular monasteries, forms of worship, and works of
literature and art, but these are all mere "fingers pointing at the moon." The moon is none
other than the unmediated experience of the absolute in which the dualism of subject
and object, observer and observed, is transcended. This view of Zen has become so well
established that many hesitate to speak of Zen at all for fear of being censured as insuf-
ficiently experienced.

Suzuki, like Radhakrishnan, places this understanding of Zen in the interests of a
transparently nationalist discourse. Suzuki insisted that Zen is the wellspring of Japanese
culture, and that the traditional arts of Japan—tea ceremony, monochrome painting,
martial arts, landscape gardening, Noh theatre, etc.—are all ultimately expressions of Zen
gnosis. Japanese culture naturally predisposes the Japanese toward Zen experience, such
that they have a deeply ingrained appreciation of the unity of subject and object, human
being and nature. This is in marked contradistinction to the excessively materialistic and
dualistic traditions of the West.

Suzuki's musings on the "Japanese mind" must be understood in the context of Japan's
sense of technological and scientific inferiority *vis-à-vis* the Occident in the earlier part
of this century. In the final analysis, Suzuki, like Radhakrishnan, attempts nothing less
than the apotheosis [or divination] of an entire people. And like Radhakrishnan, Suzuki's
emphasis on experience owes as much to his exposure to Western thought as it does to
indigenous Asian or Zen sources. In fact, Suzuki's qualifications as an exponent of Zen are
somewhat dubious. Suzuki did engage in Zen practice at Engakuji during his student days

at Tokyo Imperial University, and he enjoyed a close relationship with the abbot Shaku Soen (1859–1919). But by traditional standards Suzuki's training was relatively modest: he was never ordained, his formal monastic education was desultory at best, and he never received institutional sanction as a Zen teacher. This is not to impugn Suzuki's academic competence; he was a gifted philologist who made a lasting contribution to the study of Buddhist texts. In the end, however, his approach to Zen, with its unrelenting emphasis on an unmediated inner experience, is not derived from Buddhist sources so much as from his broad familiarity with European and American philosophical and religious writings (Sharf 1995c).

Suzuki's early interest in things Western was wide-ranging, and included such fashionable quasi-religious movements as Theosophy, Swedenborgianism, and the "Religion of Science." The latter doctrine was the brainchild of the German-American essayist Paul Carus (1852–1919), who worked as editor at the Open Court Publishing Company in La Salle, Illinois. Carus was convinced that once the "old religions" were purified of their superstitious and irrational elements, they would work in conjunction with science to bring humankind to the realization that there is no distinction between the immaterial and the material—between mind and matter. Carus was particularly attracted to Buddhism, which he felt was close in spirit to his own philosophy.

Suzuki was initially drawn to Carus after reading *Gospel of Buddha*, a compendium of Buddhist teachings compiled by Carus and published in Open Court's Religion of Science series in 1894 (see Carus 1915). Carus had taken available European translations of Buddhist scriptures and, through the use of careful selection, creative retranslation, and outright fabrication, managed to portray the teachings of the Buddha as humanistic, rational, and scientific. Suzuki, who had been asked to translate the *Gospel* into Japanese, was so impressed with Carus's work that he arranged to travel to America to study under his tutelage. Suzuki was to remain in La Salle for some eleven years, and it was toward the end of this period that he became familiar with the writings of William James.

Suzuki appears to have been responsible for introducing James' work to his high-school friend Nishida Kitaro (1870–1945). It was through Nishida, who was to emerge as Japan's leading modern philosopher, that the notion of a distinctively religious mode of experience took hold in Japan. Nishida's first philosophical monograph, published in 1911 under the title *Zen no kenkyu* ("A Study of the Good"; see Nishida 1990), was dedicated to the elucidation of *junsui keiken*, or "pure experience," a notion culled directly from James. But the context of Nishida's "pure experience" was much removed from that of James. James sought to overcome the substance ontology that continued to infect classical empiricism, and to this end he proposed a pragmatic account of experience that avoided the reification of either subject or object. Nishida, on the other hand, was interested in integrating Western philosophy with his understanding of Zen, and consequently his notion of pure experience seems to function both as an ontological ground that subsumes subject and object, and as a psychological state of heightened self-awareness.

Suzuki seized upon Nishida's notion of pure experience and made it the central element in his exposition of Zen. And it proved to be an effective hermeneutic strategy, for here was an approach to Zen that was both familiar and attractive to Suzuki's Western audience.

The irony of the situation is that the terms used by the Japanese to render "experience"—*keiken* and *taiken*—are both modern neologisms coined in the Meiji period (1868–1912) by translators of Western philosophical works. (As far as I have been able to determine, *keiken* was first used to render the English "experience," while *taiken* was used for the German *erleben* and *Erlebnis*.) There simply is no premodern Japanese lexical equivalent for "experience." Nor, I would add, is there a premodern Chinese equivalent. Chinese translators borrowed the Japanese neologisms in their own renderings of Western texts.

The interest in religious experience among twentieth-century Asian intellectuals is not difficult to fathom. Like their Western counterparts, Asian apologists were forced to respond to empiricist and pluralist critiques of their religious heritage. But Asian intellectuals had another threat with which to contend as well, namely, the affront of Western cultural imperialism, sustained as it was by the West's political, technological, and military dominance. Asian intellectuals, many of whom were educated in Christian missionary schools, were deeply aware of the contempt with which Occidentals viewed the religious culture of Asia. Castigated as primitive, idolatrous, and intellectually benighted, Asian religion was held responsible for the continent's social, political, and scientific failings. This is the context in which we must understand the Asian appropriation and manipulation of the rhetoric of experience. Men like Radhakrishnan and Suzuki would not only affirm the experiential foundation of their own religious traditions, but they would turn around and present those traditions as more intuitive, more mystical, more experiential, and thus "purer" than the discursive faiths of the West. In short, if the West excelled materially, the East excelled spiritually. This strategy had the felicitous result of thwarting the Enlightenment critique of religion on the one hand, and the threat of Western cultural hegemony on the other.

The polemics of Radhakrishnan, Suzuki, and their intellectual heirs has had a significant impact on the study of religion in the West. Few Western scholars were in a position to question the romanticized image of Asian mysticism proffered forth by these intelligent and articulate "representatives" of living Asian faiths. Besides, the discovery of common ground offered considerable comfort. The very notion that religious experience might function as a universal in the study of world religions evolved, in many respects, out of this cross-cultural encounter. In time the dialogue grew into a veritable academic industry, complete with its own professional societies, its own journals, and its own conferences and symposia, all devoted to the comparative study of "Western" and "Eastern" thought. The striking confluence of Western and Asian interests prevented those on both sides from noticing the tenuous ground on which the exchange had been built.

5.

Seemingly oblivious to matters of historical context, arguments continue over the nature of mystical experience to the present day with no resolution in sight. The issues have not changed: scholars disagree over the extent to which mystical experiences are shaped by prior culturally mediated expectations and presuppositions, over whether one can separate a mystic's description of her experiences from her interpretations, over the existence of so-called "pure consciousness" devoid of intentional objects, over competing schemes for typologizing mystical states, and over the philosophical and ethical significance, if any, of mystical experience. (The *Journal of the American Academy of Religion* alone has, of late, seen fit to publish an article a year on the topic; see Barnard 1992; Forman 1993; Shear 1994; Short 1995; and Brainard 1996.) What is curious in these ongoing discussions is not so much the points of controversy as the areas of consensus. Virtually all parties tacitly accept the notion that terms such as "religious experience," "mystical experience," or "meditative experience" function referentially, that is, their signification lies in the signifieds to which they allegedly refer. Hence scholars of mysticism are content to focus on the distinctive characteristics and the philosophical implications, if any, of religious or mystical experiences without pausing to consider what sort of thing "experience" might be in the first place.

What exactly *do* we mean by experience? The dictionaries provide several overlapping definitions, but for our purposes we can focus on two more-or-less distinct usages. The first is to "participate in," or "live through," as one might say "I have combat experience" or "I have experience with diesel engines." This use of the term is relatively unproblematic; it does not elicit any particular epistemological or metaphysical conundrums since the refer- ent of the term would seem to lie in the social or public sphere. The second more epistemo- logical or phenomenological meaning is to "directly perceive," "observe," "be aware of," or "be conscious of." Here there is a tendency to think of experience as a subjective "mental event" or "inner process" that eludes public scrutiny. In thinking of experience along these lines it is difficult to avoid the image of mind as an immaterial substrate or psychic field, a sort of inner space in which the outer material world is reflected or re-presented. Scholars leave the category experience unexamined precisely because the meaning of experience, like the stuff of experience, would seem to be utterly transparent. Experience is simply given to us in the immediacy of each moment of perception.

This picture of mind clearly has its roots in Descartes and his notion of mind as an "immaterial substance" (although few today would subscribe to Descartes's substance ontology). And following the Cartesian perspective, we assume that in so far as experience is immediately present, experience *per se* is both indubitable and irrefutable. (While the *content* of experience may prove ambiguous or deceptive, the fact that I am experiencing *something* is beyond question.) The characteristics of immediacy and indubitability gal- vanized the "hermeneutic of experience." Experience, construed as the inviolable realm of pure presence, promised a refuge from the hermeneutic and epistemological vagaries of modern intellectual life. Just as some scholars of literature would invoke "authorial intent" as a way to overcome ambiguity in the interpretation of literary works (see esp. Hirsch 1967), the notion of experience promised to ground the meaning of religious texts and performances through an appeal to the experiences to which they refer. (The analogy is more than fortuitous: "authorial intent" and "religious experience" both occupy the same highly ambiguous but ultimately unassailable "ontological space.")

Yet the problem is unavoidable: if talk of "shamanic experience," "mystical experience," "enlightenment experience," or what have you is to have any sort of determinate meaning we must construe the term "experience" in referential or ostensive terms. But to do so is to objectify it, which would seem to undermine its most salient characteristic, namely, its immediacy. So we are posed with a dilemma: experience cannot be determinate without being rendered a "thing"; if it is a thing it cannot be indubitable; but if it is not a thing then it cannot perform the hermeneutic task that religious scholars require of it—that of determining meaning. We will return to this point below.

But first I must respond to the following inevitable rebuke: the fact that a scholar such as myself should have a difficult time "situating" the locus of religious experience merely attests to his own spiritual impoverishment. If only I had a taste of the real thing I would quickly and humbly forgo my rueful attempt to explain away such phenomena. Indeed, I would sympathize with the difficulty mystics have in expressing themselves. Do not mystics repeatedly allude to precisely this problem, that is, the problem in conceptualizing that which transcends all concepts?

This objection would seem to rest on an appeal to ethnographic evidence, to the witness of real mystics or religious adepts with first-hand experience of nonconceptual states. Of course, the problem is exacerbated by the fact that, according to the historical critique summarized above, the category "experience" is itself of recent provenance, and thus the testimony of mystics of old, who talk in rather different terms (not to mention in dead languages), is going to prove ambiguous at best. So let us keep things simple and select a contemporary religious community that (1) unquestionably valorizes religious experience, and (2) possesses a sophisticated technical vocabulary with which they describe and analyze such experience.

Vipassana or "insight" practice (also known as *satipatthana* or "foundations of mindfulness") is a Buddhist form of meditation that is popular in Theravada communities in Southeast Asia. (It is also influential among Buddhist enthusiasts in the West.) It must be noted that the specific techniques propagated today under the *vipassana* rubric, with their unequivocal emphasis on exalted meditative states, cannot be traced back prior to the late nineteenth century, and thus they are an unreliable source for the reconstruction of premodern Theravada. (The techniques were reconstructed in the modern period on the basis of scriptural accounts; see Sharf 1995a.) Be that as it may, contemporary adepts believe that their experiences in meditation tally with the "descriptions" of progressive soteriological stages found in Buddhist scriptures. They thus treat the ancient scholastic terms pertaining to stages of Buddhist practice as if they designated discrete experiences accessible to contemporary practitioners. The claim that adepts in *vipassana* can clearly recognize and reproduce the various stages mentioned in canonical sources has encouraged some scholars to treat Theravada meditation theory as a sort of empirical phenomenology of altered states of consciousness that can be applied to non-Buddhist as well as Buddhist phenomena (Sharf 1995a, 261).

On closer inspection, however, we find that the scriptures upon which the *vipassana* revival is based (primarily the two *Satipatthana-suttas* and the *Visuddhimagga*) are often ambiguous or inconsistent, and contemporary *vipassana* teachers are frequently at odds with each other over the interpretation of key terms. For example, Buddhist sources categorize the range of available meditation techniques under two broad headings, *samatha* or "concentration," and *vipassana* or "insight." Judging from scriptural accounts, one would presume that it would be difficult to confuse the two; both the techniques and the goals to which the techniques are directed differ substantially. *Samatha* practices, which involve focusing the mind on a single object, are supposed to result in an ascending series of four "material absorptions" (or "trances," *rupa-jhana*) and a further series of four (or five) "immaterial absorptions" (*arupa-jhana*), that bestow upon the practitioner various supernatural powers. *Vipassana*, on the other hand, involves the disciplined contemplation of seminal Buddhist doctrines such as impermanence or nonself, and leads directly to nirvana or full liberation. Nirvana is achieved in four successive stages known as the "noble attainments" (*ariya-phala*), the first of which is called *sotapatti* or "entry into the stream." While *samatha* is an effective means to acquire specific spiritual powers, such as the ability to levitate or to read minds, only *vipassana* leads to enlightenment proper. Since the soteriological ramifications of *samatha* and *vipassana* differ so markedly, one would suppose that the experiential states with which they are associated would be easy to distinguish on phenomenological grounds.

All contemporary Theravada meditation masters accept the canonical categories outlined above. But curiously, despite the fact that these teachers have "tasted the fruits" of practice, there is little if any consensus among them as to the application of these key terms. On the contrary, the designation of particular techniques and the identification of the meditative experiences that result from them are the subjects of continued and often acrimonious debate. More often than not the categories are used polemically to disparage the teachings of rival teachers. Since all agree that *vipassana* leads to liberation while *samatha* does not, *samatha* is used to designate the techniques and experiences promoted by one's competitors, while *vipassana* is reserved for one's own teachings. Other teachers may *think* they are promoting authentic *vipassana* and realizing stages of enlightenment, but in fact they are simply mistaking *jhanic* absorption for *sotapatti*, the first stage of enlightenment achieved through *vipassana*.

I do not have the space to explore the *vipassana* controversies in detail here (see the full account in Sharf 1995a). Suffice it to say that there is simply no public consensus in the contemporary Theravada community as to the application of terms that allegedly refer to discrete experiential states. Not surprisingly, the same is found to be true in Japanese Zen. Again, it is important to remember that, *pace* much of the popular literature on Zen, premodern Zen masters rarely emphasized exotic experiential states, and terms such as *satori* ("to understand" or "to apprehend") and *kensho* ("to see one's true nature") were not construed as singular "states of consciousness." Be that as it may, some contemporary Zen teachers, notably those associated with the upstart Sanbokyodan lineage, do approach Zen phenomenologically. In other words, they unapologetically present Zen practice as a means to inculcate *kensho*, which they understand to be an unmediated and transitory apprehension of "nonduality." Some Sanbokyodan masters go so far as to present certificates to students who achieve *kensho* to validate and celebrate their accomplishment.

Even if the Sanbokyodan understanding of *kensho* does not accord with classical models, one might suppose that it is nevertheless an identifiable and reproducible experience. After all, it is verified and certified by the masters of the school. But once again the ethnographic evidence points in another direction. One quickly discovers that eminent teachers from other living Zen traditions (Rinzai, Soto, Obaku) do not accord legitimacy to Sanbokyodan claims of *kensho*. This might be dismissed as mere sectarian rivalry or sour grapes. But even within the Sanbokyodan itself there has been a long-standing controversy surrounding the verification and authentication of *kensho* experiences that has threatened to result in schism (Sharf 1995b). In modern Zen, as in Theravada, eminent meditation masters prove unable to agree on the identification of a "referent" of terms that supposedly refer to specific and replicable experiential states.

The lack of consensus among prominent Buddhist teachers as to the designation not only of particular states of consciousness but also of the psychotropic techniques used to produce them (*samatha* versus *vipassana*) belies the notion that the rhetoric of meditative experience, at least in Buddhism, functions ostensively. Critical analysis shows that modern Buddhist communities judge "claims to experience" on the basis of the meditator's particular lineage, the specific ritual practice that engendered the experience, the behavior that ensued, and so on. In other words, a meditative state or liberative experience is identified not on the basis of privileged personal access to its distinctive phenomenology, but rather on the basis of eminently public criteria. Such judgments are inevitably predicated on prior ideological commitments shaped by one's vocation (monk or layperson), one's socioeconomic background (urban middle-class or rural poor), one's political agenda (traditionalist or reformer), one's sectarian affiliation, one's education, and so forth. In the end, the Buddhist rhetoric of experience is both informed by, and wielded in, the interests of personal and institutional authority.

The modern Theravada and Zen reform movements discussed here are of particular import, as both claim to possess an elaborate technical vocabulary that refers to a set of exotic but nonetheless verifiable and reproducible experiences. Clearly, if these experiential states are not determinative, then the baroque visions, ineffable reveries, and exotic trances associated with various other mystical traditions inspire even less confidence that the rhetoric of experience functions ostensively.

6.

At this point the reader may well be growing impatient. Surely, even if mystics and meditation masters cannot always agree among themselves as to the designation or soteriological import of their experiences, it is clear that *something* must be going on. Those Buddhist meditators are clearly experiencing *something* in the midst of their ascetic ordeals, even if they cannot ultimately agree on whether it should be called *jhana*, *sotapatti*, *kensho*, or whatever. The vigorous and often exuberant language used by mystics the world over to describe their visions, trances, and states of cosmic union must refer to *something*.

This objection attests once again to our deep entanglement in the Cartesian paradigm, to the lingering allure of what Richard Rorty has called the "glassy essence" or "mirror of nature" view of mind (1979). This is not the place to plunge into the hoary controversies waged under the auspices of "philosophy of mind." Rather, I will defer once again to an ethnographic case that underscores issues of immediate relevance to the study of religion.

Consider, for a moment, a distinctly contemporary form of visionary experience: reports of alien abduction. There are now hundreds if not thousands of individuals from across America who claim to have been abducted by alien beings. A number of apparently reputable investigators have found the abductees' stories compelling, in large part because of the degree of consistency across the narratives (e.g., Mack 1995; Bryan 1995). For example, many of the abductees "independently" report encountering the "small grey"—short hairless humanoid beings with large heads, big black eyes, tiny nostrils, no discernible ears, and a thin slit for a mouth which is apparently little used. (The small greys communicate telepathically.) Their torsos are slender, with long arms and fingers but no thumb, and they sport close-fitting single-piece tunics and boots (Mack 1995, 22–3). After being transported to the alien craft, abductees report being subject to various medical examinations and procedures, many of which focus on the reproductive system. The abductees are then returned, usually to the place from which they were first spirited away.

The vast majority of the abductees have no initial recall of the episode at all. They may be aware only of an unaccountable gap of a few hours or so, and a lingering sense of anxiety, confusion, and fear. They are able to fill in the blanks and reconstruct the details of their abduction only with the help of therapy and hypnosis.

The abductees, known among themselves and in the literature as "experiencers," come from a wide variety of economic and social backgrounds. According to investigators, as a population the abductees show no significant prior history of, or propensity toward, psychopathology. Many of the abductees insist that prior to their alien encounter they had no interest in, or exposure to, reports of abductions, UFOs, or other "new age" phenomena. In fact, the one thing on which both believers and skeptics agree is that the abductees are on the whole sincere; they are not consciously fabricating the narratives for personal fame or profit. On the contrary, the abductees are convinced that their memories accord with objective events, and they stand by their stories even when ridiculed or ostracized by neighbors and relatives. Investigators sympathetic to the abductees' plight report that they manifest the sort of confusion, stress, and chronic anxiety characteristic of "post-traumatic stress syndrome." In fact, the psychological disorders suffered by the abductees, and their own steadfast belief in their stories, constitute the closest thing we have to empirical evidence for the abductions.

Despite the pleas of a few prominent investigators such as John Mack, most scholars are understandably skeptical. Skeptics can cite the striking absence of corroborating physical evidence, as well as the questionable methods used by investigators. As mentioned above, many abductees have no memory of the event until it is "recovered" by therapists who have made a specialty out of treating victims of alien abductions. Finally, folklorists are able to trace the origins of many central elements and motifs in the abduction narratives—the physiognomy of the aliens, the appearance of their spacecrafts, the ordeal of the medical examination, and so on—to popular science fiction comics, stories, and films of the past fifty years. The scholarly consensus would seem to be that the abductions simply did not take place; there is no *originary event* behind the memories.

The notion of originary event is crucial here. Clearly, we will not get far by denying the existence of the memories themselves. Our skepticism is rather directed at what, if anything, may lie behind them. We suspect that the abductees' reports do not stem from actual alien encounters, but that some other complex historical, sociological, and psychological processes are at work. Whatever the process turns out to be (and we are a long way from an adequate explanation of the phenomenon), it is reasonable to assume that the abductees' memories do not faithfully represent actual historical occurrences.

One might argue that skepticism with regard to the existence of aliens does not imply that there is no *other* determinate historical event at the root of the memories. The memories must refer back to *some* previous incident, even if the nature of this incident is systematically misconstrued by the credulous abductees. Memory is fickle.

This has been the approach of some psychoanalytically oriented observers, who treat the alien encounters as "screen memories" that cloak an early repressed trauma such as childhood sexual abuse. The problem with this hypothesis is that the epistemological problems raised by postulating repressed memories turn out to be, in many respects, of the same order as those associated with alien abductions. Childhood trauma has been the *etiology du jour*, and is typically only "recovered" in a therapeutic encounter with a specialist whose training and institutional investments predispose him to this specific diagnosis. In the end childhood trauma is as elusive a beast as the aliens themselves (see Hacking 1995).

Several scholars have drawn attention to the religious patterns and motifs running through the abduction narratives. The reports are reminiscent, for example, of tales of shamanic trance journeys, in which the subject is transported to an alien domain populated by otherworldly beings with inconceivable powers and ambiguous intentions. Many abductees are entrusted with important spiritual messages to be propagated among the human race, messages about the importance of peace, love, and universal brotherhood (Whitmore 1995). Moreover, the role of the therapists who help to elicit and shape the abduction narratives is analogous to the role played by priest or preceptor in more established religious traditions. The question is unavoidable: is there any reason to assume that the reports of experiences by mystics, shamans, or meditation masters are any more credible as "phenomenological descriptions" than those of the abductees?

It should now be apparent that the question is not merely whether or not mystical experiences are constructed, unmediated, pure, or philosophically significant. The more fundamental question is whether we can continue to treat the texts and reports upon which such theories are based as referring, however obliquely, to determinative phenomenal events at all.

7.

But I have felt so many strange things, so many baseless things assuredly, that they are perhaps better left unsaid. To speak for example of the times when I go liquid and become like mud, what good would that do? Or of the others when I would be

lost in the eye of a needle, I am so hard and contracted? No, those are well-meaning
squirms that get me nowhere.   *Malone Dies* by Samuel Beckett

Consider the taste of beer. Most would agree that beer is an acquired taste; few enjoy their
first sip. In time many come to enjoy the flavour. But what has changed? The flavour, or
merely our reaction to it? More to the point, how could one possibly decide the issue one
way or the other? Something seems fishy about the question itself.

This is one of a series of illustrations and anecdotes used by the philosopher Daniel
Dennett to undermine the concept of *qualia* (1992; see also Dennett 1991). Qualia (the
singular form is *quale*) is a term proposed by philosophers to designate those subjective
or phenomenal properties of experience that resist a purely materialistic explanation. (The
notion is an attempt to capture that aspect of consciousness that, say some, could never be
reproduced by a "thinking machine.") In short, qualia refer to the way things *seem*. "Look
at a glass of milk at sunset; *the way it looks to you*—the particular, personal, subjective
visual quality of the glass of milk is the *quale* of your visual experience at the moment.
The *way the milk tastes to you then* is another, gustatory *quale*" (Dennett 1992, 42). As it is
never possible to communicate exactly how things appear to us (how could we ever know
whether your experience of red is precisely the same as mine?), qualia are construed as
essentially private, ineffable, and irreducible properties of experience.

Dennett thinks the whole notion of qualia is wrong-headed, and employs a series of
"intuition pumps," such as his musings on the flavor of beer, in order to undermine our
confidence in the existence of intrinsic properties of experience. "If it is admitted that one's
attitudes towards, or reactions to, experiences are in any way and in any degree constitutive of their experiential qualities, so that a change in reactivity *amounts to* or *guarantees*
a change in the property, then those properties, those 'qualitative or phenomenal features,'
cease to be 'intrinsic' properties and in fact become paradigmatically extrinsic, relational
properties" (Dennett 1992, 61). And if these most salient aspects of experience are in fact
extrinsic and relational, one must relinquish one's picture of experience as a determinate
something that occurs someplace "inside the brain," in what Dennett calls the "Cartesian
theater" (Dennett 1991). In short, one must give up what, in the Cartesian view, is a fundamental attribute of experience: its privacy.

In a somewhat similar spirit I have suggested that it is ill conceived to construe the
object of the study of religion to be the inner experience of religious practitioners. Scholars
of religion are not presented with experiences that stand in need of interpretation, but
rather with texts, narratives, performances, and so forth. While these representations
may at times assume the rhetorical stance of phenomenological description, we are not
obliged to accept them as such. On the contrary, we must remain alert to the ideological
implications of such a stance. Any assertion to the effect that someone else's inner experience bears some significance for *my* construal of reality is situated, by its very nature, in
the public realm of contested meanings.

Before we throw out experience altogether, however, we must take stock of what is at
stake. The appeal of the rhetoric of experience lay in its promise to forestall the objectification and commodification of personal life endemic to modern mass society. By

147

objectification I refer to the projection of the "subject" or "self" into a centerless physical world of "objective facts" amenable to scientific study and technological mastery—a projection that threatened to efface subjectivity altogether (Nagel 1986). The flip side of objectification has been the rampant alienation that characterizes modernity—the sense of being rootless and adrift, cut off from tradition and history. Into this vacuum rushed the experts—sociologists, psychologists, anthropologists, and even scholars of religion—who claimed to understand *my* memories, *my* dreams, *my* desires, *my* beliefs, *my* thoughts, better than I. We are understandably reluctant to cede such authority to a guild of specialists, no matter how enlightened or well intentioned they may be. Our last line of defense has been the valorization of the "autonomous self," construed as a unique and irreducible center of experience.

This raises a host of complex political and philosophical issues concerned with the modern notion of selfhood and self-determination, issues that, for lack of space, I am unable to pursue here. As students of religion, our more immediate theoretical concerns are hermeneutic: How are we to understand people very different from ourselves without somehow effacing the very differences that separate us? Scholars have become acutely aware of the methodological problems entailed in using *our* conceptual categories and theoretical constructs to comprehend the world of others. In addition, recent post-colonial and feminist critiques have forced us to focus on the asymmetrical relationship between the investigator and his or her subjects. We are wary of the intellectual hubris and cultural chauvinism that often attends scholars as they claim insight into the self-representations of others, especially when those others are at a political and economic disadvantage. And again, the one defense against the tendency to objectify, to domesticate, to silence and eviscerate the other has been to sanction the other's singular and irreducible experience of the world.

Therein lies the rub. We believe it politically and intellectually essential to respect diverse "worldviews," but at the same time we are hesitant to abandon the hermeneutic suspicion that is the mark of critical scholarship. We want to valorize the self-representations of others, yet we balk when "respect for others" places undue demands upon our own credulity. Most draw the line, for example, when it comes to acceding the existence of the small greys. And well we should; a critical investigation of the abduction phenomenon can only begin once the decision has been made to look for alternative explanations—explanations that do not involve the existence of interloping aliens.

One strategy to negotiate this impasse has been to empower experience by affirming the truth of the experience narrative, but only to the one doing the narration. This strategy, which is closely allied with the phenomenological approach to religion mentioned above, tends to fragment reality into "multiple objective worlds" (Shweder 1991)—a consequence that does not seem to trouble many scholars of religion. In her book on near-death experiences, for example, Carol Zaleski engages in a critical historical analysis of the sociological and mythological factors that have contributed to near-death narratives in both medieval and modern times. But, somewhat incongruously, she concludes her sophisticated contextual analysis by insisting on the inherent truth value of the experiences themselves. Zaleski manages this by identifying the "other world" described in the near-death accounts with the "inner psychological world" of the subjects themselves. This allows her to valorize the near-death experiences as a "legitimate imaginative means through which one can instill a religious sense of the cosmos" (1987, 203). Zaleski is thus able to countenance the experiences without subscribing to the fantastic cosmologies—the baroque views of heaven, hell, and everything between—that attend them.

Felicitas Goodman, in her study of spirit possession, goes a step further, assuming a decidedly agnostic stance toward the existence of the spirits reported by her subjects. "The experience of [the] presence [of spirits] during possession is accompanied by observable physical changes. We should remember that whether these changes are internally generated or created by external agencies is not discoverable. No one can either prove or disprove that the obvious changes of the brain map in possession or in a patient with a multiple personality disorder, for that matter, are produced by psychological processes or by an invading alien being" (Goodman 1988, 126). Goodman's agnosticism is but a small step away from John Mack's qualified acceptance of the existence of alien abductors.

This methodological stance is made possible by the peculiar nature of claims to experience, particularly religious experiences that are, by definition, extraordinary. Reports of mystical or visionary experiences can be likened to reports of dreams in so far as it is difficult, if not impossible, to separate the report of the experience from the experience itself. In a philosophical examination of dreams Norman Malcolm argues that the dream report is indeed the *only* criterion for the dream, and thus to report that one has dreamed *is* to have dreamed; there is simply no other criterion for the dream's existence (Malcolm 1959). Malcolm concludes that dreams are therefore not experiences, a claim that has more to do with how he stipulates the meaning of "experience" than with the nature of dreaming itself.

Scholars such as Zaleski and Goodman (as well as Steven Katz and other "constructivists") tacitly, if not explicitly, adopt a similar perspective toward religious experience. They acknowledge that there is no way to tease apart the representation of a religious experience from the experience itself. Malcolm would argue that if the two cannot be separated—if the only criterion for the "experience" is the report itself—then one cannot claim to be dealing with an experience at all. But Zaleski and Goodman move in a different direction, treating the reports as if they provided unmediated access to some originary phenomenal event. The constructivists seem to assume that since the historical, social, and linguistic processes that give rise to the narrative representation are identical with those that give rise to the experience, the former, which are amenable to scholarly analysis, provide a transparent window to the latter.

While we might laud the humanistic impulse that motivates this line of reasoning—the desire to countenance a diversity of "worldviews"—it fails to grasp the rhetorical logic of appeals to experience. The word "experience," in so far as it refers to that which is given to us in the immediacy of perception, signifies that which by definition is nonobjective, that which resists all signification. In other words, the term experience cannot make ostensible a *something that exists in the world*. The salient characteristic of private experience that distinguishes it from "objective reality" is thus its unremitting indeterminacy. At the same time, the rhetoric of experience tacitly posits a place where signification comes to an end, variously styled "mind," "consciousness," the "mirror of nature," or what have you.

The category experience is, in essence, a mere place-holder that entails a substantive if indeterminate terminus for the relentless deferral of meaning. And this is precisely what makes the term experience so amenable to ideological appropriation.

Again, I am not trying to deny subjective experience. (Indeed, how would one do that?) I merely want to draw attention to the way the concept functions in religious discourse—in Wittgenstein's terms, its "language game." I have suggested that it is a mistake to approach literary, artistic, or ritual representations as if they referred back to something other than themselves, to some numinous inner realm. The fact that religious experience is often circumscribed in terms of its nondiscursive or nonconceptual character does not mitigate the problem: that nothing can be said of a particular experience—that is, its ineffability—cannot in and of itself constitute a delimiting characteristic, much less a phenomenal property. Thus while experience—construed as that which is "immediately present"—may indeed be both irrefutable and indubitable, we must remember that whatever epistemological certainty experience may offer is gained only at the expense of any possible discursive meaning or signification. To put it another way, all attempts to signify "inner experience" are destined to remain "well-meaning squirms that get us nowhere."

11

JOAN WALLACH SCOTT

"The Evidence of Experience," from *Critical Inquiry*

American historian Joan Wallach Scott is the Harold F. Linder Professor at the School of Social Science in the Institute for Advanced Study in Princeton, NJ. Her fields of expertise include French history and gender and feminist theories. A pioneer in challenging the methods and assumptions used in historical scholarship, Scott has been an important voice calling for the investigation and renovation of previously accepted scholarly methods and assumptions.

Although known for her authorship of a variety of books—(including *Gender and the Politics of History* (1988; 1999); *Only Paradoxes to Offer: French Feminists and the Rights of Man* (1996); *Parité: Sexual Equality and the Crisis of French Universalism* (2005); and *The Politics of the Veil* (2007))—one would be remiss not to mention the 1988 publication of her highly influential article, "Gender as a Useful Category of Historical Analysis." In that essay Scott interrogates mainstream theories of gender while simultaneously considering the utility of a gender-based analysis. What she offers the reader is a complex look at the assumptions at play in scholarly treatments of gender, many of which carry critical flaws. With an eye toward the power of discourse (a term referring to the myriad social structures that shape what gets to count as "knowledge"), Scott argues that gender is a discursive act based on notions of power and difference.

This same trend toward overturning long-held scholarly models is exacted in this present essay, entitled "The Evidence of Experience." Besides offering important methodological insights, here Scott also provides an introduction to some of the key terms of fields such as postmodernism, post-structuralism, the many forms of Marxism, and feminist theory, almost all of which fall under the wider umbrella term, "Critical Theory." Although these movements have differences, they are generally united by the desire to uncover how historical factors have led to inequality, by the assumption that truly objective knowledge does not exist, and by an understanding of all social phenomena as humanistic, or the product of humans, rather than looking to a supernatural or other non-human explanation for events. Most critical theorists assume that power and privilege are the undercurrents of human discourse.

In this present excerpt, Scott asserts that the dominant mode of doing history depends on the notion that evidence for a phenomenon comes by way of experiences, which are believed to reflect something real. The problem in making such seemingly logical assumptions is that the person who had the experience becomes the sole point of departure from which this reality is built, and little effort is given toward discussing how such experiences might be constructed, including the available language any particular person might have to describe an experience.

As such, Scott contends that when one talks about the self-evident nature of reality as found in experience, one does little to overturn the ideological systems that provided the epistemological framework (that is, the foundations of knowledge) through which experience is interpreted in the first place. Providing the history or experiences of a group or thing deemed "different" overlooks the most central questions of all—what the rules of "difference" are and how they came about.

Scott thus forces the scholar's hand, in a sense, asking for an account of what one should make of experiential claims, as well as their explanatory usefulness. In this she echoes the framework established in the essays by Wayne Proudfoot and Robert Sharf, but further complicates matters by interrogating the self-evidence of the *scholar's* position, not just the participant's account. Through this she demonstrates the universality of the critical problems that underlie labels of difference and other modes of creating identity.

"THE EVIDENCE OF EXPERIENCE," FROM *CRITICAL INQUIRY*

BECOMING VISIBLE

There is a section in Samuel Delany's magnificent autobiographical meditation, *The Motion of Light in Water* (1988), that dramatically raises the problem of writing the history of difference, the history, that is, of the designation of "other," of the attribution of characteristics that distinguish categories of people from some presumed (and usually unstated) norm.[1] Delany (a gay man, a black man, a writer of science fiction) recounts his reaction to his first visit to the St. Marks bathhouse in 1963. He remembers standing on the threshold of a "gym-sized room" dimly lit by blue bulbs. The room was full of people, some standing, the rest

> an undulating mass of naked, male bodies, spread wall to wall.
>
> My first response was a kind of heart-thudding astonishment, very close to fear.
>
> I have written of a space at certain libidinal saturation before. That was not what frightened me. It was rather that the saturation was not only kinesthetic but visible. (Delany 1988, 173)

Watching the scene establishes for Delany a "fact that flew in the face" of the prevailing representation of homosexuals in the 1950s as "isolated perverts," as subjects "gone awry." The "apprehension of massed bodies" gave him (as it does, he argues, anyone, "male, female, working or middle class") a "sense of political power":

---

1. For an important discussion of the "dilemma of difference," see Minow (1987).

what *this* experience said was that there was a population—not of individual homosexuals ... not of hundreds, not of thousands, but rather of millions of gay men, and
that history had, actively and already, created for us whole galleries of institutions,
good and bad, to accommodate our sex.   (Delany 1988, 174)

The sense of political possibility is frightening and exhilarating for Delany. He emphasizes
not the discovery of an identity, but a sense of participation in a movement; indeed, it
is the extent (as well as the existence) of these sexual practices that matters most in his
account. Numbers—massed bodies—constitute a movement and this, even if subterra-
nean, belies enforced silences about the range and diversity of human sexual practices.
Making the movement visible breaks the silence about it, challenges prevailing notions,
and opens new possibilities for everyone. Delany imagines, even from the vantage of 1988,
a future utopian moment of genuine sexual revolution, "once the AIDS crisis is brought
under control":

That revolution will come precisely because of the infiltration of clear and articulate
language into the marginal areas of human sexual exploration, such as this book
from time to time describes, and of which it is only the most modest example.
Now that a significant range of people have begun to get a clearer idea of what has
been possible among the varieties of human pleasure in the recent past, hetero-
sexuals and homosexuals, females and males will insist on exploring them even
further.   (1988, 175)

By writing about the bathhouse Delany seeks not, he says, "to romanticize that time into
some cornucopia of sexual plenty," but rather to break an "absolutely sanctioned public
silence" on questions of sexual practice, to reveal something that existed but that had
been suppressed.

Only the coyest and the most indirect articulations could occasionally indicate
the boundaries of a phenomenon whose centers could not be spoken or written
of, even figuratively: and that coyness was medical and legal as well as literary;
and, as Foucault has told us, it was, in its coyness, a huge and pervasive discourse.
But what that coyness means is that there is no way to gain from it a clear, accurate, and extensive picture of extant public sexual institutions. That discourse only
touched on highly select margins when they transgressed the legal and/or medical
standards of a populace that firmly wished to maintain that no such institutions
existed.   (1988, 175–6)

The point of Delany's description, indeed of his entire book, is to document the existence of those institutions in all their variety and multiplicity, to write about and thus to
render historical what has hitherto been hidden from history.

As I read it, a metaphor of visibility as literal transparency is crucial to his project. The
blue lights illuminate a scene he has participated in before (in darkened trucks parked

along the docks under the West Side Highway, in men's rooms in subway stations), but understood only in a fragmented way. "No one ever got *to see* its whole" (1988, 174; emphasis added). He attributes the impact of the bathhouse scene to its visibility: "You could *see* what was going on throughout the dorm" (1988, 173; emphasis added). Seeing enables him to comprehend the relationship between his personal activities and politics: "the first direct sense of political power comes from the apprehension of massed bodies." Recounting that moment also allows him to explain the aim of his book: to provide a "clear, accurate, and extensive *picture* of extant public sexual institutions" so that others may learn about and explore them (Delany 1988, 174, 176; emphasis added). Knowledge is gained through vision; vision is a direct apprehension of a world of transparent objects. In this conceptualization, the visible is privileged; writing is then put at its service.[2] Seeing is the origin of knowing. Writing is reproduction, transmission—the communication of knowledge gained through (visual, visceral) experience.

This kind of communication has long been the mission of historians documenting the lives of those omitted or overlooked in accounts of the past. It has produced a wealth of new evidence previously ignored about these others and has drawn attention to dimensions of human life and activity usually deemed unworthy of mention in conventional histories. It has also occasioned a crisis for orthodox history by multiplying not only stories but subjects, and by insisting that histories are written from fundamentally different—indeed irreconcilable—perspectives or standpoints, none of which is complete or completely "true." Like Delany's memoir, these histories have provided evidence for a world of alternative values and practices whose existence gives the lie to hegemonic constructions of social worlds, whether these constructions vaunt the political superiority of white men, the coherence and unity of selves, the naturalness of heterosexual monogamy, or the inevitability of scientific progress and economic development. The challenge to normative history has been described, in terms of conventional historical understandings of evidence, as an enlargement of the picture, a correction to oversights resulting from inaccurate or incomplete vision, and it has rested its claim to legitimacy on the authority of experience, the direct experience of others, as well as of the historian who learns to see and illuminate the lives of those others in his or her texts.

Documenting the experience of others in this way has been at once a highly successful and limiting strategy for historians of difference. It has been successful because it remains so comfortably within the disciplinary framework of history, working according to rules that permit calling old narratives into question when new evidence is discovered. The status of evidence is, of course, ambiguous for historians. On the one hand, they acknowledge that "evidence only counts as evidence and is only recognized as such in relation to a potential narrative, so that the narrative can be said to determine the evidence as much as the evidence determines the narrative" (Gossman 1989, 26). On the other hand, historians' rhetorical treatment of evidence and their use of it to falsify prevailing interpretations depends on a referential notion of evidence which denies that

---

2. On the distinction between seeing and writing in formulations of identity, see Bhabha (1987, 5–11).

it is anything but a reflection of the real.[3] Michel de Certeau's description is apt. Historical discourse, he writes,

> gives itself credibility in the name of the reality which it is supposed to represent, but this authorized appearance of the "real" serves precisely to camouflage the practice which in fact determines it. Representation thus disguises the praxis that organizes it. (de Certeau 1986, 203)

When the evidence offered is the evidence of "experience," the claim for referentiality is further buttressed—what could be truer, after all, than a subject's own account of what he or she has lived through? It is precisely this kind of appeal to experience as uncontestable evidence and as an originary point of explanation—as a foundation on which analysis is based—that weakens the critical thrust of histories of difference. By remaining within the epistemological frame of orthodox history, these studies lose the possibility of examining those assumptions and practices that excluded considerations of difference in the first place. They take as self-evident the identities of those whose experience is being documented and thus naturalize their difference. They locate resistance outside its discursive construction and reify agency as an inherent attribute of individuals, thus decontextualizing it. When experience is taken as the origin of knowledge, the vision of the individual subject (the person who had the experience or the historian who recounts it) becomes the bedrock of evidence on which explanation is built. Questions about the constructed nature of experience, about how subjects are constituted as different in the first place, about how one's vision is structured—about language (or discourse[4]) and history—are left aside. The evidence of experience then becomes evidence for the fact of difference, rather than a way of exploring how difference is established, how it operates, how and in what ways it constitutes subjects who see and act in the world.[5]

To put it another way, the evidence of experience, whether conceived through a metaphor of visibility or in any other way that takes meaning as transparent, reproduces

---

3. On the "documentary" or "objectivist" model used by historians, see LaCapra (1985b, 17–18).

4. [Ed. note] Although it commonly is taken to mean speech or an act of communication, "discourse"— under the influence of postmodern scholarship—is here used as a technical term to imply that collection of institutions, assumptions, practices, and artefacts that constitute a specific domain of knowledge. Discourses are the structures in which knowledge takes place. For instance, the discourse of academia includes libraries, tweed-jacketed professors, hierarchical relations between teachers and students, and even ivy-covered brick. With these, and much more, up and running, it is possible not only to come to know the university but, more importantly perhaps, to "feel" smart or qualified for having gone to such a place.

5. Vision, as Donna Haraway points out, is not passive reflection. "All eyes, including our own organic ones, are active perceptual systems, building in translations and specific ways of seeing—that is, ways of life" (Haraway 1988, 583). In another essay she pushes the optical metaphor further: "The rays from my optical device diffract rather than reflect. These diffracting rays compose *interference* patterns, not reflecting images.... A diffraction pattern does not map where differences appear, but rather where the *effects* of differences appear" (Haraway typescript). In this connection, see also Minnie Bruce Pratt's discussion (1984) of her eye that "has only let in what I have been taught to see," and the analysis of Pratt's autobiographical essay by Biddy Martin and Chandra Talpade Mohanty (1986).

rather than contests given ideological systems—those that assume that the facts of history speak for themselves and those that rest on notions of a natural or established opposition between, say, sexual practices and social conventions, or between homosexuality and heterosexuality. Histories that document the "hidden" world of homosexuality, for example, show the impact of silence and repression on the lives of those affected by it and bring to light the history of their suppression and exploitation. But the project of making experience visible precludes critical examination of the workings of the ideological system itself, its categories of representation (homosexual/heterosexual, man/woman, black/white as fixed immutable identities), its premises about what these categories mean and how they operate, and of its notions of subjects, origin, and cause. Homosexual practices are seen as the result of desire, conceived as a natural force operating outside or in opposition to social regulation. In these stories homosexuality is presented as a repressed desire (experience denied), made to seem invisible, abnormal, and silenced by a "society" that legislates heterosexuality as the only normal practice.[6] Because this kind of (homosexual) desire cannot ultimately be repressed—because experience is there—it invents institutions to accommodate itself. These institutions are unacknowledged but not invisible; indeed, it is the possibility that they can be seen that threatens order and ultimately overcomes repression. Resistance and agency are presented as driven by uncontainable desire; emancipation is a teleological story[7] in which desire ultimately overcomes social control and becomes visible. History is a chronology that makes experience visible, but in which categories appear as nonetheless ahistorical: desire, homosexuality, heterosexuality, femininity, masculinity, sex, and even sexual practices become so many fixed entities being played out over time, but not themselves historicized. Presenting the story in this way excludes, or at least understates, the historically variable interrelationship between the meanings "homosexual" and "heterosexual," the constitutive force each has for the other, and the contested and changing nature of the terrain that they simultaneously occupy. "The importance—an importance—of the category 'homosexual,'" writes Eve Kosofsky Sedgwick,

> comes not necessarily from its regulatory relation to a nascent or already-constituted minority of homosexual people or desires, but from its potential for giving whoever wields it a structuring definitional leverage over the whole range of male bonds that shape the social constitution.   (Sedgwick 1985, 86)

Not only does homosexuality define heterosexuality by specifying its negative limits, and not only is the boundary between the two a shifting one, but both operate within the structures of the same "phallic economy"—an economy whose workings are not taken into account by studies that seek simply to make homosexual experience visible. One way to describe this economy is to say that desire is defined through the pursuit of the phallus—that veiled and evasive signifier which is at once fully present but unattainable,

---

6. On the disruptive, antisocial nature of desire, see Bersani (1976).

7. [Ed. note] To say something is teleological is to say that it is developing toward a predetermined endpoint or goal.

and which gains its power through the promise it holds out but never entirely fulfills (see Gallop 1982; de Lauretis 1984, chapter 5; Sedgwick 1985; and Lacan 1977). Theorized this way, homosexuality and heterosexuality work according to the same economy, their social institutions mirroring one another. The social institutions through which gay sex is practiced may invert those associated with dominant heterosexual behavior (promiscuous versus restrained, public versus private, anonymous versus known, and so on), but they both operate within a system structured according to presence and lack.[8] To the extent that this system constructs desiring subjects (those who are legitimate as well as those who are not), it simultaneously establishes them and itself as given and outside of time, as the way things work, the way they inevitably are.

The project of making experience visible precludes analysis of the workings of this system and of its historicity; instead, it reproduces its terms. We come to appreciate the consequences of the closeting of homosexuals and we understand repression as an interested act of power or domination; alternative behaviors and institutions also become available to us. What we don't have is a way of placing those alternatives within the framework of (historically contingent) dominant patterns of sexuality and the ideology that supports them. We know they exist, but not how they have been constructed; we know their existence offers a critique of normative practices, but not the extent of the critique. Making visible the experience of a different group exposes the existence of repressive mechanisms, but not their inner workings or logics; we know that difference exists, but we don't understand it as relationally constituted. For that we need to attend to the historical processes that, through discourse, position subjects and produce their experiences. It is not individuals who have experience, but subjects who are constituted through experience. Experience in this definition then becomes not the origin of our explanation, not the authoritative (because seen or felt) evidence that grounds what is known, but rather that which we seek to explain, that about which knowledge is produced. To think about experience in this way is to historicize it as well as to historicize the identities it produces. This kind of historicizing represents a reply to the many contemporary historians who have argued that an unproblematized "experience" is the foundation of their practice; it is a historicizing that implies critical scrutiny of all explanatory categories usually taken for granted, including the category of "experience."

THE AUTHORITY OF EXPERIENCE

History has been largely a foundationalist discourse. By this I mean that its explanations seem to be unthinkable if they do not take for granted some primary premises, categories, or presumptions. These foundations (however varied, whatever they are at a particular moment) are unquestioned and unquestionable; they are considered permanent and transcendent. As such they create a common ground for historians and their objects of study in

---

8. Discussions with Elizabeth Weed on this point were helpful.

the past and so authorize and legitimize analysis; indeed, analysis seems not to be able to proceed without them.[9] In the minds of some foundationalists, in fact, nihilism, anarchy, and moral confusion are the sure alternatives to these givens, which have the status (if not the philosophical definition) of eternal truths.

Historians have had recourse to many kinds of foundations, some more obviously empiricist than others. What is most striking these days is the determined embrace, the strident defense, of some reified,[10] transcendent category of explanation by historians who have used insights drawn from the sociology of knowledge, structural linguistics, feminist theory, or cultural anthropology to develop sharp critiques of empiricism. This turn to foundations even by antifoundationalists appears, in Fredric Jameson's characterization, as "some extreme form of the return of the repressed" (Jameson 1991a, 199).

"Experience" is one of the foundations that has been reintroduced into historical writing in the wake of the critique of empiricism;[11] unlike "brute fact" or "simple reality," its connotations are more varied and elusive. It has recently emerged as a critical term in debates among historians about the limits of interpretation and especially about the uses and limits of post-structuralist theory for history.[12] In these debates those most open to interpretive innovation—those who have insisted on the study of collective mentalities, of economic, social, or cultural determinations of individual behavior, and even of the influences of unconscious motives on thought and action—are among the most ardent defenders of the need to attend to "experience." Feminist historians critical of biases in "malestream" histories and seeking to install women as viable subjects, social historians insisting on the materialist basis of the discipline on the one hand and on the "agency" of individuals or groups on the other, and cultural historians who have brought symbolic analysis to the study of behavior, have joined political historians whose stories privilege the purposive actions of rational actors and intellectual historians who maintain that thought originates in the minds of individuals. All seem to have converged on the argument that experience is an "irreducible" ground for history.

The evolution of "experience" appears to solve a problem of explanation for professed anti-empiricists even as it reinstates a foundational ground. For this reason it is interesting

---

9. I am grateful to Judith Butler for discussions on this point.

10. [Ed. note] Reification—the term used to name the process of treating abstract ideas and concepts as if they were actual things—is often the critique leveled at philosophical idealists.

11. [Ed. note] Empiricism is the name given to a modern philosophical and eventually scientific movement that prioritizes the observation of data that are thought to exist independently of human consciousness—data that can therefore be commonly described by people using one of their five senses. Contrasted with rationalism (the philosophical movement that prioritized pre-existent, or innate, ideas and categories of the mind that are used to understand reality), empiricists therefore claim that knowledge is derived from experience of the external world.

12. [Ed. note] Post-structuralism is often equated with the broader term postmodernism, though many would distinguish the two. Generally speaking, this names a philosophical, literary, architectural, and aesthetic movement that dates to mid-twentieth-century Europe (actually, France) and which emphasized disjunction over unity and constructedness over self-evidence. As a reaction to structuralists' attempts to develop a grand theory of society and symbol systems, post-structuralists (though exhibiting a number of important differences between themselves) sought to overthrow, by means of critique, all total systems of classification and thought.

to examine the uses of "experience" by historians. Such an examination allows us to ask whether history can exist without foundations and what it might look like if it did.

In *Keywords*, Raymond Williams sketches the alternative senses in which the term experience has been employed in the Anglo-American tradition. These he summarizes as "(i) knowledge gathered from past events, whether by conscious observation or by consideration and reflection; and (ii) a particular kind of consciousness, which can in some contexts be distinguished from 'reason' or 'knowledge'"(1983, 126 [this text is reproduced in section one of this anthology]). Until the early eighteenth century, he says, experience and experiment were closely connected terms, designating how knowledge was arrived at through testing and observation (here the visual metaphor is important). In the eighteenth century, experience still contained this notion of consideration or reflection on observed events, of lessons gained from the past, but it also referred to a particular kind of consciousness. This consciousness, in the twentieth century, has come to mean a "full and active awareness," including feeling as well as thought (1985, 127). The notion of experience as subjective witness, writes Williams, is "offered not only as truth, but as the most authentic kind of truth," as "the ground for all (subsequent) reasoning and analysis" (1983, 128). According to Williams, experience has acquired another connotation in the twentieth century different from these notions of subjective testimony as immediate, true, and authentic. In this usage it refers to influences external to individuals—social conditions, institutions, forms of belief or perception—"real" things outside them that they react to, and does not include their thought or consideration.

In the various usages described by Williams, "experience," whether conceived as internal or external, subjective or objective, establishes the prior existence of individuals. When it is defined as internal, it is an expression of an individual's being or consciousness; when external, it is the material on which consciousness then acts. Talking about experience in these ways leads us to take the existence of individuals for granted (experience is something people have) rather than to ask how conceptions of selves (of subjects and their identities) are produced.[13] It operates within an ideological construction that not only makes individuals the starting point of knowledge, but that also naturalizes categories such as man, woman, black, white, heterosexual, and homosexual by treating them as given characteristics of individuals.

Teresa de Lauretis's redefinition of experience exposes the workings of this ideology. "Experience," she writes, is the

> process by which, for all social beings, subjectivity is constructed. Through that process one places oneself or is placed in social reality, and so perceives and comprehends as subjective (referring to, originating in, oneself) those relations—material, economic, and interpersonal—which are in fact social and, in a larger perspective, historical. (de Lauretis 1984, 159)

---

13. On the ways knowledge is conceived "as an assemblage of accurate representations," see Rorty (1979, 163).

The process that de Lauretis describes operates crucially through differentiation; its effect is to constitute subjects as fixed and autonomous, and who are considered reliable sources of a knowledge that comes from access to the real by means of their experience.[14] When talking about historians and other students of the human sciences it is important to note that this subject is both the object of inquiry—the person one studies in the present or the past—and the investigator him- or herself—the historian who produces knowledge of the past based on "experience" in the archives or the anthropologist who produces knowledge of other cultures based on "experience" as a participant observer.

The concepts of experience described by Williams preclude inquiry into processes of subject-construction; and they avoid examining the relationships between discourse, cognition, and reality, the relevance of the position or situatedness of subjects to the knowledge they produce, and the effects of difference on knowledge. Questions are not raised about, for example, whether it matters for the history they write that historians are men, women, white, black, straight, or gay; instead, as de Certeau writes, "the authority of the 'subject of knowledge' [is measured] by the elimination of everything concerning the speaker" (1986, 218). His knowledge, reflecting as it does something apart from him, is legitimated and presented as universal, accessible to all. There is no power or politics in these notions of knowledge and experience.

An example of the way "experience" establishes the authority of a historian can be found in R. G. Collingwood's *The Idea of History*, the 1946 classic that has been required reading in historiography courses for several generations. For Collingwood, the ability of the historian to reenact past experience is tied to his autonomy, "where by autonomy I mean the condition of being one's own authority, making statements or taking action on one's own initiative and not because those statements or actions are authorized or prescribed by anyone else" (1946, 274–5). The question of where the historian is situated—who he is, how he is defined in relation to others, what the political effects of his history may be—never enters the discussion. Indeed, being free of these matters seems to be tied to Collingwood's definition of autonomy, an issue so critical for him that he launches into an uncharacteristic tirade about it. In his quest for certainty, the historian must not let others make up his mind for him, Collingwood insists, because to do that means

> giving up his autonomy as an historian and allowing someone else to do for him what, if he is a scientific thinker, he can only do for himself. There is no need for me to offer the reader any proof of this statement. If he knows anything of historical

---

14. Gayatri Chakravorty Spivak describes this as "positing a metalepsis":

> A subject-effect can be briefly plotted as follows: that which seems to operate as a subject may be part of an immense discontinuous network ... of strands that may be termed politics, ideology, economics, history, sexuality, language, and so on .... Different knottings and configurations of these strands, determined by heterogeneous determinations which are themselves dependent upon myriad circumstances, produce the effect of an operating subject. Yet the continuist and homogenist deliberative consciousness symptomatically requires a continuous and homogeneous cause for this effect and thus posits a sovereign and determining subject. This latter is, then, the effect of an effect, and its positing a metalepsis, or the substitution of an effect for a cause. (1988, 204)

work, he already knows of his own experience that it is true. If he does not already know that it is true, he does not know enough about history to read this essay with any profit, and the best thing he can do is to stop here and now.   (1946, 274–5)

For Collingwood it is axiomatic that experience is a reliable source of knowledge because it rests on direct contact between the historian's perception and reality, (even if the passage of time makes it necessary for the historian to imaginatively reenact events of the past). Thinking on his own means owning his own thoughts, and this proprietary relationship guarantees an individual's independence, his ability to read the past correctly, and the authority of the knowledge he produces. The claim is not only for the historian's autonomy, but also for his originality. Here "experience" grounds the identity of the researcher as a historian.

Another, very different use of "experience" can be found in E. P. Thompson's 1963 book, *The Making of the English Working Class* [1980], the book that revolutionized social and labor history.[15] Thompson specifically set out to free the concept of "class" from the ossified categories of Marxist structuralism. For this project "experience" was a key concept. "We explored," Thompson writes of himself and his fellow New Left historians,[16] "both in theory and in practice, those junction-concepts (such as 'need,' 'class,' and 'determine') by which, through the missing term, 'experience,' structure is transmuted into process, and the subject re-enters into history" (Thompson 1978, 170).

Thompson's notion of experience joined ideas of external influence and subjective feeling, the structural and the psychological. This gave him a mediating influence between social structure and social consciousness. For him experience meant "social being"—the lived realities of social life, especially the affective domains of family and religion and the symbolic dimensions of expression. This definition separated the affective and the symbolic from the economic and the rational. "People do not only experience their own experience as ideas, within thought and its procedures," he maintained, "they also experience their own experience as feeling" (Thompson 1978, 171). This statement grants importance to the psychological dimension of experience, and it allows Thompson to account for agency.[17] Feeling, Thompson insists, is "handled" culturally as "norms, familial and kinship

---

15. [Ed. note] Social history—a field to which the British historian E. P. Thompson made noteworthy contributions—is the name given to a mid- to late twentieth-century intellectual movement among historians who were interested in describing, and accounting for, the development and movement of social trends (i.e., economic, political, legal, etc.). For many social historians, this meant abandoning the so-called "great man" or "top-down" model often adopted by historians, by which history is understood as the actions of political and military figures. Instead, they wrote history "from the bottom up"—that is, prioritizing accounts of people's daily lives and seeing social trends as large-scale phenomena that trickle up, not down, the class ladder.

16. [Ed. note] The New Left, by means of the British journal associated with Thompson and his peers, *The New Left Review*, was a mid-twentieth-century intellectual and political movement in Europe that applied revised Marxist theories ("revised" implying a break with traditional or orthodox Communist thinking of that time) to the study of history, politics, and economics.

17. [Ed. note] A classic problem in the field of social theory is the tension between structure and agency—that is, scholars interested in examining, say, the effects of such things as economic or political systems often

obligations and reciprocities, as values or (through more elaborated forms) within art and religious beliefs" (1978, 171). At the same time it somehow precedes these forms of expression and so provides an escape from a strong structural determination: "For any living generation, in any 'now'," Thompson asserts, "the ways in which they 'handle' experience defies prediction and escapes from any narrow definition of determination" (1978, 171).[18]

And yet in his use of it, experience, because it is ultimately shaped by relations of production, is a unifying phenomenon, overriding other kinds of diversity. Since these relations of production are common to workers of different ethnicities, religions, regions, and trades they necessarily provide a common denominator and emerge as a more salient determinant of "experience" than anything else. In Thompson's use of the term, experience is the start of a process that culminates in the realization and articulation of social consciousness, in this case a common identity of class. It serves an integrating function, joining the individual and the structural, and bringing together diverse people into that coherent (totalizing) whole which is a distinctive sense of class.[19] "'Experience' (we have found) has, in the last instance, been generated in 'material life', has been structured in class ways, and hence 'social being' has determined 'social consciousness'" (Thompson 1978, 171). In this way unequivocal and uniform identity is produced through objective circumstances and there is no reason to ask how this identity achieved predominance—it had to.

The unifying aspect of experience excludes whole realms of human activity by simply not counting them as experience, at least not with any consequences for social organization or politics. When class becomes an overriding identity, other subject-positions are subsumed by it, those of gender, for example (or, in other instances of this kind, of history, race, ethnicity, and sexuality). The positions of men and women and their different relationships to politics are taken as reflections of material and social arrangements rather than as products of class politics itself; they are part of the "experience" of capitalism. Instead of asking how some experiences become more salient than others, how what matters to Thompson is defined as experience, and how differences are dissolved, experience becomes itself cumulative and homogenizing, providing the common denominator on which class consciousness is built.

Thompson's own role in determining the salience of certain things and not others is never addressed. Although his author's voice intervenes powerfully with moral and ethical judgments about the situations he is recounting, the presentation of the experiences themselves is meant to secure their objective status. We forget that Thompson's history, like

---

are accused of minimizing the ability of the individual human agent to effect change and act creatively. Scholarship that emphasizes the role of agency, on the other hand, is often critiqued for overlooking the manner in which social structures predetermine what sorts of actions can (and cannot) be performed. A mediating position argues that agency and structure are dialectical—that is, they presuppose and therefore require each other and neither is primary.

18. Williams's discussion of "structures of feeling" takes on some of these same issues in a more extended way. See Williams (1961) and the interview about it (1979, 133–74). I am grateful to Chun Lin for directing me to these texts.

19. On the integrative functions of "experience," see Butler (1990, 22–5).

the accounts offered by political organizers in the nineteenth century of what mattered in workers' lives, is an interpretation, a selective ordering of information that through its use of originary categories and teleological accounts legitimizes a particular kind of politics (it becomes the only possible politics) and a particular way of doing history (as a reflection of what happened, the description of which is little influenced by the historian if, in this case, he only has the requisite moral vision that permits identification with the experiences of workers in the past).

In Thompson's account class is finally an identity rooted in structural relations that pre-exist politics. What this obscures is the contradictory and contested process by which class itself was conceptualized and by which diverse kinds of subject-positions were assigned, felt, contested, or embraced. As a result, Thompson's brilliant history of the English working class, which set out to historicize the category of class, ends up essentializing it. The ground may seem to be displaced from structure to agency by insisting on the subjectively felt nature of experience, but the problem Thompson sought to address isn't really solved. Working-class "experience" is now the ontological foundation of working-class identity, politics, and history.[20]

This kind of use of experience has the same foundational status if we substitute "women's" or "black" or "lesbian" or "homosexual" for "working-class" in the previous sentence. Among feminist historians, for example, "experience" has helped to legitimize a critique of the false claims to objectivity of traditional historical accounts. Part of the project of some feminist history has been to unmask all claims to objectivity as an ideological cover for masculine bias by pointing out the shortcomings, incompleteness, and exclusiveness of mainstream history. This has been achieved by providing documentation about women in the past that calls into question existing interpretations made without consideration of gender. But how do we authorize the new knowledge if the possibility of all historical objectivity has been questioned? By appealing to experience, which in this usage connotes both reality and its subjective apprehension—the experience of women in the past and of women historians who can recognize something of themselves in their foremothers.

Judith Newton, a literary historian writing about the neglect of feminism by contemporary critical theorists, argues that women, too, arrived at the critique of objectivity usually associated with deconstruction or the new historicism. This feminist critique came "straight out of reflection on our own, that is, women's experience, out of the contradictions we felt between the different ways we were represented even to ourselves, out of the inequities we had long experienced in our situations" (Newton 1988, 93). Newton's appeal to experience seems to bypass the issue of objectivity (by not raising the question of whether feminist work can be objective) but it rests firmly on a foundational ground (experience). In her work the relationship between thought and experience is represented

---

20. For a different reading of Thompson on experience, see Sewell (1990, 50–77). I also have benefited from Sylvia Schafer's "Writing about 'Experience': Workers and Historians Tormented by Industrialization" (typescript).

as transparent (the visual metaphor combines with the visceral) and so is directly accessible, as it is in historian Christine Stansell's insistence that "social practices," in all their "immediacy and entirety," constitute a domain of "sensuous experience" (a prediscursive reality directly felt, seen, and known) that cannot be subsumed by "language" (Stansell 1987, 28).[21] The effect of these kinds of statements, which attribute an indisputable authenticity to women's experience, is to establish incontrovertibly women's identity as people with agency. It is also to universalize the identity of women and thus to ground claims for the legitimacy of women's history in the shared experience of historians of women and those women whose stories they tell. In addition, it literally equates the personal with the political, for the lived experience of women is seen as leading directly to resistance to oppression, that is, to feminism.[22] Indeed, the possibility of politics is said to rest on, to follow from, a pre-existing women's experience.

"Because of its drive towards a political massing together of women," writes Denise Riley, "feminism can never wholeheartedly dismantle 'women's experience,' however much this category conflates the attributed, the imposed, and the lived, and then sanctifies the resulting mélange" (Riley 1988, 100). The kind of argument for a women's history (and for a feminist politics) that Riley criticizes closes down inquiry into the ways in which female subjectivity is produced, the ways in which agency is made possible, the ways in which race and sexuality intersect with gender, the ways in which politics organize and interpret experience—in sum, the ways in which identity is a contested terrain, the site of multiple and conflicting claims. In Riley's words, "it masks the likelihood that … [experiences] have accrued to women not by virtue of their womanhood alone, but as traces of domination, whether natural or political" (Riley 1988, 99). I would add that it masks the necessarily discursive character of these experiences as well.

But it is precisely the discursive character of experience that is at issue for some historians because attributing experience to discourse seems somehow to deny its status as an unquestionable ground of explanation. This seems to be the case for John Toews, who wrote a long article in the *American Historical Review* in 1987 called "Intellectual History after the Linguistic Turn: The Autonomy of Meaning and the Irreducibility of Experience." The term *linguistic turn* is a comprehensive one used by Toews to refer to approaches to the study of meaning that draw on a number of disciplines, but especially on theories of language "since the primary medium of meaning was obviously language" (Toews 1987, 881). The question for Toews is how far linguistic analysis has gone and should go, especially in view of the post-structuralist challenge to foundationalism. Reviewing a number of books that take on questions of meaning and its analysis, Toews concludes that

---

21. Often this kind of invocation of experience leads back to the biological or physical "experience" of the body. See, for example, the arguments about rape and violence offered by Hawkesworth (1989).

22. This is one of the meanings of the slogan "the personal is the political." Personal knowledge, that is, the experience of oppression is the source of resistance to it. This is what Mohanty calls "the feminist osmosis thesis: females are feminists by association and identification with the experiences which constitute us as female" (1987, 32). See also an important article by Katie King (1986).

> the predominant tendency [among intellectual historians] is to adapt traditional historical concerns for extralinguistic origins and reference to the semiological challenge, to reaffirm in new ways that, in spite of the relative autonomy of cultural meanings, human subjects still make and remake the worlds of meaning in which they are suspended, and to insist that these worlds are not creations *ex nihilo* [from/ out of nothing] but responses to, and shapings of, changing worlds of experience ultimately irreducible to the linguistic forms in which they appear. (1987, 882)

By definition, he argues, history is concerned with explanation; it is not a radical hermeneutics, but an attempt to account for the origin, persistence, and disappearance of certain meanings "at particular times and in specific sociocultural situations" (Toews 1987, 882). For him explanation requires a separation of experience and meaning: experience is that reality which demands meaningful response. "Experience," in Toews's usage, is taken to be so self-evident that he never defines the term. This is telling in an article that insists on establishing the importance and independence, the irreducibility of "experience." The absence of definition allows experience to resonate in many ways, but it also allows it to function as a universally understood category—the undefined word creates a sense of consensus by attributing to it an assumed, stable, and shared meaning.

Experience, for Toews, is a foundational concept. While recognizing that meanings differ and that the historian's task is to analyze the different meanings produced in societies and over time, Toews protects "experience" from this kind of relativism. In doing so he establishes the possibility for objective knowledge and for communication among historians, however diverse their positions and views. This has the effect (among others) of removing historians from critical scrutiny as active producers of knowledge.

The insistence on the separation of meaning and experience is crucial for Toews, not only because it seems the only way to account for change, but also because it protects the world from "the hubris of wordmakers who claim to be makers of reality" (Toews 1987, 906). Even if Toews here uses "wordmakers" metaphorically to refer to those who produce texts, those who engage in signification, his opposition between "words" and "reality" echoes the distinction he makes earlier in the article between language (or meaning) and experience. This opposition guarantees both an independent status for human agents and the common ground on which they can communicate and act. It produces a possibility for "intersubjective communication" among individuals despite differences between them, and also reaffirms their existence as thinking beings outside the discursive practices they devise and employ.

Toews is critical of J. G. A. Pocock's vision of "intersubjective communication" based on rational consensus in a community of free individuals, all of whom are equally masters of their own wills. "Pocock's theories," he writes, "often seem like theoretical reflections of familiar practices because the world they assume is also the world in which many contemporary Anglo-American historians live or think they live" (Toews 1987, 893). Yet the separation of meaning and experience that Toews offers does not really provide an alternative. A more diverse community can be posited, of course, with different meanings given to experience. Since the phenomenon of experience itself can be analyzed outside the meanings given to it, the subjective position of historians then can seem to have nothing to do with the knowledge they produce.[23] In this way experience authorizes historians and it enables them to counter the radical historicist stance that, Toews says, "undermines the traditional historians' quest for unity, continuity, and purpose by robbing them of any standpoint from which a relationship between past, present, and future could be objectively reconstructed" (Toews 1987, 902). Here he establishes as self-evident (and unproblematic) the reflective nature of historical representation, and he assumes that it will override whatever diversity there is in the background, culture, and outlook of historians. Attention to experience, he concludes, "is essential for our self-understanding, and thus also for fulfilling the historian's task of connecting memory with hope" (Toews 1987, 907).[24]

Toews's "experience" thus provides an object for historians that can be known apart from their own role as meaning makers and it then guarantees not only the objectivity of their knowledge, but their ability to persuade others of its importance. Whatever diversity and conflict may exist among them, Toews's community of historians is rendered homogeneous by its shared object (experience). But as Ellen Rooney has so effectively pointed out, using the field of literary theory as her example, this kind of homogeneity can exist only because of the exclusion of the possibility that "historically irreducible interests divide and define reading communities" (Rooney 1989, 6). Inclusiveness is achieved by denying that exclusion is inevitable, that difference is established through exclusion, and that the fundamental differences that accompany inequalities of power and position cannot be overcome by persuasion. In Toews's article no disagreement about the meaning of the term experience can be entertained, since experience itself lies somehow outside its signification. For that reason, perhaps, Toews never defines it.

Even among those historians who do not share all of Toews's ideas about the objectivity or continuous quality of history writing, the defense of "experience" works in much

---

23. De Certeau puts it this way:

> That the particularity of the place where discourse is produced is relevant will be naturally more apparent where historiographical discourse treats matters that put the subject-producer of knowledge into question: the history of women, of blacks, of Jews, of cultural minorities, etc. In these fields one can, of course, either maintain that the personal status of the author is a matter of indifference (in relation to the objectivity of his or her work) or that he or she alone authorizes or invalidates the discourse (according to whether he or she is "of it" or not). But this debate requires what has been concealed by an epistemology, namely, the impact of subject-to-subject relationships (men and women, blacks and whites, etc.) on the use of apparently "neutral" techniques and in the organization of discourses that are, perhaps, equally scientific. For example, from the fact of the differentiation of the sexes, must one conclude that a woman produces a different historiography from that of a man? Of course, I do not answer this question, but I do assert that this interrogation puts the place of the subject in question and requires a treatment of it unlike the epistemology that constructed the "truth" of the work on the foundation of the speaker's irrelevance.   (1986, 217–18)

24. Here we have an example of what Foucault characterized as "continuous history":

> the indispensable correlative of the founding function of the subject: the guarantee that everything that has eluded him may be restored to him; the certainty that time will disperse nothing without restoring it in reconstituted unity.   (1977, 12)

the same way: it establishes a realm of reality outside of discourse and it authorizes the historian who has access to it. The evidence of experience works as a foundation providing both a starting point and a conclusive kind of explanation, beyond which few questions can or need to be asked. And yet it is precisely the questions precluded—questions about discourse, difference, and subjectivity, as well as about what counts as experience and who gets to make that determination—that would enable us to historicize experience and to reflect critically on the history we write about it, rather than to premise our history on it.

HISTORICIZING "EXPERIENCE"

Gayatri Chakravorty Spivak begins an essay addressed to the Subaltern Studies collective[25] with a contrast between the work of historians and literary scholars:

> A historian confronts a text of counterinsurgency or gendering where the subaltern has been represented. He unravels the text to assign a new subject-position to the subaltern, gendered or otherwise.
>
> A teacher of literature confronts a sympathetic text where the gendered subaltern has been represented. She unravels the text to make visible the assignment of subject-positions....
>
> The performance of these tasks, of the historian and the teacher of literature, must critically "interrupt" each other, bring each other to crisis, in order to serve their constituencies; especially when each seems to claim all for its own.
>
> (Spivak 1988, 241)

Spivak's argument here seems to be that there is a difference between history and literature that is both methodological and political. History provides categories that enable us to understand the social and structural positions of people (as workers, subalterns, and so on) in new terms, and these terms define a collective identity with potential political (maybe even revolutionary, but certainly subversive) effects. Literature relativizes the categories history assigns, and exposes the processes that construct and position subjects. In Spivak's discussion, both are critical operations, although she clearly favors the deconstructive task of literature.[26] Although her essay has to be read in the context of a specific debate within

---

25. [Ed. note] Subaltern Studies is a recently named intellectual field that is devoted to studying those peoples traditionally ranked by Euro-North American scholarship as being below or in an inferior position (as implied by the term "subaltern," which is used in the works of the Italian Marxist theorist Antonio Gramsci [1891–1937]); it is also a scholarly field that overlaps with post-colonial studies in examining the social processes by which populations, who traditionally do not speak for themselves inasmuch as they do not have access to scholarship, are made to seem inferior or derivative.

26. Her argument is based on a set of oppositions between history and literature, male and female, identity and difference, practical politics and theory, and she repeatedly privileges the second set of terms. These polarities speak to the specifics of the debate she is engaged in with the (largely male) Subaltern Studies collective, historians working within a Marxist, especially Gramscian, frame.

Indian historiography, its general points must also be considered. In effect, her statements raise the question of whether historians can do other than construct subjects by describing their experience in terms of an essentialized identity.

Spivak's characterization of the Subaltern Studies historians' reliance on a notion of consciousness as a "strategic use of positivist essentialism" doesn't really solve the problem of writing history either, since whether it's strategic or not, essentialism appeals to the idea that there are fixed identities, visible to us as social or natural facts (Spivak 1988, 205).[27] A refusal of essentialism seems particularly important once again these days within the field of history, as disciplinary pressure builds to defend the unitary subject in the name of his or her "experience." Neither does Spivak's invocation of the special political status of the subaltern justify a history aimed at producing subjects without interrogating and relativizing the means of their production. In the case of colonial and post-colonial peoples, but also of various others in the West, it has been precisely the imposition of a categorical (and universal) subject-status (the worker, the peasant, the woman, the black) that has masked the operations of difference in the organization of social life. Each category taken as fixed works to solidify the ideological process of subject-construction, making the process less rather than more apparent, naturalizing rather than analyzing it.

It ought to be possible for historians (as for the teachers of literature Spivak so dazzlingly exemplifies) to "make visible the assignment of subject-positions," not in the sense of capturing the reality of the objects seen, but of trying to understand the operations of the complex and changing discursive processes by which identities are ascribed, resisted, or embraced, and which processes themselves are unremarked and indeed achieve their effect because they are not noticed. To do this a change of object seems to be required, one that takes the emergence of concepts and identities as historical events in need of explanation. This does not mean that one dismisses the effects of such concepts and identities, nor that one does not explain behavior in terms of their operations. It does mean assuming that the appearance of a new identity is not inevitable or determined, not something that was always there simply waiting to be expressed, not something that will always exist in the form it was given in a particular political movement or at a particular historical moment. Stuart Hall writes:

> The fact is "black" has never been just there either. It has always been an unstable identity, psychically, culturally and politically. It, too, is a narrative, a story, a history. Something constructed, told, spoken, not simply found. People now speak of the society I come from in totally unrecognizable ways. Of course Jamaica is a black society, they say. In reality it is a society of black and brown people who lived for three or four hundred years without ever being able to speak of themselves as "black." Black is an identity which had to be learned and could only be learned in a certain moment. In Jamaica that moment is the 1970s.　　　　(Hall 1987, 45)[28]

---

27. See also Spivak and Rooney (1989, 128); on essentialism, see Fuss (1989).
28. See also Fields (1982). Fields's article is notable for its contradictions: the way, for example, that it historicizes race, naturalizes class, and refuses to talk at all about gender.

To take the history of Jamaican black identity as an object of inquiry in these terms is necessarily to analyze subject-positioning, at least in part, as the effect of discourses that placed Jamaica in a late twentieth-century international racist political economy; it is to historicize the "experience" of blackness.[29]

Treating the emergence of a new identity as a discursive event is not to introduce a new form of linguistic determinism, nor to deprive subjects of agency. It is to refuse a separation between "experience" and language and to insist instead on the productive quality of discourse. Subjects are constituted discursively, but there are conflicts among discursive systems, contradictions within any one of them, multiple meanings possible for the concepts they deploy.[30] And subjects do have agency. They are not unified, autonomous individuals exercising free will, but rather subjects whose agency is created through situations and statuses conferred on them. Being a subject means being "subject to definite conditions of existence, conditions of endowment of agents and conditions of exercise" (Adams and Minson 1978, 52).[31] These conditions enable choices, although they are not unlimited. Subjects are constituted discursively and experience is a linguistic event (it doesn't happen outside established meanings), but neither is it confined to a fixed order of meaning. Since discourse is by definition shared, experience is collective as well as individual. Experience can both confirm what is already known (we see what we have learned to see) and upset what has been taken for granted (when different meanings are in conflict we readjust our vision to take account of the conflict or to resolve it—that is what is meant by "learning from experience," though not everyone learns the same lesson or learns it at the same time or in the same way). Experience is a subject's history. Language is the site of history's enactment. Historical explanation cannot, therefore, separate the two.

The question then becomes how to analyze language, and here historians often (though not always and not necessarily) confront the limits of a discipline that has typically constructed itself in opposition to literature. (These are not the same limits Spivak points to; her contrast is about the different kinds of knowledge produced by history and literature, mine is about different ways of reading and the different understandings of the relationship between words and things implicit in those readings. In neither case are the limits obligatory for historians; indeed, recognition of them makes it possible for us to get beyond them.) The kind of reading I have in mind would not assume a direct correspondence between words and things, nor confine itself to single meanings, nor aim for the resolution of contradiction. It would not render process as linear, nor rest explanation on simple correlations or single variables. Rather it would grant to "the literary" an integral, even irreducible, status of its own. To grant such status is not to make "the literary" foundational, but to open new possibilities for analyzing discursive productions of social and political reality as complex, contradictory processes.

---

29. An excellent example of the historicizing of black women's "experience" is Carby's *Reconstructing Womanhood: The Emergence of the Afro-American Woman Novelist* (1987).
30. For discussions of how change operates within and across discourses, see Bono (1990); see also Poovey (1988, 1–23).
31. On the constitution of the subject, see Foucault (1977, 95–6); Nussbaum (1989); and de Bolla (1989).

The reading I offered of Delany at the beginning of this essay is an example of the kind of reading I want to avoid. I would like now to present another reading—one suggested to me by literary critic Karen Swann—as a way of indicating what might be involved in historicizing the notion of experience. It is also a way of agreeing with and appreciating Swann's argument about "the importance of the 'literary' to the historical project."[32]

For Delany, witnessing the scene at the bathhouse (an "undulating mass of naked male bodies" seen under a dim blue light) was an event. It marked what in one kind of reading we would call a coming to consciousness of himself, a recognition of his authentic identity, one he had always shared, would always share with others like himself. Another kind of reading, closer to Delany's preoccupation with memory and the self in this autobiography, sees this event not as the discovery of truth (conceived as the reflection of a prediscursive reality), but as the substitution of one interpretation for another. Delany presents this substitution as a conversion experience, a clarifying moment, after which he sees (that is, understands) differently. But there is all the difference between subjective perceptual clarity and transparent vision; one does not necessarily follow from the other even if the subjective state is metaphorically presented as a visual experience. Moreover, as Swann has pointed out, "the properties of the medium through which the visible appears—here, the dim blue light, whose distorting, refracting qualities produce a wavering of the visible"—make any claim to unmediated transparency impossible. Instead, the wavering light permits a vision beyond the visible, a vision that contains the fantastic projections ("millions of gay men" for whom "history had, actively and already, created ... whole galleries of institutions") that are the basis for political identification. "In this version of the story," Swann notes, "'political' consciousness and power originate, not in a presumedly unmediated experience of presumedly real gay identities, but out of an apprehension of the moving, differencing properties of the representational medium—the motion of light in water."

The question of representation is central to Delany's memoir. It is a question of social categories, personal understanding, and language, all of which are connected, none of which are or can be a direct reflection of the others. What does it mean to be black, gay, a writer, he asks, and is there a realm of personal identity possible apart from social constraint? The answer is that the social and the personal are imbricated in one another and that both are historically variable. The meanings of the categories of identity change and with them the possibilities for thinking the self:

> At that time, the words "black" and "gay"—for openers—didn't exist with their current meanings, usage, history. 1961 had still been, really, part of the fifties. The political consciousness that was to form by the end of the sixties had not been part of my world. There were only Negroes and homosexuals, both of whom—along with artists—were hugely devalued in the social hierarchy. It's even hard to speak of that world. (Delany 1988, 24)

---

32. Karen Swann's comments on this paper were presented at the Little Three Faculty Colloquium on "The Social and Political Construction of Reality" at Wesleyan University in January 1991. The comments exist only in typescript.

But the available social categories aren't sufficient for Delany's story. It is difficult, if not impossible, to use a single narrative to account for his experience. Instead he makes entries in a notebook, at the front about material things, at the back about sexual desire. These are "parallel narratives, in parallel columns" (Delany 1988, 29). Although one seems to be about society, the public, and the political, and the other about the individual, the private, and the psychological, in fact both narratives are inescapably historical; they are discursive productions of knowledge of the self, not reflections either of external or internal truth. "That the two columns must be the Marxist and the Freudian—the material column and the column of desire—is only a modernist prejudice. The autonomy of each is subverted by the same excesses, just as severely" (1988, 212). The two columns are constitutive of one another, yet the relationship between them is difficult to specify. Does the social and economic determine the subjective? Is the private entirely separate from or completely integral to the public? Delany voices the desire to resolve the problem: "Certainly one must be the lie that is illuminated by the other's truth" (1988, 212). And then he denies that resolution is possible since answers to these questions do not exist apart from the discourses that produce them:

> If it *is* the split—the space between the two columns (one resplendent and lucid with the writings of legitimacy, the other dark and hollow with the voices of the illegitimate)—that constitutes the subject, it is only after the Romantic inflation of the private into the subjective that such a split can even be located. That locus, that margin, that split itself first allows, then demands the appropriation of language now spoken, now written—in both directions, over the gap.   (1988, 29–30)

It is finally by tracking "the appropriation of language ... in both directions, over the gap" and by situating and contextualizing that language that one historicizes the terms by which experience is represented, and so historicizes "experience" itself.

CONCLUSION

Reading for "the literary" does not seem at all inappropriate for those whose discipline is devoted to the study of change. It is not the only kind of reading I am advocating, although more documents than those written by literary figures are susceptible to such readings. Rather it is a way of changing the focus and the philosophy of our history, from one bent on naturalizing "experience" through a belief in the unmediated relationship between words and things, to one that takes all categories of analysis as contextual, contested, and contingent. How have categories of representation and analysis—such as class, race, gender, relations of production, biology, identity, subjectivity, agency, experience, even culture—achieved their foundational status? What have been the effects of their articulations? What does it mean for historians to study the past in terms of these categories and for individuals to think of themselves in these terms? What is the relationship between the salience of such categories in our own time and their existence in the past? Questions such as these open consideration of what Dominick LaCapra has referred to as the "transferential" relationship between the historian and the past, that is, of the relationship between the power of the historian's analytic frame and the events that are the object of his or her study (LaCapra 1985a, 71–94).[33] And they historicize both sides of that relationship by denying the fixity and transcendence of anything that appears to operate as a foundation, turning attention instead to the history of foundationalist concepts themselves. The history of these concepts (understood to be contested and contradictory) then becomes the evidence by which "experience" can be grasped and by which the historian's relationship to the past he or she writes about can be articulated.

This is what Foucault meant by genealogy:

> If interpretation were the slow exposure of the meaning hidden in an origin, then only metaphysics could interpret the development of humanity. But if interpretation is the violent or surreptitious appropriation of a system of rules, which in itself has no essential meaning, in order to impose a direction, to bend it to a new will, to force its participation in a different game, and to subject it to secondary rules, then the development of humanity is a series of interpretations. The role of genealogy is to record its history: the history of morals, ideals, and metaphysical concepts, the history of the concept of liberty or of the ascetic life; as they stand for the emergence of different interpretations, they must be made to appear as events on the stage of historical process. (1977, 151–2)

Experience is not a word we can do without, although, given its usage to essentialize identity and reify the subject, it is tempting to abandon it altogether. But experience is so much a part of everyday language, so imbricated in our narratives that it seems futile to argue for its expulsion. It serves as a way of talking about what happened, of establishing difference and similarity, of claiming knowledge that is "unassailable" (see Pierson typescript). Given the ubiquity of the term, it seems to me more useful to work with it, to analyze its operations and to redefine its meaning. This entails focusing on processes of identity production, insisting on the discursive nature of "experience" and on the politics of its construction. Experience is at once always already an interpretation and something that needs to be interpreted. What counts as experience is neither self-evident nor straightforward; it is always contested, and always therefore political. The study of experience, therefore, must call into question its originary status in historical explanation. This will happen when historians take as their project not the reproduction and transmission of knowledge said to be arrived at through experience, but the analysis of the production of that knowledge itself. Such an analysis would constitute a genuinely nonfoundational history, one which retains its explanatory power and its interest in change but does not stand on or reproduce naturalized categories.[34] It also cannot guarantee the historian's neutrality, for deciding which categories to historicize is inevitably political, necessarily tied to

---

33. See LaCapra 1985a, 71–94

34. Conversations with Christopher Fynsk helped clarify these points for me.

the historian's recognition of his or her stake in the production of knowledge. Experience is, in this approach, not the origin of our explanation, but that which we want to explain. This kind of approach does not undercut politics by denying the existence of subjects; it instead interrogates the processes of their creation and, in so doing, refigures history and the role of the historian and opens new ways for thinking about change.[35]

---

35. For an important attempt to describe a post-structuralist history, see de Bolla (1986).

© Jeremy Horner/iStockphoto

CONCLUSION

THE CAPITAL OF "EXPERIENCE"

12

WILLIAM JAMES IN LATE CAPITALISM: OUR RELIGION OF THE STATUS QUO

Craig Martin

"[T]ell me how you classify and I'll tell you who you are." (Barthes 1972, 175)

According to William James and the intellectual tradition of which he is a part, institutional religion is the "excrescence" (James 2004, 432) built on religious experience. While much has been written on "religious experience," there is less critical scholarship on the idea of "institutional religion" or "organized religion." However, both sets of terms belong together in a pervasive and broadly persuasive contemporary discourse—a discourse that, ironically, informs those very religious traditions it was designed in part to criticize—and a consideration of one should involve a consideration of the other. In this essay I will explain how this contemporary discourse operates and how it belongs to a dominant folk theory of religion that dovetails well with consumerism under late capitalism.[1] In sum, I will argue

This essay was improved immeasurably as a result of feedback provided by Jeremy Vecchi, Nathan Rein, Bill Arnal, Aldea Mulhern, Brad Stoddard, and Tim Morgan. In addition, special thanks go to Neerja Chaturvedi and C. J. Churchill, who organized the St. Thomas Aquinas College faculty research retreat in May of 2010, where I initially tried out some of these ideas. Last, I want to thank the students in my fall 2010 course, "The Evolution of Jesus," and my spring 2011 course, "Religions of the East," who forced me to clarify my argument at key points. As always, the views expressed in the paper may not reflect the views of those who helped me to improve it.

1. I am not, strictly speaking, using either Ernest Mandel's (1999) or Fredric Jameson's (1991b) definitions of "late capitalism," although my use of the term overlaps with theirs in a number of ways. By "late capitalism" I mean the neoliberal capitalist regime currently dominant in the so-called Western world, which is marked by at least four key elements: first, the prominence of finance capital markets and cross-national investment, often resulting in exploitation of so-called "underdeveloped nations" (see Harvey 2005 and 2007; Naomi Klein offers a somewhat popularized version of Harvey's thesis in Klein 2007); second, neoliberal forms of governmentality (in the Foucauldian sense), under which citizens are encouraged to pursue their own freedom, and where "freedom" turns out to dovetail with consumerism (see Giddens 1991, Rose 1998 and 1999, and Rose and Miller 1998); third, forms of cultural production whereby social

that the experience/institution distinction is a building block of a modern, domesticated religion of the status quo, which has incarnations in both modern "spirituality," as well as liberal forms of Christianity. I do not claim that all uses of "religious experience" and "institutional religion" advance late capitalism, but that they are easily and often aligned with late capitalist norms.

EXPERIENCE VS. INSTITUTION[2]

I want to set the stage with a brief anecdote about teaching William James's *Varieties of Religious Experience*, shared by J. Z. Smith in *Relating Religion*:

> What my college students derive from [James's *Varieties*] is their own take on religion read back to them: the priority of the individual, the centrality of experience and feeling, a vague but palpable sense of transcendence, a distrust of thought about religion (especially from "afar"), and the necessity of raising questions of ethical implications. None of these are helpful to a science of religion. If Harvard is to be our guide in the construction of such a science, I far prefer the lectures of James's colleague and critic, Josiah Royce. In his *The Problem of Christianity* Royce privileged both a theory of language and of community—two essential elements in any theoretical proposal concerning religion. Both are lacking in James.
>
> (Smith 2004, 162)

What is it about James's approach that makes it so easily appropriated by contemporary students (as well as others—often those who enjoy publishing success in popular literature on religion, such as Karen Armstrong)?[3] Of course Smith's students' "take on religion" is not simply the result of the vast influence of William James; it is not that his ideas have been so widely disseminated that their interest in him is merely the result of the "trickle-down" effect of his theories into popular culture. James is only one person in a long line of thinking about religion that utilizes an inward/outward dichotomy, opposing

---

identities and differences are manufactured, marketed, and consumed (Marshall Sahlins calls it "bourgeois totemism"—see Sahlins 1976, Bourdieu 1984, 1993, 1998, and 2003, and Halter 2000); fourth, a neoliberal ideology that legitimates "free markets" with talk of "the self-made man" and "individual responsibility" while obscuring the extent to which social conditions, social networks, and classes of origin are keys to success in a capitalist regime (see Carrette and King 2005, and Bourdieu 1998 and 2003; also related is Emerson and Smith 2000).

2. Although I do not cite or quote from these secondary sources, my analysis throughout this section is dependent on the insights of Russell McCutcheon (2001, 2003, and 2005), Tim Murphy (2007), and Jeremy Carrette and Richard King (2005).

3. Although it might seem from this and what follows that I have no respect for William James, I want to point out that I have a great deal of appreciation for his pragmatism and similar philosophical writings— just not for his theory of religion.

inward "spirituality" to "institutional religion." Talk of "institutional religion" has a long history that can be traced from Erasmus' inside/outside distinction, to appeals for tolerance following the Protestant Reformation (according to which the magistrate should leave religion alone because the essence of religion was the connection between God and the individual soul), to anti-Catholic sentiment in general, to Protestant Pietism, to French anti-clericalism, to James's focus on religious experience as at the core of religion, up to today's "I'm spiritual, but not religious" (SBNR) movement.

James offers us an important example of this discourse in practice. Historically speaking, as a philosopher his writings on religion lent an air of authority and credibility to the experience/institution distinction. "James's stature as a 'highbrow' intellectual has cast an aura of respectability over the continuing public fascination" with religious experience (Fuller 2001, 58). Indeed, "Academic departments of psychology, philosophy, and religious studies consider him one of the most influential thinkers in the history of their disciplines" (134). Both inside and outside of the discipline of religious studies, James is held up as an important theorist of religion. His work is therefore important both because his model for thinking about religion was widely influential and because he provides a particularly clear example of this broader experience/institution discursive tradition being put to work.

In this broader tradition—again, of which James is but a part—we can trace the following distinctions, each of which builds on the prior associations.

Primary term	Secondary term
Inside	Outside
Inward religion	Outward religion
Faith	Works
Inward sincerity	Outward dead ritual
Christianity	Judaism
Protestantism	Catholicism
True religion	False religion
Soul	Body
Spiritual	Temporal
Invisible church	Visible church
Religion	Civil society
Religion	Magic
Religious experience	Institutional religion
Personal religion	Organized religion
Religion	Fundamentalism
Spirituality	Religion[4]

Of course, the term "religion" appears on both sides of this set of homologies, but even when it swaps sides the same primary/secondary distinction is maintained: when people

---

4. For an extensive account of how these distinctions were put to use in liberal discourses following the Protestant Reformation, see Martin 2010, especially chapters 2 and 3.

say "I'm spiritual, but not religious" they are playing off the existing primary/secondary rhetorical associations, not reversing them.

This discursive tradition often depends upon a supernatural ontology and anthropology, according to which all humans have souls and bodies, and true religion (or spirituality) is linked to the soul stuff, not the body stuff. Getting caught up in the external, second-ary, bodily stuff is ultimately to miss the authentic, inward experience of the divine. Thus Luther could call Judaism a religion of works righteousness disconnected from sincere faith in God; Protestants could say the same of Catholicism; James could consider all institutional religions secondary accretions built on personal religious experiences; and the SBNR groups can say that all organized religions are unnecessary diversions from authentic experiences of transcendence.

As a pragmatist, James tends to be wary of such supernaturalist ontologies, and we can see his suspicion in *The Varieties of Religious Experience*. He makes it clear that he does not intend to give much "ontological umpf" (a phrase I've stolen from Russell McCutcheon) to the distinction between "personal" and "institutional" religion. He writes:

> Now in these lectures I propose to ignore the institutional branch entirely, to say nothing of the ecclesiastical organization, to consider as little as possible the sys-tematic theology and the ideas about the gods themselves, and to confine myself as far as I can to personal religion pure and simple. To some of you personal religion, thus nakedly considered, will no doubt seem too incomplete a thing to wear the general name. ...
>
> But if you say this, it will only show the more plainly how much the question of definition tends to become a dispute about names. Rather than prolong such a dispute, I am willing to accept almost any name for the personal religion of which I propose to treat. Call it conscience or morality, if you yourselves prefer, and not religion—under either name it will be equally worthy of our study.
>
> (James 2004, 37–8)[5]

This is a typical pragmatist (and nominalist) gesture. In sum, James is suggesting some-thing like the following: "We are not talking about 'personal religion' in the sense of some Kantian 'noumena'—rather, I'm using the phrase 'personal religion' to pick out something in the world of interest to me. We could just as well divide the world up differently by using different words or by using the same words differently." This nominalist gesture is one with which I have a great deal of sympathy. However, in the following paragraph James goes on to put the "ontological umpf" back in:

> In one sense at least the personal religion will prove itself more fundamental than either theology or ecclesiasticism. Churches, when once established, live at

---

5. If here and in what follows I extensively quote James and representatives of those with similar views, it is because I do not want to be accused of constructing a "straw man."

second-hand upon tradition; but the *founders* of every church owed their power originally to the fact of their direct personal communion with the divine. Not only the superhuman founders, the Christ, the Buddha, Mahomet [sic], but all the originators of Christian sects have been in this case;—so personal religion should still seem the primordial thing, even to those who continue to esteem it incomplete. (38)

Later in the book he suggests that the religious experiences he has put his finger on are the "nucleus" (432) or the "essence" (433) of religion. He therefore reclaims the ontological ground he gave up in the previous paragraphs. This "personal religion" *is* primary or fundamental just as the soul is primary in the soul/body supernatural ontology. That is, James is making precisely the sort of ontological distinction he claims not to be making.

This ontologizing of the distinction leads to dehistoricization (i.e., mystification) in two ways. First, because the distinction is ontologized, it is difficult for people to see that the very distinction is a social construction, the product of a history for which we can perform a genealogy. Much like the public/private distinction unique to modern Western thought (see McCutcheon 2003 and 2005, and Martin 2010), this distinction is taken for granted as if it were a feature of the universe, rather than a product of human thought. As such, it is taken to be "discovered" in the world rather than "created." Because of this, its social or ideological effects are underanalyzed—or, rather, they aren't analyzed at all. (I'll return to the consequences of this naïve empiricism below.)

Second, and more importantly, the ontologizing of this distinction prevents the historicization of what the distinction presumes to identify or discover in the world: both "religious experience" *and* "religious institutions." On the surface, it would seem to prevent the historicization of only the former: the distinction implies that religious experience is pure, direct, unmediated, outside the effects of time, space, and history, whereas institutions are precisely those things that are mediated, inside time, space, and history, and can be analyzed using the methods of history (unlike experience itself). That is, in a way that hearkens back to the spiritual/temporal distinction used in the sixteenth, seventeenth, and eighteenth centuries, what the latter term identifies is subject to history and therefore can in principle be historicized, while the former cannot. By contrast, I'm arguing that while it obviously renders "experience" outside the realm of history—for it is of "the transcendent"—it simultaneously renders "religious institutions" outside of history. By ontologizing "institutions" as opposite to "experiences," they are rendered unchanging and unalterable in key ways: institutions are universally *secondary, derivative*. Institutions are just as ahistorical as experiences here: no matter where you look in time and space, religious institutions will be the same.

The SBNR discourse has displaced James's use of "religion"; for this discourse, "religion" is the second term rather than the first term in the dichotomy, and James's "religion" has been replaced with "spirituality." Hence we get the following (which I've taken from a discussion board on Facebook's SBNR group, and which I take to be a paradigmatic example of the discourse I'm examining [I've left the capitalization, spelling, grammar, and punctuation as it was in the original]):

To me Religion is a set of rules set down by man and it is Man, through Man, through god. Religion has always been the bane of mans existence. Look at Europe during the Reformation where Christian was killing Christian of minor differences in religion. Whether to baptize a baby or wait until adult hood, whether to pay for indulgences or not. Let alone how many non-Christians were brutalized and killed during these times because of religious ideas.

Look at the Middle East where Muslim is killing Muslim over who the successor of Mohammed is when ultimately that shouldn't really matter, the words of the Prophet are what matters and the spirit of Islam not the personal interpretations of particular individuals.

Spiritualism or faith is something directly between you and your God or Gods, it is a pure set of ideas which come from your mind and heart and not from the rules of a man made church, it comes from your interpretations of your Scriptures not taking the words of another man who is no better then you. It comes from you and you lone with your relationship with the spirit.

religion empowers evil men to do evil things in the name of benevolent beings for religion does not allow from deviation from interpretation. Religion does not allow one to freely think hence the term Heresy which when broken down to its original etymology means "Free thinker"

Spiritualism allows a person to think for themselves to make their own choices in faith based off their own observations. It is a pure and direct link to god where one is governed by their conscience which is the voice of The One, not governed by the Religions which is the voice of man.

Even the Bible will tell you we are self guided as we ate of the Tree of Knowledge of Good and Evil, whereby we are now born with the innate knowledge of both. The original sin is when knowing naturally what is right or wrong we choose wrong. You are more apt to choose wrong if you let others tell you what Right is.

Your are your own Judge

This author reproduces the elements we find in James's ontology[6] (while adding some matters James would not) and essentializes each term in the dichotomy: on the one hand is spiritualism or faith, purity, individuality,[7] direct connection with divinity, freedom,

---

6. I do not mean to suggest that this author incorporated these discursive elements after having read James directly—these are elements of a dominant discourse of which both James and this individual are only particular examples.

7. There is of course one exception: the author of this post associates *individual* interpretations of Muhammad with the second, derivative set of associations, presumably because some individuals interpret Muhammad's message or experience inauthentically.

thinking-for-oneself, innate knowledge (specifically of good and evil), rightness, and on the other hand is religion (i.e., institutional religion), violence, mediated connection with divinity (through "man" and man's "interpretation"), secondary knowledge, evil and wrongness, and the imposition of the group on the individual (possibly "groupthink" or "herd mentality"). There is no room for historical variability—the second term has essential features that are unchanging.

To reiterate: whereas one might think that James's distinction might lead to the historicization of "institutional religion" if not "religious experience," it seems that his legacy has been aligned with forbidding the historicization of either term: "institutional religion" is always and ever degraded, secondary, and imposing on human individual and freedom. As a result of the ontologization of the experience/institution dichotomy, neither are truly subjected to historical analysis. (This ahistorical essentialization is part of a teleological folk theory of religion, which I will discuss further below.)

"INSTITUTIONAL RELIGION" AS A NAÏVE, CRYPTO-NORMATIVE RHETORICAL DEVICE

Because James's rhetoric and the SBNR discourse are ontological and essentialist, they lend themselves to naïve empiricism. Academic scholars are, in a sense, all Foucauldians now: the world is not simply "there" to be discovered; not only do we constitute the world through language, but we can also investigate what historical conditions led to us constituting the world the way that we do. By contrast, the naïve empiricism of the ontologized spirituality/institutional religion dichotomy results in subjects just "finding" spirituality and "finding" religion in the world, with nary a concern about how this way of dividing the world is historically constituted.

A byproduct of this naïve empiricism is that it becomes that much easier to use the phrase "institutional religion" as a pejorative term. In fact, the phrase is used precisely because of the negative associations that have come to be connected to it. *This rhetoric is intrinsically polemical.* "Institutional religion" is inherently a *bad thing*, and as such it is deployed as an insult, like the word "cult." One need not show what is bad about a so-called "cult"—the mere application of the word calls forth a negative evaluation and a set of social prescriptions. In addition, outside of those rare occasions where "fundamentalism" is used to refer to early twentieth-century evangelical Christian movements that emphasized the "five fundamentals," the word "fundamentalism" is similarly pejorative. When my students refer to a group as "fundamentalist," I need not inquire into how they might evaluate such a group—I already know they view such a group negatively. When words such as these are used, careful description is traded for what amounts to name-calling. One pretends to find institutional religion in the world, but one is in fact passing off one's own evaluations under the guise of description.

Together these two elements—naïve empiricism and the crypto-normative nature of the phrase "institutional religion"—end up functioning much like conservative Christian hermeneutics. Conservative Christians sometimes "interpret" the world using a certain hermeneutic that, once it gets off the ground, is self-confirming and impregnable. We see this in analyses of their god's presence in the world. When something good happens, that is interpreted as the hand of their god. When something bad happens, that is interpreted as the work of the devil. This hermeneutic works through projection of a subject's assumptions onto the world: what makes something "God's hand" or "the devil's hand" is not some objective feature of an event or object in the world itself, but the subject's view of what is good or bad. Anything the subject sees as good could be God's hand; anything the subject views as bad could be the devil's hand. The hermeneutic turns not on the world but on the subject's background assumptions about what is good or bad. The hermeneutic doesn't evaluate evidence so much as merely sort evidence. Bad things are slotted into the category "the devil's work." As such, counterfactuals are simply unthinkable—once a subject internalizes this hermeneutic, it is possible that nothing could contradict it.[8]

The "institutional religion" rhetoric is not identical, but it works similarly. What an individual takes to be "organized religion" as opposed to "true spirituality" will follow not from some objective features of things in the world but from the subject's background assumptions. One might think that "organization" is the key, but it is not—there are several SBNR organizations.[9] Rather, the word "organized" in "organized religion" is emptied of its usual content; what makes some instance of religion "organized" is not its features, but rather the fact that the subject making the identification does not like it. If one likes zazen, it is likely a portal to pure, internal religious experience; if one doesn't like zazen, it is probably a secondary ritual performance utilized by religious practitioners who are just "going through the motions" in an institutional setting. In addition, not only is this process invisible to the subjects employing this hermeneutic—that is, the subjects think they are discovering something in the world rather than projecting themselves onto it— but the fact that their background assumptions themselves are socially constituted will likely remain invisible.[10]

---

8. I see this when my conservative Christian family members interpret events in their lives as evidence that their god is answering their prayers—any positive life event that can be linked to a prayer request is the work of their god, and any apparent failure to answer a prayer is either the work of the devil or part of the inscrutable long-term plans of their god. Apparently counterfactual evidence to the claim that "God answers prayers" is easily slotted into one of these latter categories and thereby neutralized. We arguably find this naïve hermeneutic not only in conservative Christianity, but in conservative Judaism, conservative Islam, etc. In addition, we can find it in liberal forms of these religious traditions as well—although the events taken to be signs of "God's hand" are swapped to reflect left-leaning social views.

9. This is not indicative of bald hypocrisy; here the word "organization" is used like a symbol. In fact, the colloquial meaning of the term is probably largely irrelevant; what chiefly matters is that the term carries pejorative connotations. We see the same thing with the way the term "Nazi" is applied to people or groups—even Jews—who have absolutely no connection with Nazism and who the Nazis would have hated.

10. Armed with an impervious hermeneutic, and one whose function is invisible, the author of the quotation above (from the SBNR Facebook page) can sort anything he doesn't like into the category "organized religion" and anything he does like into the category "true spirituality." The fact that he is projecting a reality rather than discovering one is unlikely to be noticed, and the fact that his background assumptions about what is good or bad are products of his own social, cultural, and institutional context remains

Those who utilize the SBNR rhetoric are not the only ones unable to historicize their own common sense. In *The Scandal of the Evangelical Mind*, Mark A. Noll criticizes American evangelicals' almost complete inability to historicize their own position and their own hermeneutic. In part his criticism is directed at the fact that evangelical populism is heavily dependent on the projection of their own "common sense" as if it were universally common sense. Noll locates this in the American evangelicals' appropriation of Scottish enlightenment thought, which emphasized "that all humans possessed, by nature, a common set of capacities … through which they could grasp the basic realities of nature and morality" (Noll 1994, 85). This appeal to their own inner common sense as common sense *tout court* had the effect of authorizing their values as universal. The naïve empiricism of the SBNR discourse works much the same way, and therefore it is no surprise that the author quoted above appealed to a universal common sense in justification for his position. For him, objective right and wrong are no different than what he discovers to be right and wrong when he turns to his own inner conscience—which he views as "pure" and as the direct result of thinking for oneself.[11] In addition, his inherited rhetoric is easily historically locatable in a particular social context, but it is precisely that which prevents him from seeing his institutional context.

It is worthwhile returning to Noll's evangelicals at this point. He argues that their biblical hermeneutic in the first half of the twentieth century was linked to a certain form of creation science, which was obviously a historical response to the rise of evolutionary accounts of human origins. However, the historical location of their particular biblical hermeneutic was lost on them: "millions of evangelicals think they are defending the Bible by defending creation science, but in reality they are giving ultimate authority to the merely temporal, situated, and contextualized interpretations of the Bible that arose from the mania for science of the nineteenth century" (Noll 1994, 199). That is, they misrecognize their local hermeutic as *the* hermeneutic of the Bible, and misunderstand the Bible as a result. I am arguing similarly: the application of the experience/institution distinction as ontologically built into the nature of the universe allows individuals to take their own local values and local hermeneutic (embedded of course in local interests and local battles), project them onto the world or interpret the world in terms of them, and as such mistake their creation for reality itself. This is naïve empiricism at its best: "individuals" opposed to "institutions" are unable to see themselves and their world as historically constituted by particular institutions (discursive and otherwise). In addition, their crypto-normative evaluation of "institutional religion" passes as objective because they are incapable of seeing the extent to which their evaluation is the result of a projective hermeneutic—and

---

invisible. Ironically, his institutional context (which has given him his background assumptions as well as the rhetoric he uses to sort the world) manifests itself in his scheme as pure, inward spirituality: his institutionally and socially produced "common sense" is taken to be inward truth. That is, what he takes to be "inside" is precisely what is from the "outside."

11. He misses the irony that this claim is being used to advance a certain morality at the same time that he argues that listening to "others" about what is right and wrong is bound to be "wrong." That is, he calls for a universal moral individualism at the same time that he advances this as a moral imperative for other individuals.

one that is, ironically, relatively identical to the hermeneutic of the "religious" people—that is, Noll's evangelicals—to which they rhetorically oppose themselves.

One might argue that I've strayed too far from James; the SBNR discourse is not *The Varieties of Religious Experience*. But we find the same crypto-normative language passing itself off as a description of the facts of the matter in James's *Varieties*. He talks about "institutional religion" with the following normative rhetoric: "corporate ambitions," "the spirit of politics and the lust of dogmatic rule," "hypocrisy and tyranny and meanness and tenacity of superstition" (2004, 293), "baseness," "bigotries," and "the spirit of dogmatic dominion" (296), "corruption by excess" (297), and "fanaticism" (298). James goes on to note that religious wars are not caused by true religious experience but by xenophobic tribalism inherent in the human spirit but distinct from true piety.[12] How does one know that true piety has passed into corruption or excess? "Common sense must judge" (297). Little attempt is made to situate the social-cultural infrastructure that informs moral judgment and "common sense," and James does not take note of the fact that what he takes to be "common sense" might very well have been taken by others as "fanatical," and vice versa— and it is at this point that James's own ahistorical naïve empiricism shines through.[13]

A FOLK THEORY OF RELIGION

James's discourse, in so far as it privileges a religious experience at the foundation of every religion, encourages a return-to-origins narrative that distorts history and prevents useful analysis of religious traditions. James's theory of religion is extremely superficial; it goes something like this: a divine power strikes like lightning, giving an individual a pure experience he then shares with others. His teachings are, however, degraded when they are taken up by followers interested merely in power. While elements of the original, pure

---

12. "I beseech you never to confound the phenomena of mere tribal or corporate psychology which it presents with those manifestations of the purely interior life which are the exclusive object of our study. The baiting of Jews, the hunting of Albigenses and Waldenses, the stoning of Quakers and ducking of Methodists, the murdering of Mormons and the massacring of Armenians, express much rather that aboriginal human neophobia, that pugnacity of which we all share the vestiges, and that inborn hatred of the alien and of eccentric and nonconforming men as aliens, than they express the positive piety of the various perpetrators. Piety is the mask, the inner force is tribal instinct" (James 2004, 296).

13. So our poster to the Facebook SBNR page is not at all far from the discourse James too has incorporated. He insists that outward religion is responsible for Muslim internecine warfare ("Look at the Middle East where Muslim is killing Muslim over who the successor of Muhammad is when ultimately that shouldn't really matter, the words of the Prophet are what matters and the spirit of Islam not the personal interpretations of particular individuals"); he insists that true religion is pure, unmediated ("Spiritualism or faith is something directly between you and your God or Gods") and individual ("Spiritualism allows a person to think for themselves to make their own choices in faith based off their own observations"); and outward religion is best judged by universal common sense ("Even the Bible will tell you we are self guided as we ate of the Tree of Knowledge of Good and Evil, whereby we are now born with the innate knowledge of both"; "Your are your own Judge").

message—derived from the experience—can be found in the teaching that is passed down by his followers, it is used—wrongly—to control others. The institutional religions that result from this degradation are extremely authoritarian and require strict obedience from all members. Religious practitioners are little different from automatons. The development of all religions follows this same trajectory.[14]

But this is not a social theory of religion—it is an ahistorical teleology that presumes all religious traditions form in exactly the same way. It suffers from the teleological excesses for which Hegel's theory of religion is rightly rejected. On this theory, historical differences do not matter, since all institutional religions are essentially the same. As I noted above, the religious experience/institutional religion dichotomy contributes to the dehistoricization of both "experience" and "institutions." It is only through this dehistoricization that James can mention Jesus, the Buddha, and Muhammad in the same breath, as if they functionally had the same experiences that gave rise to essentially identical, second-hand, authoritarian institutions. This is a popular, folk theory of religion, and it is a superficial one.

What this folk theory allows, however, is for people to tell a narrative into which they can slot their own favorite "good guys" and "bad guys." If we don't like al Qaeda, we can articulate this story onto the group. Our story will go something like this: at the origin of Islam, Muhammad had an experience with the divine, but his followers degraded that message and wrote things into the Qur'an about killing infidels; Al Qaeda has taken that degraded message and formed an extremist, authoritarian institution, according to which all who do not agree with their strict views should be killed; they are killing in the name of God because they misunderstand the true message of the Prophet.

This sort of popular folk narrative—which will likely be familiar to those who work with popular rhetoric about Islam[15]—provides an explanation for al Qaeda's actions that need not bear any relationship to historical or empirical research. Because all organized religions are more or less fundamentally identical, we need investigate neither what al Qaeda actually says nor the socio-political context in which they are situated. We need not think

---

14. Lest readers think I've distorted James's view in *Varieties*, here is the evidence: (1) All religions start with a "direct personal communication with the divine" (James 2004, 38); (2) the experiences constitute the "essential" (433) "nucleus" (432) of religion; (3) institutional religion is a secondary thing created by "disciples" and "sympathizers" with a "lust for dogmatic rule" (293); (4) institutional religion "contaminate[s] the originally innocent thing," and becomes tied up with "hypocrisy and tyranny and meanness" (293); (5) institutional religion expresses a "tribal instinct," and all "fanaticism" produced by this is external to "the purely interior life" (296); (6) institutional religion requires "exclusive devotion" and "idealizes the devotion itself" (298); (7) the excessiveness or fanatical nature of institutional religion can be judged by "common sense" (297); (8) institutional religion is the same for "every church" (38), for these things are "almost always the same" (433).

15. Here is one example: a high school student's PowerPoint slideshow on "The Dangers of Organized Religion," made available on the web, shows a picture of the World Trade Center towers burning, and the following bullet points lie in the foreground: "Today, modern theology differs greatly from its foundations"; "However, traditional interpretation of holy texts often leads to violent, terrorist behavior"; "Needless to say, this behavior is harmful to humanity, causing death, destruction, and terror"; "This is because organized religion today provides multiple justifications of murder and destruction" (Moran 2009).

about all of the following matters: the United States' alliances with Saudi Arabia from the end of World War II onward; the United States' military involvement in Saudi Arabia—an absolute monarchy with ongoing human rights violations—from the early 1990s to 2003; the United States' unwavering support of Israel and its repression of Palestine; the United States' alliance with the mujahedin and the use of Afghanistan to fight a proxy war with the USSR, a war that resulted in the deaths of hundreds of thousands of Afghani civilians; the United States' participation in sanctions against Iraq that resulted in deaths of an estimated half a million Iraqi children; etc. The social, cultural, and political context that might give rise to al Qaeda is irrelevant; an eternally recurring storyline is substituted for historical investigation.

If all organized religions are the same, the following contemporary blogger can negatively characterize al Qaeda, the IRA, and the medieval Catholic church in the same breath:

> War is an obvious effect of organized religion, and there are many examples of this. The Catholic Protestant war in Ireland is a perfect example of this. The crusades are another fine example of organized religion creating havoc. The most recent example is the World Trade Center and the Iraq war. It is supposedly because of religion.[16] ... [O]ur government makes it seem like something new when it is not. Organized religion is meant to unite people, but in many cases it has only accomplished separation, stereotypes, and war amongst peoples. (Ganly 2007)

Al Qaeda, the IRA, and the medieval Catholic church go together because the story of "organized religion" is not new; on the contrary, here we are dealing with the eternal recurrence of "good guys vs. bad guys." And James's view is little different; as I noted above, for James these things are "almost always the same."

This superficial theory is understandable when it comes from novices uninitiated in the methodologies and theories of those in religious studies or the social sciences generally, but it is unacceptable from a Harvard scholar with access to an Ivy League university library—leafing through the stacks for an hour or two would reveal that one must do a great deal of data manipulation to get all those traditions we call religious to fit into this straitjacket.

"INSTITUTIONAL RELIGION," LATE CAPITALISM, AND CONSUMERISM

How is this dehistoricizing discourse easily aligned with late capitalism? If this rhetoric masks the source of social norms by positing them as springing from the soul or from

---

16. Here the author says "supposedly because of religion," which might be interpreted to contradict my thesis; however, from the surrounding passage I take the author to mean something like this: it is supposedly because of religion, but it is *really* because of *organized* religion.

common sense, from where do those norms come? What follows is a tentative attempt to address these questions.

I want to begin by situating James's view and the SBNR discourse alongside other modern, liberal religious traditions. Liberal forms of Western religions are often distinguished from premodern forms by using the category of "privatization," but I believe Bruce Lincoln's maximalist/minimalist distinction is more useful for understanding some of the changes that came about in the Western world during the modern period. For Lincoln, in Europe prior to modernity, Christianity was the "central domain of culture" (Lincoln 2006, 59). The social order was ordered, legitimated, sustained, and contested through the use of Christian vocabulary, Christian stories, Christian institutions, and so on. Lincoln uses the term "maximalist" to identify this state of affairs—during this period religion had a "maximal" relation to social order.

By contrast, Lincoln suggests that after the rise of capitalism the economy becomes the "central domain of culture" (59). The world at large becomes ordered, legitimated, sustained, and contested by economic rationalities, discourses, and practices. When this happens, economics in a sense becomes "maximalist," while religion is moved to a "minimalist" position.

For Lincoln, when religion is in the "maximalist" position, "cultural preferences [are] constituted largely as morality and stabilized by religion"; in addition, religious minimalism is "experienced as powerful and intrusive; a serious temptation for would-be elites and a dangerous threat to all" (59). When religious minimalism is hegemonic, however, "cultural preferences [are] constituted largely as fashion and open to market fluctuations"; in addition, religious maximalism is "experienced in two ways: a quaint, seductive diversion for some, and as a resentful atavism, capable of reactionary counterattacks" (59). By this I take Lincoln to mean, for instance, that for people who adopt religious minimalism, those who do not—like the American Amish or al Qaeda—are taken to be either "quaint" (interesting for sightseers) or dangerous.[17]

What do we gain by replacing the public religion/privatized religion dichotomy with the maximalist/minimalist one? We can recognize that those institutions we colloquially call religions have clearly taken a subordinate role to modern Western capitalism: for most of us in the modern Western world, our lives are ordered more by our jobs, our taxes, our retirement accounts, our mortgages, our car payments, and our credit card debts—all in pursuit of social distinction that bears a capitalist flavor, if Pierre Bourdieu and Marshall Sahlins are to be believed (Bourdieu 1984 and Sahlins 1976)—than we are by the moral norms of Judaism, Christianity, or Islam. However, this need not imply that there is something "private" about Judaism, Christianity, or Islam. For instance, evangelical Christians

---

17. I am somewhat uncomfortable with Lincoln's distinction between religion and economics; while I would not say they are identical, I'm not sure it makes sense to register an ontological distinction between them (and perhaps Lincoln would not). Why not just say that Christianity went from being a maximalist discourse and set of practices to a minimalist position, but capitalism then replaced Christianity as the maximalist discourse and set of practices? Doing so would not result in positing some sort of fundamental distinction between "religion" and other forms of culture.

are highly active politically—to call their form of Christianity a "private matter" is to say something relatively nonsensical and vacuous of critical import.[18]

As capitalism becomes the dominant discourse and set of practices that order modern Western life, minimalist forms of previously maximalist traditions emerge. We see the development of forms of liberal Christianity, for instance, that make fewer and fewer demands on the lives of its practitioners. Despite contemporary Evangelicals' insistence that one should not be a Christian only on Sunday morning, most Christians *are*, in a manner of speaking. Groups like the Amish, whose members' lives are primarily ordered, legitimated, and maintained through their form of Christianity, are a rarity today. By contrast, subjects whose lives are ordered by capitalism think such groups quaint or extremist, as Lincoln rightly suggests. Any group that would demand that adherents actually *adhere* to a habitus at odds with Western consumerism is almost by definition "fanatical."[19] By contrast, religious groups that make few if any demands on members' lives—or at least demands that might conflict or chafe against late capitalism and its consumer culture—have grown in popularity.[20] As capitalism has replaced Christianity's hegemonic position, most contemporary American Christians spend more time in shopping malls than in church, more time watching commercials than reading the Bible.[21]

Christian Smith and Melinda Lundquist Denton demonstrate in *Soul Searching: The Religious and Spiritual Lives of American Teenagers* (2005) that the majority of contemporary American teenagers—from many different religious traditions—are, for all practical purposes, minimalist deists. They do not reject the religious traditions of their parents— they are neither anti-clerical nor do they identify as "spiritual but not religious"—but when asked to describe their religion, it amounts to the belief that God exists, he wants everyone to be happy and good, and if we are good he will reward us by sending us to heaven. Smith

---

18. However, although talk about religion as a "private matter" might be devoid of critical import, it is not devoid of significance—arguments about the essentially private nature of religion advance social agendas even when they are not strictly true.

19. And if one's religious tradition requires one to move into shared living space, it's probably a "cult." According to Terry Eagleton—in a discussion of the rise of the popularity of atheism—more and more people are paying attention to religion, "even in England, where religion is in general a rather moderate, discrete, slightly shamefaced affair—and ... where people are likely to believe that when religion starts interfering with your everyday life that it's time to give it up. In that sense it resembles alcohol, I suppose." As long as one can hold a job and remain a consumer—thereby responsibly contributing to the economy— religion and alcohol are acceptable; once they begin interrupting one's responsible contributions to the economy, that is when people start to raise eyebrows. See "The God Debate," part of the Gifford lecture series at Edinburgh University (available at http://www.youtube.com/watch?v=QCqHnwIR1PY).

20. Evangelical Christianity and Mormonism have also grown in this time period, although for reasons independent of those discussed in this essay. I recognize they are an exception to what I am arguing here, and note that an account of their popularity would require a consideration of a separate set of discursive strategies and sociological issues.

21. Such Christians are often called "nominally" Christian, but the word "nominally" makes a (dubious) judgment of orthodoxy: it implies they are *not really* Christians. Although I'm guilty of using the word "nominally" myself, here I would argue that such Christians are not "false" but merely different from, for instance, more maximalist evangelical Christians.

and Denton call this "moralistic, therapeutic deism" (MTD) because of its thin content about the nature of the god identified and the emphasis on morality and happiness.

MTD is extremely minimalist, in Lincoln's sense of the term. Smith and Denton write,

> We talked with the teens we interviewed about what they get enthusiastic about, what pressing issues they are dealing with, and what forces and experiences and routines seem to them most important and central to their lives. Most teenagers talk about friends, school, sports, television, music, movies, romantic interests, family relationships, dealing with issues of drugs and alcohol, various organized activities with which they're involved, and specific fun or formative events they have experienced. (Smith and Denton 2005, 130)

That is, they paint a picture of what life is like for a teenager in a late capitalist consumer society. "What rarely arises in such conversations are teens' religious identities, beliefs, experiences, or practices. Religion just does not naturally seem to appear much on most teenagers' open-ended lists of what really matters in their lives" (130). This is precisely what one would expect where consumer capitalism takes the "maximalist" position—one's Christian, Jewish, or Muslim identity is simply not demanding on or formative of one's life. "[M]ost teens seem content to live with a low-visibility religion that operates somewhere in the mental background of their lives" (137).[22] It is therefore no surprise that the teenagers interviewed do not find "religion" to be a point of conflict in their lives (cf. 122 ff.); one's religious identity would only be a point of conflict if it informed one's behavior in a way that caused friction with the behavior of others. If one's religious identity makes no demands on one's behavior, then "religious conflict" would be relatively inconceivable.

For many of the teens, MTD was paired with a rejection of any maximalist religious tradition: if one's religious tradition makes substantial demands on one's behavior, particularly demands that conflict with modern consumerism (like one's clothing practices), it is fanatical or extreme. An important category for them was the category of people who are "too religious" (141). When describing those who Lincoln might call maximalist, these

---

22. Although most of these teens often explicitly said their religious tradition was really important to them, it appeared not to be when they were pressed for examples. Their religious identities were so minimalist that it was almost impossible for teens to articulate *any* practical consequence of their tradition for their lives. One girl suggested that her faith prevents her from hanging out with Satanists, and another boy suggested that his religion teaches important moral prohibitions, "like murder or something" (139). Smith and Denton comment: "perhaps this boy does struggle with murderous tendencies, but more probably, this explanation merely establishes religious influences in a way that is not too demanding or threatening to his routine life" (139). If their religious identity *does* make demands on them, those demands are noticeable due to the way they conflict with consumerism. "One sixteen-year-old Seventh Day Adventist girl, for instance, explained the difference her faith makes in this way: 'Well, without my faith, my life would be different, um, I'd go shopping on Saturday 'cause they always have sales on Saturdays'" (139). This is minimalism indeed: "our impression is that ... the teens are simply groping for something, anything that might confirm their claim that religion is indeed important in their lives. And sometimes they seem to have to grope hard *because it actually is not very important*" (140).

teens started using the following pejorative vocabulary, phrases, and comparisons: holier than thou, sanctimonious, holy roller, Ned Flanders, weird, church-y, following everything to a T, fanatic, annoying, Jesus freak, overboard, extreme (141–3).[23]

If religion is tied up with morality, what is moral? "One of the key teenage assumptions in this religion–morality equation is that right and wrong are simply common sense, something everyone just knows. For most teens, morality is not something that requires much thought or discernment. "Everyone knows it" (155). The fact that "common sense" is both variable and a product of socialization is nowhere recognized. As a result, the local social and moral norms pass as if they were universal. Although these teens are socialized by a capitalist and consumerist social, cultural, and institutional context—all of which informs their ideas of what is morally right and wrong—they misidentify the moral norms they accept as springing from deep within the self.

In one particularly telling interview, a "fourteen-year-old conservative Protestant girl" reveals how God's goodness is tied up with modern capitalist life:

[Interviewer]: When you think of God, what image do you have of God?
[Teenager]: [yawning]
I: What is God like?
T: Um, good. Powerful.
I: Okay, anything else?
T: Tall.
I: Tall?
T: Big.
I: Do you think God is active in people's lives or not?
T: Ah, I don't know.
I: You're not sure?
T: Different people have different views of him.
I: What about your view?
T: What do you mean?
I: Do you think God is active in your life?
T: In my life? Yeah.
I: Yeah, hmmm. Would you say you feel close to God or not really?
T: Yeah, I feel close. [yawns]
I: Where do you get your ideas about God?
T: The Bible, my mom, church. Experience.
I: What kind of experience?
T: He's just done a lot of good in my life, so.
I: Like, what are examples of that?
T: I don't know.

---

23. One teen puts it well: "Sometimes people that are more religious take it to an extreme, like sure, but after a point, when are you going to finally live your life?" (143) I take it that "live your life" implies living life as a consumer in late capitalism—anything else would amount to *not* living one's life.

I: Well, I'd love to hear. What good has God done in your life?

T: I, well, I have a house, parents, I have the Internet, I have a phone, I have cable.

(Smith and Denton 2005, 135)

In sum, this teenager's god is active in so far as he provides the amenities of bourgeois life in late capitalism. Apparently "good" means "middle-class." What is taken to be good is not derived from Protestantism but invisibly comes from late capitalist middle-class norms—but the latter are passed off as what God wants for us.[24]

Unlike the SBNR discourse, this MTD does not have a substantial anti-clerical strain to it (i.e., of the sort we see associated with talk of "institutional religion"). I would suggest that this deism need not have one, as these teenagers' "clerics" make no substantial demands on their behavior. The anti-clericalism of the SBNR discourse "kicks in," so to speak, when clerics make demands. Indeed, Robert C. Fuller argues that one thing that makes the SBNR discourse so appealing to its adherents is the fact that it makes no demands. "[A]lthough [spiritual] phenomena are intriguing, they don't affect the way most people go about their daily lives. … [T]he paranormal doesn't impose any religious demands" (Fuller 2001, 68).[25] However, Smith and Denton's MTD versions of Christianity, Judaism, and Islam rarely make any substantial demands. If Christianity has taken a form that is so easily articulated onto late capitalism that clerics make no demands that would conflict with it, then there would be no call for anti-clericalism. In addition, as Smith and Denton note, as soon as the teenagers are presented with forms of religious traditions where substantial demands are in fact made on adherents, they begin using the language of fanaticism and extremism. These teenagers, it seems, implicitly deploy a mainstream/extremist distinction that performs that same rhetorical function that the spirituality/religion distinction does for the SBNR groups. These religious teenagers are not anti-clerical, but they are just as opposed as the SBNR crowd to religious groups that demand anything of substance from adherents. *Their "religious" cultural tradition has been completely domesticated by the norms of late capitalism.*

We can therefore think of religious maximalism and minimalism along a continuum, where MTD is in the penultimate position, and the SBNR discourse is at the apogee of the minimalist pole. Both are features of late capitalism: most subjects' lives—whether they are "deist" or "spiritualist"—are directed by norms and practices related to late capitalism and consumerist culture. What perhaps distinguishes MTD from the SBNR discourse is that MTD suggests that one's values are derived from one's religious tradition: Smith's study

---

24. No doubt the Amish's rejection of the Internet or cable is taken as "extreme" or "fanatical."

25. It is therefore not surprising to find one opponent of "organized religion" say, "If you devote serious time to the practice of religion, it's safe to say you practice *toilet-bowl time management,* flushing much of your precious life down the drain with little or nothing to show for it…. [Y]ou can expect to waste even more time on repetitive ritual and ceremony, such as attending mass, learning prayers, and practicing unproductive meditations. …If I add up the time I attended mass and Sunday school, studied religion in school as if it were a serious subject, and memorized various prayers, I count thousands of hours of my life I'd love to have back…. The more time you devote to religious practice, the more you waste your life on pointless, dead-end pursuits" (Pavlina 2008).

shows that the teenagers interviewed—whether Jewish, Christian, Muslim, etc.—seemed to believe that their values and morals were derived from their traditions and sacred texts, although they also believed that the moral norms found, for instance, in the Bible, were identical to the universal moral norms of common sense (Smith and Denton 2005, 155). In a sense, the following equation is at work, with the terms on the left taking priority:

modern consumerist culture = common sense = what it says in the Bible

As a result, anything in the Bible that conflicts with consumerist culture or capitalist values must be a fanatical, secondary degradation or insertion.[26]

By contrast, the SBNR discourse jettisons even this minimal appeal to (or projection upon) tradition or scripture: values come from direct, pure experience with the divine or with spirits, not from degraded historical messages; we can all have the experiences of God that Jesus had, for instance, without having to pass through the Christian institution. In the end, however, it appears that the values of each are the values of late capitalism. The values of the teens studied by Smith and Denton are late capitalist consumerist values. In addition, most contemporary participants in the SBNR discourse are college educated and work in white-collar jobs (see Fuller 2001, 7); the SBNR discourse is a *middle-class discourse*.

While MTD and SBNR do not directly legitimate capitalism—i.e., they do not offer some sort of narrative according to which capitalism or class difference is divine (as did John Withrop in his "Model of Christian Charity" sermon, or Henry Ward Beecher in his "Individual Responsibility" sermon [see McCloud 2007, 109 ff.])—but they are aligned with it in so far as these discourses use the spirituality/institutional religion dichotomy (or some variant) in order to sanction any religious tradition that makes demands on practitioners that conflict with late capitalism: "institutional religion" that makes demands on subjects is fanatical or extremist. In the end, this discourse indirectly legitimates late capitalist norms and sanctions what falls outside of them—all the while mystifying those values by making it seem as if they spring from one's soul or common sense. The religious experience/institutional religion and spiritual/religious distinctions are perfect for this because they are more or less intrinsically ahistorical; they lend themselves to passing off the local as the universal and preventing one from historicizing the local. Late capitalism provides people with their values, but the spirituality/religion discourse makes it seem as if those values sprang directly from the soul.

It is for these reasons that the religious experience/institutional religion distinction can have the effect of maintaining the status quo in late capitalism. What better way to legitimate capitalism than to suggest that its values are universal, and spring from deep within one's pure soul—and that anyone who challenges late capitalism is obviously an extremist or dogmatist? Again, I do not mean to suggest that William James was a propagandist for

---

26. As a student once told me, Jesus *would never* say that one should hate one's family (cf. Luke 14 and Matthew 10); when asked how he could justify such a claim, he told me because it was because the "hate" comments conflicted with the Jesus he simply *knew*. Apparently "Jesus" was the variable term that turned on his own, local common sense. That people's account of what their gods think about social and political issues hangs on their own personal views has been demonstrated in scientific studies; see Epley *et al.* 2009.

late capitalism. However, his experience/institution distinction and the coordinate folk theory of religion is a convenient one for sanctioning any religious practices that create friction when they rub up against contemporary consumerism.

CAVEAT

Before concluding, I want to make an important caveat. Very simply, the minimalist/maximalist distinction ultimately breaks down for two interrelated reasons. First, it can implicitly carry a judgment of orthodoxy: it tends to imply that maximalist Christianity, for instance, is true Christianity, and that minimalist Christianity is an inauthentic deviation. The claim that minimalist Christians do not allow Christianity to make demands on their life only makes sense if we assume in advance that Christianity is a tradition that places demands on individuals that fundamentally conflict with capitalism or consumerism. However, if what I have called minimalist Christianity is not an illegitimate or inauthentic form of Christianity, then minimalist Christians may very well accept the demands made on them *by minimalist Christianity*.

Second, and more importantly, up to now I have suggested that Christian maximalism (i.e., in the European Middle Ages) has been replaced by capitalist maximalism today: capitalism orders the lives of minimalist Christians more than Christianity does. But in so far as minimalist Christianity has been domesticated by capitalism, this version of Christianity is maximalist: minimalist Christianity is ultimately maximalist because *it does order the lives of minimalist Christians*. To put it otherwise, minimalist Christianity is implicitly capitalist Christianity, and those I've been calling minimalist Christians may very well have their entire lives organized in ways that are complicit with capitalist Christianity. This discourse on religious experience is a technology of the self that is simultaneously and necessarily a *general social technology*. The discourse on religious experience normatively prescribes for us where religion belongs, what religion should and should not do, and so on; and in so far as our "religions" incorporate this discourse, they too are social technologies with a reach beyond the self. The idea of "minimalist religion" is subtly seductive—like the discourse of individualism, it organizes the social sphere as a whole while pretending to organize only a part of it. It prevents us from thinking about how "minimalist religion" has social effects far beyond the so-called "religious sphere."

For these reasons I think the minimalist/maximalist distinction has a temporary heuristic value, but should be abandoned for more sophisticated terminology, although I am as yet uncertain what might provide us with more analytical precision.

CONCLUSION

In this essay I have argued that the experience/institution distinction we find in James's *Varieties* and adapted by others is well-suited to being adapted for capitalist or consumerist social norms; while these discursive elements may not intrinsically or directly advance or legitimate consumerism, they are easily made to dovetail with it.

I find it ironic that those who prioritize personal, individual religion appear to adhere so strictly to a common script. But it is clear to see why they do so: the ahistorical universalism of the experience/institution and the coordinate folk theory of religion rhetoric require them to project unity where none exists, in so far as they take it for granted that these things are "almost always the same." My conclusion is therefore not different from Russell McCutcheon's, in his review of Karen Armstrong's *A History of God*:

> *A History of God* is yet another instance of the liberal attempt to unify diversity by glossing over concrete differences of culture, politics, economics, and so on, in favor of a presumably abstract, nonhistorical—and, in this case—so-called religious or spiritual sameness. Amstrong's best seller is not a history of the concept of God but is an unknowing history, and practical example, of the on-going human effort to create social identity and homogeneity by means of the rhetorics of unity, a rhetoric that purchases social identity at the expense of those who do not quite fit the pattern. (2001, 55)

I would argue that the popular schema James and others use is part and parcel of an ostensibly minimalist religion that is in fact maximalist in so far as it "purchases" a pervasively ordering "social identity at the expense of those who do not quite fit" the consumerism of late capitalism.

While it may be the case that there could be *something* of value in James's *Varieties* or James's legacy for religious studies in general, I propose that his canonical status be retired at present; given the ease with which his work is appropriated into what amounts to vulgar rhetoric, it should be relegated to the status of Hegel's philosophy of religion: a historical curiosity that is interesting in so far as it has informed the field of religious studies in the past, but—due to its embedded ideological assumptions—presently not of much use to critical scholarship on religion. The pseudo-scholarly accounts of religion that rely on James's vocabulary and teleology should be recognized for what they are: sophisticated propaganda.

SOME AFTERWORDS ...

13

I HAVE A HUNCH

Russell T. McCutcheon

I have hunches; I experience them sweeping through me, registering deep in me.[1] My hunches are about moments in some possible future and they cause me to adjust my behavior in the present. It's difficult to put into words, but I have hunches and I live my life accordingly; in fact, I'm having one right now: I have a hunch that you know what I'm talking about.

It was my belief in the universal nature of the hunch which first suggested that a scientific study of hunches was worth pursuing, a field both diachronic (i.e., I believe that hunches have evolved over time) and synchronic (i.e., cross-cultural comparison can determine the deep structure of the hunch). But I can guess what you're going to say—and by the way, substituting that utterly dismissive term "guess," which is nothing more than an ignorant stab in the dark, is an insult to those who have hunches—you might say: "Russ, cognitive scientists already study these sorts of things. Why do we need to establish a phenomenology and a hermeneutics of hunches?"

My reply? I believe that we are ethically compelled to correct the over-emphasis on the cognitive content of the hunch, for it overlooks the lived experience of those who have them. This is why I distinguish hunches not just from guesses but also from hypotheses that can be tested empirically. Certainly, parts of the hunch can be reduced to a prediction, but, in my experience, reductionists fail to take seriously that, even when a hunch is incorrect, it nonetheless teaches us something about ourselves—indicating that the truth of the hunch lies in its value and not in its accuracy. For having a hunch is a deeply emotive thing, a form of unmediated, non-cognitive communication—what Carl Jung famously described as "perception via the unconscious" (Jung 1968). So, while there may be dimensions to the hunch that those in other fields can study, their work does not fully explain this trans-human experience. Studying the hunch in its fullest sense can therefore only be achieved by a cross-cultural and comparative science.

---

1. This short piece was written for the Yale Seminar in Religious Studies' First Annual Workshop, entitled "What is Belief?" and delivered at Yale University, April 15, 2011. My thanks to Prof. Kathyrn Loften for the kind invitation to participate in this event.

But despite many of us believing in hunches, and believing in them in precisely the same way that we believe our beliefs motivate our behaviors, there is a small group of critics who would argue that I am confusing description with analysis, thereby reproducing (and thus legitimizing) folk psychology. The problem, they claim, is that scholarly paraphrases of common sense accounts of the world fail to examine the wider, non-intentional structures that made talk of hunches, beliefs, and experiences possible and credible in the first place. Failing to take seriously our shared belief in, and experience of, the private, interior world, these scholars explain it away as derivative of what, for them, are their more primary, public conditions. I think here of four examples: Donald Lopez, Robert Sharf, Joan Wallach Scott, and Slavoj Žižek. Due to my limited space, consider merely the following four representative quotations, in which these writers socialize, politicize, and thereby dismiss the irreducibly originary, causal nature of the interior world.

First, consider Lopez's and Sharf's essays in *Critical Terms for Religious Studies*; from his essay entitled "Belief," Lopez concludes:

> the statement "I believe in...," is sensible only when there are others who "do not"; it is an agonistic affirmation.... Thus a statement of belief is a convention appropriate to a specific situation, sanctioned by a history and a community. As Wittgenstein notes, "the expression of belief ... is just a sentence;—and the sentence has sense only as a member of a system of language; as one expression within a calculus."
> (Lopez 1998)

And from his essay, "Experience," Sharf argues:

> The rhetoric of experience tacitly posits a place where signification comes to an end, variously styled "mind," "consciousness," "the mirror of nature," or what have you. The category is, in essence, a mere placeholder that entails a substantive if indeterminate terminus for the relentless deferral of meaning. And this is precisely what makes the term experience so amenable to ideological appropriation.
> (Sharf 1998)

Both Lopez and Sharf agree that conceiving of the individual as motivated by an active and autonomous inner life is a political strategy whereby the contingent situations that determine such things as who gets to count as an individual are erased, leaving only their discursive products, as if they were naturally occurring, stand-alone facts—much as a properly performed point draws your eye to a newly curious object instead of toward the one doing the pointing. Demeaning the inherent value of objects that attract our attention, reductionists like Lopez and Sharf instead see such gestures as an attempt by one speaker to coercively override the standards of others, leading us to conclude that those who adjust their bodies in response to a gesture are simply exhibiting their docile participation in an authority system—a system and a participation that evade analysis when we merely focus on the object and not the act that made it an item of discourse.

What's more, such writers argue that simply reproducing local discursive products fails to count as scholarship. For example, Wallach Scott ends a long review essay on the use of the category experience as follows:

> What counts as experience is neither self-evident nor straightforward; it is always contested and always therefore political. The study of experience, therefore, must call into question its originary status in historical explanation. This will happen when historians take as their project *not* the reproduction and transmission of knowledge said to be arrived at through experience but the analysis of the production of that knowledge itself. (Scott 1991)

And what might this analysis look like? Slavoj Žižek sketches its outlines in the opening to his anthology on ideology:

> Religious belief, for example, is not merely or even primarily inner conviction, but the Church, as an institution, and its rituals..., far from being a mere secondary externalization of the inner belief, stand for *the very mechanisms that generate it.* When Althusser repeats after Pascal: "Act as if you believe, pray, kneel down, and you shall believe, faith will arrive by itself," he delineates an intricate reflective mechanism... That is to say, the implicit logic of his argument is: kneel down and *you shall believe that you knelt because of your belief*—... in short, the "external" ritual performatively generates its own ideological foundation. (Žižek 1997)

Simply put, to the question, "Why do you believe that the University of Alabama's football team is worth cheering for," a student of mine once answered: "Because my grandfather made me watch the games with him." In shifting our focus from the worth of the team to the social situation that made the team worth watching we see the great tragedy of social theory: the inherent value of the free-floating object is lost—whether it is a compelling piece of art, the deep meaning of a text, or the intentions and agency of the author. For now value, truth, and meaning, as Émile Durkheim persuaded some, are no longer expressions of a unique inner identity but, instead, an internalized residue of contingent social situations into which we have been placed by others.

I therefore hope that it is not too much of a stretch to conclude that Western civilization itself—for example, our notions of canon, meaning, justice, property, the free market, national identity, privacy, intentionality, and even the individual which is the foundation of it all—rises or falls by our ability to combat this currently fashionable type of scholarship. For by concluding that talk about belief, faith, feeling, experience, intention, and meaning is no different whatsoever from talking about hunches, and by arguing that scholars ought to do something other than adopt local, folk notions and then use them as if they were cross-cultural universals, such scholarship makes a mockery of the lived experiences of the people we study by suggesting that they are not the final authority on how their own worlds work.

If we are to recover the dignity of our research subjects, and thereby recognize that scholars are but one voice in the human conversation, then we must place the phenomenology and the hermeneutics of hunches alongside those already recognized fields which see such things as beliefs and experiences as substantive, causal forces that are manifested throughout human history.[2]

2. Thanks goes to William Arnal, Willi Braun, Bruce Lincoln, Robert Sharf, Merinda Simmons, and Vaia Touna for their helpful comments on an earlier draft of this paper.

BIBLIOGRAPHY

Adams, Parveen and Jeff Minson. 1978. "The 'Subject' of Feminism." *m/f* 2: 43–61.

Alexander, Hartley. 1937 [1916]."North American Mythology." In *The Mythology of All Races*, Louis H. Gray, George Foot Moore, J. A. MacCulloch (eds). Boston, MA: Archaeological Institute of America/Marshall Jones Co.

Andresen, Jensine (ed.). 2001. *Religion in Mind: Cognitive Perspectives on Religious Belief, Ritual, and Experience*. Cambridge: Cambridge University Press.

Anscombe, Gertrude Elizabeth Margaret. 1958. "Modern Moral Philosophy." *Philosophy* 33: 1–19.

Auerbach, Erich. 1953. *Mimesis: The Representation of Reality in Western Literature*. Princeton, NJ: Princeton University Press.

Ayto, John. 1990. *Bloomsbury Dictionary of Word Origins*. London: Bloomsbury.

Ayto, John. 2001. *Dictionary of Word Origins*. London: Bloomsbury.

Barnard, G. William. 1992. "Explaining the Unexplainable: Wayne Proudfoot's *Religious Experience*." *Journal of the American Academy of Religion* 60(2): 231–56.

Barnhart, Robert. 1988. *The Barnhart Dictionary of Etymology*. New York: H. W. Wilson.

Barthes, Roland. 1972. *Critical Essays*. Evanston, IL: Northwestern University Press.

Becker, A. L. (ed.). 1979. "Text-Building, Etymology, and Aesthetics in Javanese Shadow Theatre." In *The Imagination of Reality: Essays in Southeast Asian Coherence Systems*, A. L. Beck and Aram A. Yengoyan (eds), 211–43. Norwood, NJ: Ablex.

Bersani, Leo. 1976. *A Future for Astyanax: Character and Desire in Literature*. Boston, MA: Little, Brown.

Bevan, Edwyn R. 1938. *Symbolism and Belief*. London: Allen and Unwin.

Bhabha, Homi K. 1987. "Interrogating Identity." In *Identity: The Real Me*. Lisa Appignanesi (ed.), 5–11. ICA Documents, 6. London: Institute of Contemporary Arts.

Blake, William. 1982 [1795–1804]. "The Four Zoas." In *The Complete Poetry and Prose of William Blake*, David W. Erdman (ed.), 300–407. New York: Anchor Books.

Boas, Franz. 1940 [1887]. "The Study of Geography." In his *Race, Language, and Culture*. New York: Macmillan.

Bono, James J. 1990. "Science, Discourse, and Literature: The Role/Rule of Metaphor in Science." In *Literature and Science: Theory and Practice*, Stuart Peterfreund (ed.), 59–89. Boston, MA: Northeastern University Press.

Bourdieu, Pierre. 1984. *Distinction: A Social Critique of the Judgment of Taste*. Richard Nice (trans.). Cambridge, MA: Harvard University Press.

Bourdieu, Pierre. 1993. "Outline of a Sociological Theory of Art Perception." In his *The Field of Cultural Production*. New York: Columbia University Press.

Bourdieu, Pierre. 1998. *Acts of Resistance: Against the Tyranny of the Market*. New York: New Press.

Bourdieu, Pierre. 2003. *Firing Back: Against the Tyranny of the Market 2*. New York: New Press.

Brainard, F. Samuel. 1996. "Defining 'Mystical Experience.'" *Journal of the American Academy of Religion* 64(2): 359–93.

Brown, Wendy. 2006. *Relating Aversion: Tolerance in the Age of Identity and Empire*. Princeton, NJ: Princeton University Press.

Bruner, Jerome. 1986. *Acts of Meaning*. Cambridge, MA: Harvard University Press.

Bryan, C. D. B. 1995. *Close Encounters of the Fourth Kind: A Reporter's Notebook on Alien Abduction, UFOs, and the Conference at M.I.T.* New York: Arkana.

Bryson, Lyman. 1948. *The Communication of Ideas*. New York: Harper.

Burke, Edmund. 2001 [1790]. *Reflections on the Revolution in France and on the Proceeding in Certain Societies in London Relative to That Event in a Letter Intended to Have Been Sent to a Gentleman in Paris,* J. C. D. Clark (ed.). Stanford, CA: Stanford University Press.

Butler, Judith. 1990. *Gender Trouble: Feminism and the Subversion of Identity*. New York: Routledge.

Caillois, Roger. 1939. "L'homme et le sacre." In his *Mythes et religions*. Paris: Leroux.

Carby, Hazel. 1987. *Reconstructing Womanhood: The Emergence of the Afro-American Woman Novelist*. New York: Oxford University Press.

Carr, David. 1986. *Time, Narrative, and History*. Bloomington, IN: Indiana University Press.

Carrette, Jeremy and Richard King. 2005. *Selling Spirituality: The Silent Takeover of Religion*. London: Routledge.

Carus, Paul. 1915. *The Gospel of Buddha*. Chicago, IL: Open Court.

Cassirer, Ernst. 1923. *Philosophie der symbolischen Formen*. Berlin: B. Cassirer.

Childe, V. Gordon. 1950. *Magic, Craftsmanship, and Science*. Liverpool: University of Liverpool Press.

Chisholm, Roderick M. 1950. "The Theory of Appearing." In *Philosophical Analysis*, Max Black (ed.), 102–18. Ithaca, NY: Cornell University Press.

Cholvy, Gerald and Yves-Marie Hillaire. 1985. *Histoire religieuse de la France contemporaine: 1800–1880*. Paris: Privat.

Clark, Walter Houston. 1970. "The Psychedelics and Religion." In *Psychedelics: The Uses and Implications of Hallucinogenic Drugs*. B. Aaronson and H. Osmond (eds), 182–95. New York: Doubleday.

Clifford, W. K. 1947. *The Ethics of Belief and other Essays*, Leslie Stephen and F. Pollock (eds). London: Watts.

Cobb, Jr., John B. 1982. *Beyond Dialogue: Toward a Mutual Transformation of Christianity and Buddhism*. Philadelphia, PA: Fortress Press.

Collingwood, R. G. 1946. *The Idea of History*. Oxford: Oxford University Press.

Connerton, Paul. 1989. *How Societies Remember*. Cambridge: Cambridge University Press.

Crapanzano, Vincent. 1977. "Introduction." In *Case Studies in Spirit Possession*, V. Crapanzano and V. Garrison (eds), 1–40. New York: John Wiley.

Cullmann, Oscar. 1949. *The Earliest Christian Confessions*, J. K. S. Reid (trans.). London: Lutterworth.

Danielou, Jean. 1950. "The Problems of Symbolism." *Thought* 25: 423–40.

de Bolla, Peter. 1986. "Disfiguring History." *Diacritics* 16: 49–58.

de Bolla, Peter. 1989. *The Discourse of the Sublime: Readings in History, Aesthetics, and the Subject*. Oxford: Blackwell.

de Certeau, Michel. 1986. "History: Science and Fiction" In *Heterologies: Discourse on the Other*, Brian Massumi (trans.), 199–221. Minneapolis, MN: University of Minnesota Press.

de Lauretis, Teresa. 1984. *Alice Doesn't: Feminism, Semiotics, Cinema*. Bloomington, IN: Indiana University Press.

de Martino, Ernesto. 1948. *Il Mondo Magico*. Florence: Giulio Einaudi.

Delany, Samuel R. 1988. *The Motion of Light in Water: Sex and Science Fiction Writing in the East Village, 1957–1965*. New York: Arbor House.

DelVecchio Good, Mary Jo, Paul Brodwin, Byron Good, and Arthur Kleinman. 1992. "Epilogue." In *Pain as Human Experience: An Anthropological Perspective*, M-J. DelVecchio Good, P. Brodwin, B. Good, and A. Kleinman (eds), 198–207. Berkeley, CA: University of California Press.

Dennett, Daniel C. 1991. *Consciousness Explained*. Boston, MA: Little, Brown.

Dennett, Daniel C. 1992. "Quining Qualia." In *Consciousness in Contemporary Science,* A. J. Marcel and E. Bisiach (eds), 42–77. Oxford: Oxford University Press.

Desjarlais, Robert. 1992. *Body and Emotion: The Aesthetics of Illness and Healing in the Nepal Himalayas*. Philadelphia, PA: University of Pennsylvania Press.

Dewey, John. 1926. *Experience and Nature*. Chicago, IL: Open Court.

Duranti, Alessandro. 1994. *From Grammar to Politics: Linguistic Anthropology in a Western Samoan Village*. Berkeley, CA: University of California Press.

Durkheim, Emile. 1947 [1912]. *The Elementary Forms of the Religious Life*, J. W. Swain (trans.). Glencoe, IL: Free Press.

Durkheim, Emile. 1995 [1912]. *The Elementary Forms of Religious Life*, Karen Fields (trans.). New York: Free Press.

Eck, Diana. 1982. *Banaras: City of Light*. New York: Alfred A. Knopf.

Eck, Diana. 2001. *A New Religious America: How a "Christian Country" Became the World's Most Religiously Diverse Nation*. New York: HarperSanFrancisco.

Eliade, Mircea. 1949. *Le mythe de l'eternal retour*. Paris: Gallimard.

Eliot, Thomas Sterns. 1950 [1921]. "The Metaphysical Poets." In *Selected Prose of T. S. Eliot*, 241–50. New York: Harcourt, Brace, Jovanovich.

Emerson, Michael O. and Christian Smith. 2000. *Divided by Faith: Evangelical Religion and the Problem of Race in America*. Oxford: Oxford University Press.

Epley, Nicholas, Benjamin A. Converse, Alexa Delbosc, George A. Monteleone, and John T. Cacioppo. 2009. "Believers' Estimates of God's Beliefs Are More Egocentric than Estimates of Other People's Beliefs." *Proceedings of the National Academy of Sciences of the United States of America* 106/51: 21533–38. Available at http://www.pnas.org/content/106/51/21533 (accessed June 2012).

Ewer, M. A. 1933. *A Survey of Mystical Symbolism*. London: S.P.C.K.

Faulkner, William. 1986 [1936]. *Absalom, Absalom!* New York: Vintage.

Fields, Barbara J. 1982. "Ideology and Race in American History." In *Region, Race and Reconstruction: Essays in Honor of C. Vann Woodward*, J. Morgan Kousser and James M. McPherson (eds), 143–77. New York: Oxford University Press.

Forman, Robert K. C. (ed.). 1990. *The Problem of Pure Consciousness: Mysticism and Philosophy*. New York: Oxford University Press.

Forman, Robert K. C. 1993. "Mystical Knowledge: Knowledge by Identity." *Journal of the American Academy of Religion* 61(4): 705–38.

Foucault, Michel. 1977. *The Archaeology of Knowledge*, A. M. Sheridan Smith (trans.). New York: Pantheon.

Foucault, Michel. 1978. *A History of Sexuality, Vol. 1. An Introduction*, R. Hurley (trans.). New York: Pantheon.

Foure, Rene. 1964. *Krishnamurti: The Man and His Teaching*. Bombay: Chetana.

Franke, Otto. 1928. "Der Kosmische Gedanke in der Philosophie und dem Staat der Chinesen." In *Vorträge der Bibliothek Warburg*, Fritz Saxl (ed.). Leipzig: Teubner.

Frankfort, Henri, H. A. Frankfort, John A. Wilson, Thorkild Jacobsen, and William A. Irwin. 1946. *The Intellectual Adventure of Ancient Man: An Essay of Speculative Thought in the Ancient Near East*. Chicago, IL: University of Chicago Press.

Fuller, Robert C. 2001. *Spiritual, but not Religious: Understanding Unchurched America*. Oxford: Oxford University Press.

Fuss, Diana. 1989. *Essentially Speaking: Feminism, Nature and Difference*. New York: Routledge.

Gadamer, Hans Georg. 1975. *Truth and Method*, Joel Weinsheimer (trans.). New York: Crossroad.

Gallop, Jane. 1982. *The Daughter's Seduction: Feminism and Psychoanalysis*. Ithaca, NY: Cornell University Press.

Ganly, Sarah. 2007. "The Negative Impact of Organized Religion." Associated Content. Available at: http://www.associatedcontent.com/article/372622/the_negative_impact_of_organized_religion.html (accessed June 2012).

Geertz, Clifford. 1986. "Making Experience, Authoring Selves." In *The Anthropology of Experience*, V. Turner and E. Bruner (eds). Urbana, IL: University of Illinois Press.

Geertz, Clifford. 2000. "The Pinch of Destiny: Religion as Experience, Meaning, Identity, Power." In his *Available Light*, 167–86. Princeton, NJ: Princeton University Press.

Gennep, Arnold van. 2004 [1960]. *The Rites of Passage*, M. B. Vizedom and G. L. Caffee (trans.). London: Routledge.

Giddens, Anthony. 1991. *Modernity and Self-Identity: Self and Society in the Late Modern Age*. Stanford, CA: Stanford University Press.

Good, Byron. 1993. "Culture and Psychopathology: Directions for Psychiatric Anthropology." In *New Directions in Psychological Anthropology*. T. Schwartz, G. White, and C. Lutz (eds). Cambridge: Cambridge University Press.

Goodman, Felicitas D. 1988. *How About Demons? Possession and Exorcism in the Modern World*. Bloomington, IN: Indiana University Press.

Gossman, Lionel. 1989. *Towards a Rational Historiography*. Philadelphia, PA: American Philosophical Society.

Hacking, Ian. 1995. *Rewriting the Soul: Multiple Personality and the Sciences of Memory*. Princeton, NJ: Princeton University Press.

Halbfass, Wilhelm. 1988. "The Concept of Experience in the Encounter between India and the West." In his *India and Europe: An Essay in Understanding*, 378–402. Albany, NY: SUNY Press.

Hall, Stuart. 1987. "Minimal Selves." In *Identity: The Real Me*, Lisa Appignanesi (ed.), ICA Documents, 6: 44–6. London: Institute of Contemporary Arts.

Hallowell, A. Irving. 1955. "The Self and Its Behavioral Enviroment." In his *Culture and Experience*, 172–83. Philadelphia, PA: University of Pennsylvania Press.

Halter, Marilyn. 2000. *Shopping for Identity: The Marketing of Ethnicity*. New York: Schocken.

Haraway, Donna. 1988. "Situated Knowledges: The Science Question in Feminism and the Privilege of Partial Perspective." *Feminist Studies* 14: 575–99.

Haraway, Donna. nd. "The Promises of Monsters: Reproductive Politics for Inappropriate/d Others." Typescript.

Harvey, David. 2005. *The New Imperialism*. Oxford: Oxford University Press.

Harvey, David. 2007. *A Brief History of Neoliberalism*. Oxford: Oxford University Press.

Hawkesworth, Mary E. 1989. "Knowers, Knowing, Known: Feminist Theory and Claims of Truth." *Signs* 14: 533–57.

Heidegger, Martin. 1962. *Being and Time*. New York: HarperCollins.

Heidegger, Martin. 1971 [1959]. *On the Way to Language*. New York: Harper and Row.

Hirsch, E. D. 1967. *Validity in Interpretation*. New Haven, CT: Yale University Press.

Howes, David. (ed.). 1991. *The Varieties of Sensory Experience: A Sourcebook in the Anthropology of the Senses*. Toronto: University of Toronto Press.

Huxley, Aldous. 1945. *The Perennial Philosophy*. London: Chatto and Windus.

Jackson, Michael. 1989. *Paths Toward a Clearing: Radical Empiricism and Ethnographic Inquiry*. Bloomington, IN: Indiana University Press.

James, William. 1902. *The Varieties of Religious Experience*. New York: Longmans, Green.

James, William. 1912. *Essays in Radical Empiricism*. New York: Longmans, Green.

James, William. 1961 [1902]. *The Varieties of Religious Experience: A Study in Human Nature*. New York: Collier.

James, William. 1977 [1909]. *A Pluralistic Universe*. Cambridge, MA: Harvard University Press.

James, William. 1982 [1902]. *The Varieties of Religious Experience*. Harmondsworth: Penguin.

James, William. 2004 [1902]. *The Varieties of Religious Experience*. New York: Barnes and Noble.

Jameson, Fredric. 1991a. "Immanence and Nominalism in Postmodern Theory." In *Postmodernism: Or, the Cultural Logic of Late Capitalism*, 181–259. Durham, NC: Duke University Press.

Jameson, Fredric. 1991b. *Postmodernism: Or, the Cultural Logic of Late Capitalism*. Durham, NC: Duke University Press.

Jantzen, Grace M. 1995. *Power, Gender, and Christian Mysticism*. Cambridge: Cambridge University Press.

Jay, Martin. 2005. *Songs of Experience: Modern American and European Variations on a Universal Theme*. Berkeley, CA: University of California Press.

Johnson, Paul E. 1945. *Psychology of Religion*. New York: Abingdon Cokesbury Press.

Jung, Carl G. 1968. "Conscious, Unconscious, and Individuation." In Carl G. Jung, *Collected Works of C. G. Jung*. 2nd ed. Vol. 9, part 1: 275–89. Princeton, NJ: Princeton University Press.

Katz, Steven T. 1978. "Language, Epistemology, and Mysticism." In *Mysticism and Philosophical Analysis*, Steven T. Katz (ed.), 22–74. New York: Oxford University Press.

Katz, Steven T. 1983. "The 'Conservative' Character of Mystical Experience." In *Mysticism and Religious Traditions*, Steven T. Katz (ed.), 3–60. New York: Oxford University Press.

Katz, Steven T. 1992. "Mystical Speech and Mystical Meaning." In *Mysticism and Language*, Steven T. Katz (ed.), 3–41. New York: Oxford University Press.

King, Katie. 1986. "The Situation of Lesbianism as Feminism's Magical Sign: Contests for Meaning and the U.S. Women's Movement, 1968–1972." *Communication* 9: 65–91.

Klein, Naomi. 2007. *The Shock Doctrine: The Rise of Disaster Capitalism*. New York: Picador.

Kleinman, Arthur and Joan Kleinman. 1995. "Suffering and its Professional Transformation: Toward an Ethnography of Interpersonal Experience." In *Writing at the Margins: Discourse Between Anthropology and Medicine*, Arthur Kleinmann. Berkley, CA: University of California Press.

Kluckholm, Clyde. 1942. "Myths and Rituals: A General Theory." *Harvard Theological Review* 35(1): 45–79.

Lacan, Jacques. 1977. "The Signification of the Phallus." In *Ecrits: A Selection*, Alan Sheridan (trans.), 281–91. New York: Norton.

LaCapra, Dominick. 1985a "Is Everyone a *Mentalité* Case? Transference and the 'Culture' Concept." In his *History and Criticism*, 77–94. Ithaca, NY: Cornell University Press.

LaCapra, Dominick. 1985b. "Rhetoric and History." In his *History and Criticism*, 15–44. Ithaca, NY: Cornell University Press.

Langer, Susanne K. 1942. *Philosophy in a New Key: A Study in the Symbolism of Reason, Rite, and Art*. New York: Penguin.

Lash, Nicholas. 1986. *Easter in Ordinary*. Notre Dame, IN: University of Notre Dame Press.

Leenhardt, Maurice. 1979 [1947]. *Do Kamo: Person and Myth in the Melanesian World*, B. Miller Gulati (trans.). Chicago, IL: University of Chicago Press.

Lévy-Bruhl, Lucien. 1938. *L'expérience mystique et les symbols chez les primitives*. Paris: Alcan.

Lienhardt, Godfrey. 1961. *Divinity and Experience: The Religion of the Dinka*. Oxford: Clarendon Press.

Lincoln, Bruce. 2006. *Holy Terrors: Thinking about Religion after September 11*. Chicago, IL: University of Chicago Press.

Lind, Robert W. 1992. *Brother Van: Montana Pioneer Circuit Rider*. Helena, MT: Falcon Press.

Lopez, Donald S. 1998. "Belief." In *Critical Terms for Religious Studies*, Mark C. Taylor (ed.), 21–35. Chicago, IL: University of Chicago Press.

Mack, John E. 1995. *Abduction: Human Encounters with Aliens*. Rev. ed. New York: Ballantine Books.

Malcolm, N. 1959. *Dreaming: Studies in Philosophical Psychology*. London: Routledge and Kegan Paul.

Malinowski, Bronislaw. 1948. *Magic, Science, and Religion and Other Essays*. Glencoe, IL: Free Press.

Mandel, Ernest. 1999. *Late Capitalism*. London: Verso.

Marks, Morton. 1974. "Uncovering Ritual Structures in Afro-American Music." In *Religious Movements in Contemporary America*, Irvin I. Zaretsky and Mark P. Leone (eds). 6–134. Princeton, NJ: Princeton University Press.

Marrett, Robert Randolph. 1932. *Faith, Hope, and Charity in Primitive Religion*. Oxford: Clarendon Press.

Marrett, Robert Randolph. 1933. *Sacraments of Simple Folk*. Oxford: Clarendon Press.

Martin, Biddy and Chandra Talpade Mohanty. 1986. "Feminist Politics: What's Home Got to Do with It?" In *Feminist Studies/Critical Studies*, Teresa de Lauretis (ed.), 191–212. Bloomington, IN: Indiana University Press.

Martin, Craig. 2010. *Masking Hegemony: A Genealogy of Liberalism, Religion and the Private Sphere*. London: Equinox.

McCloud, Sean. 2007. *Divine Hierarchies: Class in American Religion & Religious Studies*. Chapel Hill, NC: University of North Carolina Press.

McCutcheon, Russell. 2001. "Writing a History of God: 'Just the Same Game Wherever You Go.'" In his *Critics Not Caretakers: Redescribing the Public Study of Religion*. Albany, NY: SUNY Press.

McCutcheon, Russell. 2003. *The Discipline of Religion*. London: Routledge.

McCutcheon, Russell. 2005. *Religion and the Domestication of Dissent*. London: Equinox.

McManners, John (ed.). 1993. *The Oxford History of Christianity*. Oxford: Oxford University Press.

Minow, Martha. 1987. "Justice Engendered." Foreword to "The Supreme Court, 1986 Term," *Harvard Law Review* 101: 10–95.

Mohanty, Chandra Talpade. 1987. "Feminist Encounters: Locating the Politics of Experience," *Copyright* 1: 30–44.

Moore, John M. 1938. *Theories of Religious Experience*. New York: Round Table Press.

Moran, Kenny. 2009. "The Dangers of Organized Religion." Formerly available at: http://www.scribd.com/doc/15631116/The-Dangers-of-Organized-Religion. Archived at: http://fliiby.com/file/593834/7rkis1fxwj.html.

Murphy, Tim. 2007. *Representing Religion: Essays in History, Theory and Crisis*. London: Equinox.

Murray, James A. H. 1933. *New English Dictionary on Historical Principles*. Oxford: Clarendon Press.

Nagel, T. 1986. *The View from Nowhere*. Oxford: Oxford University Press.

Needham, Rodney. 1972. *Belief, Language, and Experience*. Chicago, IL: University of Chicago Press.

Newton, Judith. 1988. "History as Usual? Feminism and the 'New Historicism.'" *Cultural Critique* 9: 87–121.

Niebel, Esther C. (ed.). 1966. *A Century of Service: History of the First Methodist Church, Bozeman, Montana, 1866–1966*. Bozeman, MT: First Methodist Church.

Nilsson, Martin P. 1949. "Letter to Professor A. D. Nock." *Harvard Theological Review* 42. 71–107.

Nishida, K. 1990. *An Inquiry into the Good*, M. Abe and C. Ives (trans.). New Haven, CT: Yale University Press.

Noll, Mark. 1994. *The Scandal of the Evangelical Mind*. Grand Rapids, MI: Wm. B. Eerdmans.

Nussbaum, Felicity A. 1989. *The Autobiographical Subject: Gender and Ideology in Eighteenth-Century England*. Baltimore, MD: Johns Hopkins University Press.

Oakshott, Michael. 1985 [1933]. *Experience and its Modes*. Cambridge: Cambridge University Press.

Ochs, Elinor. 1988. *Culture and Language Development: Language Acquisition and Language Socialization in a Samoan Village*. Cambridge: Cambridge University Press.

Otto, Rudolf. 1958 [1917]. *The Idea of the Holy: An Inquiry into the Non-Rational Factor in the Idea of the Divine and its Relation to the Rational*, J. W. Harvey (trans.). London: Oxford University Press.

Otto, Rudolph. 1938. *The Kingdom of God and the Son of Man*, Floyd V. Filson and B. L. Lee (trans.). London: Lutterworth.

Pahnke, Walter N. 1970. "Drugs and Mysticism." In *Psychedelics: The Uses and Implications of Hallucinogenic Drug*, B. Aaronson and H. Osmond (eds), 145–65. New York: Doubleday.

Paton, W. (ed.). 1939. *The Authority of the Faith*. London: Oxford University Press.

Pavlina, Steve. 2008. "10 Reasons You Should Never Have a Religion." StevePavlina.com. Available at: http://www.stevepavlina.com/blog/2008/05/10-reasons-you-should-never-have-a-religion/.

Pierson, Ruth Roach. "Experience, Difference, and Dominance in the Writings of Women's History." Typescript.

Pittenger, W. Norman. 1949. *Sacraments, Signs and Symbols*. Chicago, IL: Wilcox and Follet.

Poovey, Mary. 1988. *Uneven Developments: The Ideological Work of Gender in Mid-Victorian England*. Chicago, IL: University of Chicago Press.

Pratt, Minnie Bruce. 1984. "Identity: Skin Blood Heart." In *Yours in Struggle: Three Feminist Perspectives on Anti-Semitism and Racism*, Elly Bulkin Pratt and Barbara Smith Brooklyn (eds), 9–66. New York: Long Haul Press.

Proudfoot, Wayne. 1985. *Religious Experience*. Berkeley, CA: University of California Press.

Radhakrishnan, Sarvepalli. 1937. *An Idealist View of Life*. The Hibbert Lectures for 1929, rev. 2nd ed. London: Allen and Unwin.

Radin, Paul. 1938. *Primitive Religion: Its Nature and Origin*. London: Hamish Hamilton.

Ratschow, C. H. 1947. *Magic und Religion*. Giitersloh: Bertelsmann.

Rhys-Davids, T. W. 1917. "Cosmic Law in Ancient Thought." In *Proceedings of British Academy VIII*. Oxford: Oxford University Press.

Ricoeur, Paul. 1970. *Freud and Philosophy: An Essay on Interpretation*, D. Savage (trans.). New Haven, CT: Yale University Press.

Riley, Denise. 1988. *"Am I That Name?": Feminism and the Category of "Women" in History*. Minneapolis, MN: University of Minnesota.

Robinson, John A. T. 1962. *Honest to God*. Philadelphia, PA: Westminster Press.

Rooney, Ellen. 1989. *Seductive Reasoning: Pluralism as the Problematic of Contemporary Theory*. Ithaca, NY: Cornell University Press.

Rorty, Richard. 1979. *Philosophy and the Mirror of Nature*. Princeton, NJ: Princeton University Press.

Rosaldo, Renato. 1986. "Ilongot Hunting as Story and Experience." In *The Anthropology of Experience*, V. Turner and E. Bruner (eds). Chicago, IL: University of Illinois Press.

Rose, Nikolas. 1998. *Inventing Our Selves: Psychology, Power, and Personhood*. Cambridge: Cambridge University.

Rose, Nikolas. 1999. *Governing the Soul: The Shaping of the Private Self*. London: Free Association Books.

Rose, Nikolas and Peter Miller. 1998. *Governing the Present*. Cambridge: Polity.

Rouget, Gilbert. 1985. *Music and Trance: A Theory of the Relations between Music and Possession*. Chicago, IL: University of Chicago Press.

Sacks, Oliver. 2007. "A Bolt from the Blue." *New Yorker* (July 23), 38–42.

Sahlins, Marshall. 1976. *Culture and Practical Reason*. Chicago, IL: University of Chicago Press.

Schleiermacher, Friedrich Daniel Ernst. 1958 [1831]. *On Religion: Speeches to its Cultured Despisers*, J. Oman (trans.). New York: Harper and Row.

Schleiermacher, Friedrich. 1928 [1820–1]. *The Christian Faith*, 2nd ed., H. R. Mackintosh and J. S. Stewart (trans.). Edinburgh: T & T Clark.

Scholem, Gershom Gerhart. 1969. *On the Kabbalah and Its Symbolism*, R. Manheim (trans.). New York: Schocken Books.

Scholem, Gershom (1973). *SabbataiSevi: The Mystical Messiah*, R. J. Z. Werblowski (trans.). Princeton, NJ: Princeton University Press.

Scott, Joan Wallach. 1991. "The Evidence of Experience," *Critical Inquiry* 17: 773–97.

Sedgwick, Eve Kosofsky. 1985. *Between Men: English Literature and Male Homosocial Desire*. New York: Columbia University Press.

Sewell, William H. Jr. 1990. "How Classes Are Made: Critical Reflections on E. P. Thompson's Theory of Working-class Formation." In *E. P. Thompson: Critical Debates*, Harvey J. Kay and Keith McClelland (eds), 50–77. Philadelphia, PA: Temple University Press.

Sharf, Robert H. 1995a. "Buddhist Modernism and the Rhetoric of Meditative Experience." *Numen* 42(3): 228–83.

Sharf, Robert H. 1995b. "Sanbokyodan: Zen and the Way of the New Religions." *Japanese Journal of Religious Studies* 22(3/4): 417–58.

Sharf, Robert H. 1995c. "The Zen of Japanese Nationalism." In *Curators of the Buddha: The Study of Buddhism Under Colonialism*, Donald S. Lopez, Jr. (ed.), 107–60. Chicago, IL: University of Chicago Press.

Sharf, Robert H. 1998. "Experience." In *Critical Terms for Religious Studies*, Mark C. Taylor (ed.), 94–116. Chicago, IL: University of Chicago Press.

Shear, Jonathan. 1994. "On Mystical Experiences as Empirical Support for the Perennial Philosophy." *Journal of the American Academy of Religion* 62(2): 319–42.

Shore, Brad. 1982. *Sala'ilua: A Samoan Mystery*. New York: Columbia University Press.

Short, Larry. 1995. "Mysticism, Mediation, and the Non-linguistic." *Journal of the American Academy of Religion* 63(4): 659–75.

Shweder, Richard A. 1991. *Thinking Through Cultures*. Cambridge: Harvard University Press.

Smart, Ninian. 1973. *The Science of Religion and the Sociology of Knowledge: Some Methodological Questions*. Princeton, NJ: Princeton University Press.

Smith, Christian and Melinda Lundquist Denton. 2005. *Soul Searching: The Religious and Spiritual Lives of American Teenagers*. Oxford: Oxford University Press.

Smith, J. Z. 2004. *Relating Religion: Essays in the Study of Religion*. Chicago, IL: University of Chicago Press.

Smith, Morton. 1973. *The Secret Gospel*. New York: Harper and Row.

Spivak, Gayatri Chakravorty. 1988. *In Other Worlds: Essays in Cultural Politics*. New York: Routledge.

Spivak, Gayatri Chakravorty and Ellen Rooney. 1989. "In a Word. Interview." *Differences* 1: 124–54.

Stace, W. T. 1960. *Mysticism and Philosophy*. London: Macmillan.

Stansell, Christine. 1987. "A Response to Joan Scott." *International Labor and Working-Class History* 31: 24–29.

Stocking, George (ed.). 1989. *Romantic Motives: Essays on Anthropological Sensibility*. Madison, IL: University of Wisconsin Press.

Stoller, Paul. 1989. *The Taste of Ethnographic Things: The Senses in Anthropology*. Philadelphia, PA: University of Pennsylvania Press.

Streeter, Burnett Hillman. 1932. *The Buddha and the Christ*. London: Macmillan.

Sunderland, LaRoy. 1868. *Trance and Correlative Phenomena*. Chicago, IL: J. Walker.

Taves, Ann. 2005. "Religious Experience." In *Encyclopedia of Religion*, vol. 11, Lindsay Jones (ed.-in-chief), 7736–50. Detroit, MI: Thomson Gale.

Taylor, Charles. 1989. *Sources of the Self: The Making of the Modern Identity*. Cambridge, MA: Harvard University Press.

Taylor, Charles. 2002. *Varieties of Religion Today: William James Revisited*. Cambridge, MA: Harvard University Press.

Temple, William. 1935. *Nature, Man, and God*. London: Macmillan.

Thompson, E. P. 1978. "The Poverty of Theory or an Orrery of Errors." In his *The Poverty of Theory and Other Essays*, 1–210. New York: Monthly Review Press.

Thompson, E. P. 1980 [1963]. *The Making of the English Working Class*. Harmondsworth: Penguin.

Tillich, Paul. 1947. "The Problem of Theological Method." *Journal of Religion* 27: 16–26.

Tillich, Paul. 1948. *The Protestant Era*. Chicago, IL: University of Chicago Press.

Tillich, Paul. 1955. *The Shaking of the Foundations*. New York: Charles Scribner's Sons.

Toews, John. 1987. "Intellectual History after the Linguistic Turn: The Autonomy of Meaning and the Irreducibility of Experience." *American Historical Review* 92: 879–907.

Tombs, Robert. 1996. *France: 1814–1914*. London: Longman.

Turner, Victor. 1982. *From Ritual to Theatre*. New York: Performing Arts Journal Press.

Underhill, Evelyn. 1930. *Mysticism*, 12th ed. London: Methuen.

Underhill, Evelyn. 1936. *Worship*. New York: Harper and Row.

Urban, Wilbur Marshall. M. 1939. *Language and Reality: The Philosophy of Language and the Principles of Symbolism*. London: Allen and Unwin.

van der Leeuw, Gerardus. 1938. *Religion in Essence and Manifestation*, J. E. Turner (trans.). London: Allen and Unwin.

Wach, Joachim. 1945. "Sociology of Religion," In *Symposium on Twentieth-Century Sociology*, Georges Gurvitch and Wilbert E. Moore (eds). New York: Philosophical Library.

Wach, Joachim. 1947. *Sociology of Religion*. London: Kegan Paul.

Wach, Joachim. 1951. *Types of Religious Experience: Christian and Non-Christian*. Chicago, IL: University of Chicago Press.

Weber, Max. 1922. *Wirtschaft und Gellschaft*. Tübingen: Mohr.

Weber, Max. 1947. *The Theory of Social and Economic Organization*, A. M. Henderson and T. Parsons (trans.). London: W. Hodge.

Wesley, John. 1988. *The Works of John Wesley. Vol. 18. Journals and Diaries I (1735–38)*, W. Reginald Ward and Richard P. Heitzenrater (eds). Nashville, TN: Abingdon Press.

Whitmore, J. 1995. "Religious Dimensions of the UFO Abductee Experience." In *The Gods Have Landed: New Religions from Other Worlds*, James R. Lewis (ed.). Albany, NY: SUNY Press.

Wieman, Henry N. 1946. *The Source of Human Good*. Chicago, IL: University of Chicago Press.

Wikan, Unni. 1991. "Toward an Experience-Near Anthropology." *Cultural Anthropology* 6: 285–305.

Williams, Raymond. 1958. *Culture and Society, 1780–1950*. London: Chatto and Windus.

Williams, Raymond. 1961. *The Long Revolution*. New York: Columbia University Press.

Williams, Raymond. 1979. *Politics and Letters: Interviews with New Left Review*. London: New Left Books.

Williams, Raymond. 1983. *Keywords: A Vocabulary of Culture and Society*. Oxford: Oxford University Press.

Williams, Raymond. 1985. *Keywords: A Vocabulary of Culture and Society*, rev. ed. New York: Oxford University Press.

Wittgenstein, Ludwig. 1965 [1958]. *The Blue and Brown Books: Preliminary Studies for the "Philosophical Investigations."* New York: Harper Torchbooks.

Wuthnow, Robert. 1998. *After Heaven: Spirituality in America since the 1950s*. Berkeley, CA: University of California Press.

Zaleski, Carol. 1987. *Otherworld Journeys: Accounts of Near-Death Experience in Medieval and Modern Times*. Oxford: Oxford University Press.

Žižek, Slavoj. 1997. "Introduction: The Spectre of Ideology." In *Mapping Ideology*, Slavoy Žižek (ed.), 1–33. London: Verso.

INDEX

al-Ghazzali, Abu Hamid Muhammad ibn
  Muhammad 64
alien abductions 145–6, 148–9
Althusser, Louis 201
Anscombe, Elizabeth 120
Aristotle 33, 82, 118, 120
Armstrong, Karen 178, 196
Auerbach, Erich 30–31
Aurelius, Marcus 45, 48–9
Augustine 29, 31, 45, 62, 85

Barthes, Roland 177
Bataille, Georges 132
Boas, Franz 26
Bourdieu, Pierre 178, 189
Brown, Wendy 12–13
Burke, Edmund 20–21
Butler, Judith 158, 162

Cambridge Platonists 61–2
capitalism 177–8, 188–96
Carlyle, Thomas 45, 47
Carrette, Jeremy 178
Cassirer, Ernst 79
charisma 38, 63, 86–7, 113
cognitive science 2, 122, 199
Collingwood, R. G. 160–61
Comte, Auguste 81

de Certeau, Michel 155, 160, 166
de Chardin, Teilhard 96
Delany, Samuel 152–4, 170–71
de Lauretis, Teresa 157, 159–60

Dennett, Daniel 147
Denton, Melinda Lundquist 190–94
dependence, feeling of 39, 53–4, 117, 119, 121, 136
Descartes, Rene 31, 141
Desjarlais, Robert x, 24–5, 55–6, 110
Dewey, John 27, 32, 37
Dilthey, Wilhelm 26, 31–2
Dogmatism 57, 66, 183, 186–8, 191–4
Durkheim, Emile v, 12, 74, 85, 201

Eagleton, Terry 190
Eck, Diana x, 88–9, 131
Eckhart, Meister 76
Edwards, Jonathan 22
Eliade, Mircea ix, 10, 72, 76–80, 82, 115
Eliot, T. S. 21
Emerson, Ralph Waldo 41–3, 47, 50
Erasmus 179
essences 9–10, 72, 168
experience
  as authentic 22–7, 29–30, 33, 38, 123, 128, 159,
    164
  as authoritative/authorizing 154–67
  direct ix, 3–4, 27, 40, 134–5, 153–4, 161, 164,
    181–2, 194
  as empirically inaccessible 31–2, 147
  epistemic vs. ontic concerns 25–8
  "experience past" vs. "experience present" 7–8,
    20–23, 28–9, 141, 159
  as foundation 157–67, 171–3
  lived 26–7, 32, 102, 133, 164, 199, 201
  and reference 2–15, 154–5
  requires explanation 155–7, 173

Faulkner, William 32
Foucault, Michel 33, 72, 153, 166, 169, 172, 177
Fox, George 63–4
Frazer, James G. 41
Freud, Sigmund 32
Fuller, Margaret 47
Fuller, Robert C. 179, 193–4
fundamentalism *see* dogmatism

Gadamer, Hans-Georg 26, 31–2, 132
Geertz, Clifford 26, 28, 30–32, 63
Gandhi, Mohandas K. 94, 98
Goethe, Johann Wolfgang von 53
Goodman, Felicitas 149
Gramsci, Antonio 167
Great Awakening, the 22, 61

Hacking, Ian 125, 146
Hall, Stuart 168
Harnack, Adolf von 63
Hegel, Georg Wilhelm Friedrich 66, 187, 196
Heidegger, Martin 28, 32–3
hermeneutics 30–31, 98, 136, 141–2, 148, 183–6,
    199, 202
Hölderlin, Friedrich 31
Holy, the idea of the 11, 72, 77–8, 118, 133–4
Homer 30–31
Hume, David 120–21
Husserl, Edmund 31–2
Huxley, Aldous 76, 134–5

intuition ix, 80, 120

James, William 27, 32, 37–8, 55–6, 74, 85, 109,
    122–4, 128
  criticisms of 56–67, 177–83, 186–9, 194–6
  influence of ix–x, 10, 134–7, 139
  use of Bradley 110–11, 119
Jameson, Frederic 158, 177
Jantzen, Grace 135–6
Joyce, James 32

Kant, Immanuel ix, 29, 61, 180
Katz, Steven 1 35, 149
Kempis, Thomas à 50
Kierkegaard, Soren 85, 116, 118
King, Richard 178
Kitaro, Nishida 139
Krishnamurti, Jiddu 95–6

LaCapra, Dominick 155, 172
Lincoln, Bruce 189–91, 195
Lopez, Donald 200
Luther, Martin 1, 49, 180

Mack, John 145, 149
magic vs. religion 41, 78–9, 179
Malcolm, Norman 149
Malinowski, Bronislaw 75, 79, 81, 83
Mandel, Ernest 177
map vs. territory 15
Marx, Karl 16, 19–20
Marxism 19–20, 103, 151, 161, 171
McCloud, Sean 194
McCutcheon, Russell T. 178, 180–81, 196
Merleau-Ponty, Maurice 32
Mohanty, Chandra Talpede 155, 164
Montaigne 31
Moore, G.E. 120
moralistic therapeutic deism 190–94
Murphy, Tim 178
mysterium tremendum 77–8
mysticism or mystical experience 110–14, 132–5,
    140–44
  Eastern or Asian 136–40

Narrative 1, 33, 128, 149, 154–5, 168, 187–8
near-death experiences 148–9
Newton, Judith 163–4
Nietzsche, Friedrich 45
Noll, Mark A. 185–6
Numinous 10, 75, 77–8, 80, 82, 84–6, 116, 118,
    121, 150

Oakshott, Michael 27, 32
Otto, Rudolph ix, 10–12, 72, 75, 77–8, 86–7, 118,
    121, 134–5

Parsons, Talcott 83
Pascal, Blaise 201
phenomenology 9, 26, 28–9, 32, 64, 71–3, 89,
    116–19, 128, 131, 133, 147–8
Phillips, D. Z. 115
Peirce, C.S. 37
Pietism 30, 63, 179
Plato 29, 62, 76
pluralism 88–9, 99–104
Pocock, J. G. A 165
pragmatism 37–8, 55, 109, 178

Proudfoot, Wayne x, 109–10, 122, 135–6, 152
Proust, Marcel 32

qualia 147
Quine, W. V. O. 115–16

Radhakrishnan, Sarvepalli 106, 137–8, 140
radical empiricism 37, 55
Reformation, the 59, 61, 65, 119, 179, 182
religion
    individual vs. institutional ix–x, 38, 40–41,
        58–67, 177–88, 194–6
    Joachim Wach's definition of 73–5
    vs. magic 41, 78–9, 179
    minimalism vs. maximalism 189–91, 194–6
    primitive 41, 75, 77–8, 80, 82–4, 86, 140
    sui generis 71–4, 109
    and ultimate reality 27, 74, 77, 80, 85–7, 134
    William James' definition of 38–52, 57, 180–81
    William James' theory of 186–8
Religionswissenschaft 71–2
religious experience
    attribution of causes 111–14
    as authoritative/authorizing 131–2, 134, 136–7,
        147–8
    causes of 2, 22, 67, 110–14, 116–20, 123, 125–7,
        131, 134–5
    comparison of 125–6, 128, 134–5
    Eastern vs. Western 136–40
    as empirically inaccessible 7–11, 76, 131–2, 147,
        149
    essence of 50, 74, 134–5, 181
    as essence of religion ix–x, 10, 39–41, 57, 96, 98,
        100, 133, 136–8, 140, 181
    explanation of 114–21, 126–7
    vs. expression 3, 9–10, 40–41, 57, 59–60, 63,
        75–6, 79–87, 89, 98, 177
    as invented 145–6
    Joachim Wach's definition of 74–5
    and language 66–7, 110–13, 116–18, 121
    and meditation 136–7
    as mysterious 10–11, 118
    and reference 2–15, 141–50
    routinization of 63–4
    as a socially constructed concept 124–5, 181
Renan, Ernest 44–5
Ricoeur, Paul 31, 33
Riley, Denise 164
Romanticism 11, 26, 29–30, 63, 171

Rooney, Ellen 166, 168
Rorty, Richard 144, 159
Rumi, Jalal Al-Din Muhammad 62

Sahlins, Marshall 178, 189
Schleiermacher, Friedrich ix–x, 10, 117–21, 136
Schopenhauer, Arthur 45
Scott, Joan Wallach x, 27–8, 151–2, 200–201
secularization 55, 60–61, 63–5, 84, 90
Sedgwick, Eve Kosofsky 156–7
Sharf, Robert H. 123, 131–2, 152, 200
Smith, Christian 190–94
Smith, Jonathan Z. 178
Smith, Wilfred Cantwell 10
Spinoza, Baruch 119
"spiritual but not religious" 179–86, 189–90, 193–4
    see also religion, individual vs. institutional
Spivak, Gayatri Chakravorty 160, 167–9
Stansell, Christine 164
Stoicism 47–9
Suzuki, D.T. 138–40
Swann, Karen 170

Taves, Ann x, 2, 122–3, 131
Taylor, Charles x, 26, 29–31, 33, 55–6
Theresa of Avila 65–6
thick description 31–2
Thompson, E.P. 15–16, 26, 161–3
Tillich, Paul 74, 81, 84, 96
Toews, John 164–6
tolerance 12–13
Transcendentalism 47
Tylor, E.B. 77

van der Leeuw, Gerardus 76, 78, 80
van Gennep, Arnold 83
Voltaire 44

Wach, Joachim ix–x, 71–2, 89, 118, 131
Weber, Max 59, 63, 87
Wesley, John 1–4, 6–9, 12, 15–16, 22, 62–4
Williams, Raymond x, 7, 9, 19–20, 24–5, 27, 30,
    55–6, 159–60, 162
Wittgenstein, Ludwig 4–5, 8, 12, 15, 66, 150, 200
Wordsworth, William 31
Wuthnow, Robert 67

Zaleski, Carol 148–9
Žižek, Slavoj 200–201